THE STANDOUT
BUSINESS PLAN

THE
STANDOUT
BUSINESS
PLAN

Make It Irresistible—and Get the Funds You
Need for Your Startup or Growing Business

VAUGHAN EVANS

AND

BRIAN TRACY

AMACOM AMERICAN MANAGEMENT ASSOCIATION

New York □ Atlanta □ Brussels □ Chicago □ Mexico City
San Francisco □ Shanghai □ Tokyo □ Toronto □ Washington, D.C.

Bulk discounts available. For details visit:
www.amacombooks.org/go/specialsales
Or contact special sales:
Phone: 800-250-5308 / E-mail: specialsls@amanet.org
View all the AMACOM titles at: www.amacombooks.org
American Management Association: www.amanet.org

This publication is designed to provide accurate and authoritative information in regard to the subject matter covered. It is sold with the understanding that the publisher is not engaged in rendering legal, accounting, or other professional service. If legal advice or other expert assistance is required, the services of a competent professional person should be sought.

Library of Congress Cataloging-in-Publication Data

Evans, Vaughan, 1951–
The standout business plan : make it irresistible, and get the funds you need for your startup or growing business / Vaughan Evans and Brian Tracy. — 1 Edition.
      pages cm
Includes index.
ISBN-13: 978-0-8144-3411-6
ISBN-10: 0-8144-3411-8
1. Business planning. 2. Stockholders. I. Tracy, Brian. II. Title.
HD30.28.E937 2014
658.4'01—dc23
                                                                      2014002099

About AMA
American Management Association (www.amanet.org) is a world leader in talent development, advancing the skills of individuals to drive business success. Our mission is to support the goals of individuals and organizations through a complete range of products and services, including classroom and virtual seminars, webcasts, webinars, podcasts, conferences, corporate and government solutions, business books, and research. AMA's approach to improving performance combines experiential learning—learning through doing—with opportunities for ongoing professional growth at every step of one's career journey.

Printing number
10 9 8 7 6 5 4 3 2 1

To Barbara, Kamontip, and our families

CONTENTS

□ · · □ · · □

INTRODUCTION

YOU HAVE A terrific idea for a new business. Everybody loves it and offers encouraging words, but words are cheap. You need cash. You don't have enough in the bank to launch a start-up yourself, nor does your family. You need a backer, perhaps an angel investor or venture capitalist, possibly a banker. For whomever, you need a business plan.

Or you may run your own company. You need to expand. You could just about finance it from your balance sheet or through your existing bank facilities, but you could do with some extra cushion. You need a backer, most likely your bank. You too need a plan.

Or maybe you're planning serious expansion, possibly acquisition. You'll need backing from a development capital house. You need a plan.

Perhaps you work for a company and your boss collars you at the water-cooler: "Charlie, we need a business plan. Can I leave it with you?" You're pretty good at your job in marketing or finance. But you've never written a business plan. Where do you start?

Or maybe you're planning a management buyout. Boy, do you need a plan! And it will have to be robust, nay, rock solid, because your backers will hold you accountable if the deal goes through.

In all these cases, let *The Standout Business Plan* be your guide. It is written from the perspective of a backer. Every word on every page is designed to help your business get the backing you seek.

You don't need an encyclopedia for a business plan. And you don't need an encyclopedic guide to help you write one. Your backer would walk out of the room if you presented her with such a plan. She wants the meat; having to chew through the fat will make her back off, not back you.

It's the message that counts, not the detail. Size is not important.

You need a plan that is clear and concise, easy for your backer to read and understand. You need a plan that is coherent, consistent, and convincing, furnishing your backer with the evidence and the argument needed for the go-ahead.

You need the essentials of a business plan.

This is the book for you. It is tailored to meet the needs of your backer. Many business planning guides lead you through the process from the perspective of what you, as a manager or entrepreneur, would wish to say about your business.

Not this guide. It is customer-driven, not supplier-driven. It works backward from the backer to the planner—from what your backer needs to know about your business to what you need to research and analyze to address your backer's needs.

And who is this book for—that is, who is this "planner"? It's anyone who has to produce a *backable* business plan. You may be an entrepreneur starting out on a new venture. You may be a manager in a medium-size business who's been handed the task by the managing director. Or you are the owner of a smaller business and you have delegated the task . . . to yourself.

You may even be a manager in a large company who wants to cut to the chase and draw up a short, sharp, backable plan, rather than a long-winded, interminable tome complete with pages of spreadsheets that will be out of date by the time the report lands on the boss's desk.

This book is laid out in a format designed carefully to help you write a backable business plan.

Chapter 1 is about what you need to do before you get going on your business plan, in terms of purpose, research, and organization; Chapter 1 of your plan meanwhile will be an executive summary of your Chapters 2–9.

Chapters 2–9 of this book have exactly the same titles as Chapters 2–9 of your business plan will have; this book's Chapter 3, for example, is titled "Market Demand," as will be Chapter 3 of your business plan; likewise for subsequent chapters on competition, strategy, resources, forecasts, and risk.

Chapter 10 of this book is about what you will need to do having written your business plan, namely, its future monitoring and evaluation.

This book also has highly practical appendices on how to derive your competitive position and how to undertake structured interviewing of customers. Appendix C has a set of template slides for you to copy and fill in for your own business plan. And, finally, Appendix D sets out in slide format two exemplary business plan case studies—one for a startup in manufacturing and the other for an established business in the service sector—indeed, the very same business, The Gorge Inn and Oriental Spa, that features as the central case study through every chapter of this book.

Appendices in your business plan will of course differ from those of this book. No two business plans will have the same sets of appendices, but most should contain further detail on your products/services, the markets they serve, the company's positioning, customers, marketing, facilities, IT, management

FIGURE I–1. Your backer wants to see your ducks in a row.

etc. It is up to each planner/writer to assess what elements of further detail should best be placed in an appendix—with the sole and specific purpose of transferring further evidence and comfort to the backer.

Finally, and importantly, remember that your business plan will have every chance of winning the backing it merits if it is coherent, consistent, and credible—if all your ducks are in a row (see Figure I–1).

If your ducks are all over the place, incoherent, inconsistent, and incredible, your backer, as he or she has done on hundreds of previous such occasions, will show you the door (see Figure I–2).

This book will show you how to get your ducks in a row. It will guide you on how to write a business plan that will wow your backers and get you the funding you need for your business to succeed.

FIGURE I–2. If they are all over the place, you have no backer.

1

THE GROUNDWORK

The only thing we know about the future is that it will be different.   —Peter Drucker

BEFORE YOU start to write your business plan, you must do some essential preparation. This means gathering the information you'll need to impress your potential backers and getting things organized so that you can prepare a plan that is clear, concise, and convincing. But let's start with the most basic questions concerning a business plan.

The Purpose

What's the purpose of a business plan? Why do you need it? Who's it for? Some guides devote page after page to all the possible permutations of the answers to those questions. That's a waste of time. The essential answers are straightforward: *You need a business plan to obtain backing. It is written for your backer.*

It's as simple as that. If you are in need of backing, for whatever reason, a business plan is essential. And you'll craft that plan to address all the key issues likely to be raised by that backer.

You may need backing because you are launching a startup. Or your company is set for a liftoff in growth. Or it is facing rough times and needs a cash injection.

In each case you need backing, so you'll need a business plan. Of course, it can be more complicated than that, but only a little. Here are some purposes for a business plan worthy of special mention:

- For a startup

- For raising equity finance

- For raising debt

- For board approval

- For a joint venture partner

- For sale of the business

- For differentiating from a project plan

- For use as a managerial tool

Let's look briefly at each of these purposes in turn.

A BUSINESS PLAN FOR A STARTUP

This plan is not that different from a business plan for an established business seeking growth finance. The chapter headings will be the same, but, as you will see later in this book, certain additional questions must be addressed—for example, the identification of prospective customers, the crafting of a distinctive value proposition, a pilot survey, and an assessment of competitive response.

The business plan for a startup (or an established business) will be tailored according to whether you are seeking equity or debt finance.

A BUSINESS PLAN FOR RAISING EQUITY FINANCE

Your backer is an investor. Investors look for a return on their investment—as high a return as possible with as little risk as possible. Investors place as much emphasis on opportunity to exceed plan as the risk of falling short of plan. Each chapter of your business plan must be written with that perspective in mind, exploring upsides creatively but realistically.

A BUSINESS PLAN FOR RAISING DEBT FINANCE

Your backer is a banker. Bankers will be looking to earn fees on the transaction and interest on the loan extended. They want assurance that your business will generate sufficient cash to cover interest payments. And bankers will want some form of guarantee, some security, that they will get their money back, all in one piece, at the end of the loan period.

And remember this: Your banker may not make the decision. That may be for the bank's credit committee members, and they won't meet you. They won't have the benefit of hearing your upbeat version of the future. They'll just examine a cold document: your business plan. So you had better address all the downsides in your plan and convincingly dismiss them. The credit committee won't be remotely interested in the upside—that won't benefit them one penny. They only want to know what could go wrong, with what likelihood, and what you will be able to do to mitigate the damage once things have gone wrong.

The whole tenor of a business plan for a banker will be different from a plan written for an equity investor. You will be conservative, cautious, and risk averse. Forecasts must be readily achievable. Risks to such unambitious forecasts must be extremely unlikely.

One of the authors worked in an investment bank for a number of years and had many a memorable session with credit officers. Take it from experience: No matter how conservative you are in your downside case, the credit guy will always go a shade or two more conservative—however unlikely it is. So be prepared and well-armed with the counterargument.

A BUSINESS PLAN FOR BOARD APPROVAL

The majority of business plans fall into this category. You can imagine the scene in the boardroom a month or two beforehand, with the chairman expostulating: "Charlie, you and your team have so many exciting ideas for moving this wonderful company of ours forward—but, you know, I'm a bit confused. Where are we going to aim first? Where are our best bets? Which is the more risky path? What could go horribly wrong? Will we have enough cash to fund all this expansion? We need a plan!"

The circumstances may differ, but the business plan itself, when written for board approval, will be no different from a plan written for an external investor. The board is effectively an investor—an internal investor—and should be treated with the same respect.

A BUSINESS PLAN FOR A JOINT VENTURE PARTNER

Joint ventures are like any relationship, commercial or personal—success rests entirely on both parties continuing to benefit from it. If one party obtains a seemingly unfair advantage over the other upon formation of the alliance, it will not last and the breakup will be painful on both sides.

Thus the initial success of a JV depends on the terms agreed on at the outset—and these terms, in turn, depend on both parties drawing up and exchanging robust business plans. These plans will be written as if for an investor, because in effect your partner is investing in your business and you are investing in your partner's business.

A BUSINESS PLAN FOR SALE OF THE BUSINESS

Many business plans are written for the sale of a business, but too many plans read as if written purely for an equity investor. That's fine if the buyer is a "trade buyer" (that is, another company in the same or related line of business), a joint venture partner, or a venture capitalist.

But it's not so good if private equity firms are among the prospective buyers. They will want to structure the transaction with as little equity as they can get away with, and with as much debt as possible without endangering the financial stability of the company.

This means that the financing will require the approval not just of the investment committee at the private equity house, but also the credit committee at the bank—and maybe also the credit committee at the mezzanine provider (i.e., a financier of high-yield unsecured debt with an equity kicker). So, in this circumstance, the business plan should be written to address both the upside for the investor and the downside for the banker. It needs to be cleverly balanced.

A BUSINESS PLAN VS. A PROJECT PLAN

A project plan is similar to, but differs from, a business plan. A project plan makes the business case for a specific investment project. It isolates revenue streams and costs directly attributable to the project and recommends "go" or "no go" decisions accordingly. The decision is typically taken at the board level and is separated for external finance only rarely and on very large projects.

A business plan considers the future of the whole business. That business may be a division or subsidiary of a much larger company, but it has its own income statement and will be forecast in full.

THE BUSINESS PLAN AS A MANAGERIAL TOOL

Annual business planning, while often a most useful discipline in large, multi-divisional, multinational organizations, is largely a waste of time for small and medium-size businesses (SMBs). In theory, it is a great idea. Every year the managing director appoints a capable manager to review last year's three-year plan and prepare this year's plan. Lessons are learned and steps taken to improve performance.

In practice, insufficient time and effort will be invested in the market research and strategy development parts of the annual plan, rendering the three-year forecasts unsubstantiated, often wildly optimistic, and potentially misleading. The only part of the plan for which managers will be accountable (and that's typically reflected in their pay package) will be the next-year budget numbers. So why invest serious time every September producing robust three-year forecasts against which you are not going to be monitored?

The authors have seen medium-size businesses turning over $150 million preparing rolling annual business plans that are meaningless. No manager believes in them, not even the managing director, but some adviser, some time ago, told them that annual business plans are a useful discipline. They are not, unless they are done properly.

And doing an annual business plan properly means investing time and effort—resources that are in short supply in a thriving SMB and generally better directed toward serving customers and improving performance.

The time for an SMB to do a business plan properly is when there is a specific need, such as when the board asks for one, when an investor seeks one, when the bank demands one, or when the business is for sale. Otherwise, management time is better focused elsewhere.

For whichever of these purposes you are writing a business plan, this book will be your indispensable guide. It is a guide designed to address the needs of different types of backers.

The End Result

What should a good business plan look like? Let's get the answer to that question firmly planted in the brain before we delve into other details.

Where do you need to get to? What is the end result of this process? What does a good, winning plan look like and how does a good plan differ from a bad, losing plan?

In short, what is the essential outcome?

Let's look at the outcomes under two scenarios:

- A plan for an established business

- A plan for a startup business

We'll start with the established business, because it's easier to gather the necessary facts and figures for an ongoing enterprise. The business has a track record, both operational and financial, achieved within a historical, recorded context of market demand, industry competition, strategic positioning, and resource deployment. Forecasts will be based as much on fact as judgment.

If you are planning for a startup, you should still read this section because it will help you become familiar with the various components that go into creating a strong business plan. And keep in mind that an established business scenario is where you are aiming to be in a few years' time, when your startup has made a reputation for itself and is poised for the next level.

AN ESTABLISHED BUSINESS

What does a successful business plan look like for an established business?

We'll take a fictional case study of The Gorge Inn and Oriental Spa and run with it throughout this book. Hopefully it will be a case you can relate to, because we're confident everyone has felt the urge, now and again, to flee the rat race and set up a business in some idyllic patch of this earth.

This particular piece of North American paradise is located in the Columbia River Gorge, which carves its dramatic, imposing way between Washington State and Oregon. The Gorge Inn and Oriental Spa is owned and run by Rick and Kay Jones. Rick is a former management consultant, and Kay is a stress management counselor of Eurasian heritage.

The business has been operating for three years and has just started to turn a profit. Rick and Kay have secured planning permission to build a 16-bedroom extension and swimming pool—an investment they believe will transform the profitability of the business. But they have run down their personal funds over the last few years and need a further injection of external finance.

In short, they need a backer. So they need a plan. Here's their executive summary, where you'll see that in a mere couple of pages most of the key questions a backer needs to know can be satisfactorily addressed.

THE GORGE INN AND ORIENTAL SPA BUSINESS PLAN, 2014: EXECUTIVE SUMMARY

The Gorge Inn and Oriental Spa ("The Gorge") is a destination with a difference. It is set overlooking the stunning Columbia River Gorge in the Pacific Northwest of the United States and yet offers visitors a touch of the Orient in its room decor, cuisine, and spa. It has 17 rooms for rent, most with views over the canyon, with spa and restaurant facilities offering a menu of Western and Oriental selections to both overnight and day visitors.

It turned over $513,000 in 2013, having grown by 36 percent/year since 2011, and the operating margin is expected to top 20 percent in 2014. Further investment of $1.05 million in a 16-room extension and swimming pool is forecast to double sales by 2018 and boost operating margin to 34 percent. Opportunities to exploit a proven concept outshine risks of cost overrun or slower buildup of occupancy.

The Gorge has three main business segments—rooms, catering, and spa. Room revenues have been growing fastest, at 45 percent/year, with spa revenues (20 percent of total) slower (at 18 percent/year) because of the increasing patronage of nonresident visitors from the start and subsequent capacity limitations, to be eased with the planned Phase II development.

The overnight visitor market in the Columbia River Gorge has bounced back from the 2009 downturn to an estimated $86 million in 2013 and is forecast to grow at around 4 percent/year to $105 million by 2018. Key long-term drivers are the growth in the U.S. population and per capita incomes, the propensity of Americans to take multiple short breaks, investment in state visitor attractions, such as scenic road and off-road cycling routes, and targeted marketing spend led by Travel Oregon. The main short-term driver is the economic cycle.

There are many excellent resorts, hotels, inns, B&Bs, and spas throughout Oregon. The industry is competitive, with low barriers to entry, but with the most highly differentiated businesses thriving and enjoying repeat customers. Occupancy rates in Columbia River Gorge hotels are a shade higher than elsewhere in Oregon. Spa facilities are not widespread in rural Oregon and are found primarily at the luxury resorts, but there are many good spas in Portland, the "City of Roses," which is just 35 miles from The Gorge. Restaurants offering Oriental cuisine, particularly Chinese, Thai, and Vietnamese, can also be found in Portland, along with its famed food cart pods and microbreweries.

The Gorge Inn is distinctive in two main ways: It enjoys a spectacular location atop one of the most beautiful canyons in North America, and it has an Oriental theme. The theme is understated, with a hint of the Orient applied to the bedroom decor and Oriental treatments available, in addition to standard ones, at the spa. Oriental cuisine is offered in the restaurant, but so too is Western fare. The customer is given the choice. In the three years since opening in December 2010, occupancy rates at The Gorge have grown from 39 percent to 56 percent to 71 percent and are budgeted conservatively for 75 percent in 2014. Restaurant take-up by overnight visitors has risen to 35 percent of visitor nights and spa occupancy 26 percent, both above budget.

Rick and Kay Jones bought the property in 2009 for $715,000, against which they took on a mortgage of $500,000 and spent a further $280,000 of their own funds on renovation. The owners work full-time in the business and employ a staff of three full-time workers, with part-time help added as appropriate. Spa professionals are contracted as required.

The business broke even at the operating profit level during 2012, the second year of operations, and achieved a profit before tax of 11 percent in 2013, budgeted to rise to 15 percent this year. The owners believe that profitability will be greatly boosted with the planned Phase II expansion, costing $1,050,000 for a new building with 16 rooms and an outside heated swimming pool. Overheads, other than financing costs, will rise by 50 percent, but revenues, once occupancy rates return to today's levels by (conservatively) 2018, will have almost doubled. Operating margin, assuming no change in directors' remuneration, is forecast to reach 34 percent by 2018 and profit before tax 24 percent. The speed of growth will continue to yield challenges of cash flow, and the owners will look to their backer to provide the necessary flexibility of finance.

The key risks to this plan are a slower buildup of occupancy, perhaps occasioned by a double-dip recession; the opening of direct competition; a peaking of interest in the offering or insufficient awareness; slippage in construction work; and the health of the owners—all of which are examined in depth in the plan and found to be containable.

Upside opportunities lie in raising occupancy rates higher than in the plan through marketing that's focused on exploiting a proven concept; the introduction of new, complementary services or products; liftoff in the spa segment's profitability; and the acquisition of another site (Phase III), like one provisionally identified in the North Cascades National Park in Washington State, to replicate the Oriental spa concept in the state next door.

In conclusion, The Gorge has established itself as a serious player in the Oregon tourist industry, offering visitors something very special. It is now poised, through this expansion, to become a leading player in spa services in Oregon and to achieve healthy profitability. Its owners seek a financial partner who shares this vision.

So what makes this a good business plan? First, it is clear and concise. Second, it is coherent and consistent—the story line hangs together well. Third, it tackles risk. As you will see later in this book, a backer is primarily concerned with four areas of risk, all of which seem to be covered adequately in the business plan:

- *Market demand risk* (see Chapter 3): There is strongly growing demand overall, even countercyclically during a severe economic recession.

- *Competition risk* (Chapter 4): Industry competition is tough, but less so when the offering is distinctive.

- *Strategic risk* (Chapters 5 and 6): The Gorge has gained share through its distinctive offering and seems well placed to gain further share through this strategically sound expansion.

- *Financial risk* (Chapter 7): The forecast numbers seem consistent with the market and within the competitive and strategic context.

That's it, then. The Gorge looks like a backable business—subject, of course, to due diligence.

> **TOP TIP:** *Your business plan journey should traverse the seven Cs: A good plan is* clear, crisp, concise, consistent, coherent, *and* credible. *But above all it is* convincing, *particularly in its assessment of risk. Its sole reason for being is to convince your backer. Remember all seven Cs, but especially the last.*

So what does a bad plan look like? Even a bad plan on a good company?

Suppose The Gorge's business plan had been drawn up not by Rick Jones, BA, MBA, who's proficient in management and management consulting, as well as strategic and financial analysis, but instead by some puffed-up know-it-all who is skeptical of the need for a business plan at all. This fellow thinks it's unnecessary to explain his dead-certainty case to a bunch of chinless, beardless financiers who have pockets stuffed with cash but no clue as to the nitty-gritty of the business world.

Here goes.

The Gorge Inn and Oriental Spa Business Plan, 2014: A Bad Executive Summary

The Gorge Inn and Oriental Spa is a top location in the Pacific Northwest for chilling out, with a super view, fabulous home cuisine, and an exotic treatment of guests. Revenues are growing fast and it is profitable.

Oregon is a thriving visitor destination in the USA and The Gorge is the best place to stay in the state.

It is owned and managed by Rick and Kay Jones, and they employ some help for the reception, bedrooms, kitchen, restaurant, spa, and gardens.

They plan to build an extension and a pool, which will make the business even more profitable.

There are no serious risks, but plenty of scope to roll out the model at similar locations.

In conclusion, this is your chance to back The Gorge and make some easy money.

Convinced? We suspect not. But why not? Have a go yourself at applying some red ink to the so-called plan. We could list scores of things wrong with it, but let's stick to seven, which happen to reflect the headings of each chapter in the business plan, as set out in subsequent chapters of this book:

◻ There are no key numbers on sales, growth, sales by segment, margin, market size, or market share. This atrocious executive summary only exaggerates to make the point. You'd be surprised how many business plans offer no numbers at all on sales by segment (see Chapter 2), let alone on market size or share.

◻ There is no discussion on market demand drivers, which should underpin any discussion on market demand growth. (See Chapter 3.)

◻ Competitors are dismissed, treated as an irrelevance. Far too many business plans fail to address convincingly the capabilities of competitors, and very, very few analyze the dynamics of competitive intensity. (See Chapter 4.)

◻ "The Gorge is the best. . . ." You would be surprised, perhaps horrified, but such broad-brush, unjustified, bar-talk claims are commonplace in business plans. (See Chapter 5.)

▫ So there are some employees, great, thanks, but how many? (See Chapter 6.)

▫ How much will the extension project cost, and what will be the subsequent uplift in profitability? (See Chapter 7.)

▫ What, no risk? (See Chapter 8.)

That's how *not* to write a business plan. We'll return to what it is you should be doing in the rest of the book, but first let's check on what the result should look like in a startup.

A STARTUP BUSINESS

What is the difference in a startup business plan, as compared with a plan for an established business?

Not much, in truth. The structure of the plan remains the same; there must be an introduction to the business (i.e., a proposition) and information on market demand, competition, strategic position, resources, financials, and risk—except that it will be set largely in the *future tense*.

What changes most is the level of uncertainty throughout, and in particular in the market reception to your business proposition. In a startup, the reception in the marketplace is largely unknown. However, it can be researched, assessed, and estimated in advance, as you will see in some detail in Chapter 3.

Let's suppose that Rick and Kay Jones needed to raise external financing for their startup in 2008, rather than finance the investment through the sale of their Boston home and a mortgage. Suppose they had to draw up a business plan. Here it is.

THE GORGE INN AND ORIENTAL SPA BUSINESS PLAN
AT STARTUP, 2009: EXECUTIVE SUMMARY

The Gorge Inn and Oriental Spa ("The Gorge") will be a destination with a difference. It will be set overlooking the stunning Columbia River Gorge in the Pacific Northwest of the United States and yet offer visitors a touch of the Orient in its room decor, cuisine, and spa. It will have 17 rooms for hire, most with views over the canyon, with spa and restaurant facilities offering a menu of Western and Oriental selections to both overnight and day visitors.

The overnight visitor market in the Columbia River Gorge is estimated to have reached $82 million in 2008. It has been growing strongly at around 10 percent/year for the last five years, but has probably taken a step back, perhaps by 3 percent to 4 percent, as a result of the current recession, induced by the financial crisis of last year. Key long-term drivers are the growth in the U.S. population and per capita incomes, the propensity of Americans to take multiple short breaks, investment in state visitor attractions, such as scenic road and off-road cycling routes, and targeted marketing spend led by Travel Oregon. The main short-term driver is the economic cycle. Market growth is expected to resume in 2010 and is forecast to grow at an average 5 percent per year, 2009–13.

There are many excellent resorts, hotels, inns, B&Bs, and spas throughout Oregon. The industry is competitive, with low barriers to entry, but with the most highly differentiated businesses thriving and enjoying repeat custom. Occupancy rates in Columbia River Gorge hotels are a shade higher than elsewhere in Oregon. Spa facilities are not widespread in rural Oregon and are found primarily at the luxury resorts, but there are many good spas in Portland, the "City of Roses," which is just 35 miles from The Gorge. Restaurants offering Oriental cuisine, particularly Chinese, Thai, and Vietnamese, can also be found in Portland, along with its famed food cart pods and microbreweries.

The Gorge will be distinctive in two main ways: It enjoys a spectacular location atop one of the most beautiful canyons in North America, and it will have an Oriental theme. The theme will be understated, with a hint of the Orient applied to the bedroom decor and Oriental treatments available, in addition to standard treatments, at the spa. Oriental cuisine will be offered in the restaurant, but so too will European fare. The customer will have the choice. We expect the inn to open in late 2010, and conservatively forecast occupancy rates to grow from 25 percent to 30 percent in 2011, to 60 percent in 2013. Restaurant take-up is forecast to rise to 25 percent of visitor nights and spa occupancy to 20 percent in this period.

These forecasts are underpinned by substantial market research and some test marketing. We have compiled a report on the location, offerings, and resources of a dozen competing three- to four-star hotels in the region, and an inventory of competing spa facilities. We have also visited and enjoyably experienced the facilities of two similar "Oriental spas" in North America, one in the San Francisco Bay Area and one in Las Vegas. And we spent two days talking to visitors in the Multnomah Falls area, armed with a clipboard and short questionnaire, and found that 82 percent of those currently staying in similarly positioned and priced accommodations would be happy to give a concept like The Gorge a try.

We have an offer to purchase the property for $715,000 and plan to spend $240,000 on conversion and renovation to 17 bedrooms with en suite bathrooms, a new kitchen, and spa facilities—including an outside spa tub, a sauna/steam massage shower, two treatment rooms, and a meditation room. We shall work full-time in the business and employ a staff of three full-time equivalents, with part-time help added as appropriate. Spa professionals will be contracted as required.

We plan to keep a tight control on operating costs, such that operating profit breakeven can be achieved at 40 percent occupancy and net profit breakeven at 55 percent. We forecast that the latter should be achieved by 2013, with net profit rising to 5 percent to 10 percent beyond that. The speed of growth will yield challenges of cash flow, and we shall look to our backer to provide the necessary flexibility of finance.

The key risks to this plan are insufficient business, with occupancy falling below even the 40 percent breakeven, slippage and/or cost escalation in renovation works, the opening of direct competition, and the health of the owners—all of which are examined in depth in the plan and found to be containable.

The main upside lies in raising the scale of this venture in a Phase II development. If we can gain planning permission, the construction of 12 to 16 extra rooms in a purpose-built extension, along with an aesthetically harmonious outside swimming pool, would permit a greater contribution to site overheads and result in much higher profitability. We plan to commence the planning application as soon as Phase I renovation work is underway.

In conclusion, The Gorge can become a serious, profitable player in the Oregon tourist industry, offering visitors something very special. We seek a financial partner who shares this vision.

Apart from the future tense, what's the main difference? You spotted it. It's the additional paragraph that explains the basis of the plan's forecast, where you have to convince your backer that this is not just a punt, but an investment grounded on empirical or observational market research.

We'll return to the market research you need for a startup in Chapter 3.

The Preparation

There are things you need to do in advance, before you put pen to paper and write your business plan. In essence, this essential preparation can be split into two areas:

- Research

- Organization

Let's explain them, one at a time.

RESEARCH

You might think you know your business, but how much do you know about what's driving your customers' behavior? And what your competitors are up to?

If there are gaps in your knowledge, you might find yourself making "soft" assumptions in the business plan. Then, just wait until you face cross-examination from your backer!

There are three areas of research you should either undertake or feel confident that you and your colleagues know enough about already before starting your plan. Each of these areas will be covered in detail in the relevant chapters, but in brief they are:

- Data on market demand, size, drivers, and growth trends (see Chapter 3).

- Data on competitors (Chapter 4).

- Customer data (Chapter 5). Whether you survey actual customers, if yours is an established business, or prospective customers in a startup, you must find out what customers expect from your business, both now and in the future.

Allow yourself a month or so to gather all this information. Hopefully, much of it will be at hand already, squirreled away in some filing cabinet, real or virtual, as marketing-related material. But filling in the data gaps can be time-consuming.

The customer survey tends to be the most time-consuming area of research. You should allow two or three weeks to put together a questionnaire, call customers, and assemble the results. For details on questions to ask customers, please turn to Chapter 5 and also Appendix B.

> **TOP TIP:** A business plan with little research behind it is a flimsy affair. At best it might be clear, crisp, concise, consistent, and coherent. But it is unlikely to satisfy the sixth C, which is to be credible. Your backer will ask questions such as, "How did you arrive at that market growth estimate?" and "How are your competitors responding?" and "What makes you think customers would pay for that?" You had better have credible answers rooted in research or you'll have no backer.

ORGANIZATION

There are various organizational items that are best sorted out in advance, specifically:

- The planning team
- The timetable
- The tools
- The contents
- The appendices
- The length
- The drafting process

Here are some tips on each of these elements of the business plan.

THE PLANNING TEAM. It goes without saying that one person must be tasked with full responsibility for leading the planning team. Not a team of two or three with equal responsibility, but one manager, backed up by an e-mail from the managing director delegating responsibility to that one person.

In a small business or startup, of course, that "manager" will be the owner—you! You may be the only person involved in the business plan, and you will write the whole thing. One person must take charge, not only for purposes of assembling all the data and analysis that needs to feed into each chapter of the business plan, but for establishing a consistent, coherent style and message throughout the main document. Only the appendices can get away with giving the appearance that they have been written by someone else.

In a somewhat larger business, the team leader may need to call upon two or three complementary team members, depending on the complexity of the business. One person, possibly the leader, should come from the sales and marketing team and assume responsibility for the market and competitor analysis and the customer survey. Another could come from operations and be assigned to put together all the technical information needed on the company's assets, people, systems, and processes. A third contributor could come from finance to take charge of the financial forecasts.

For a medium-size business, say, with revenues over $25 million, the team leader should expect to devote at least 50 percent of his or her time over a one-month period. Combined inputs of the others on the team could well come to two or three person-months, again depending on the complexity of the business.

THE TIMETABLE. If your boss says he wants a business plan done by the end of the week, so be it. It can be done, but the boss can't expect a properly researched plan. There will certainly be no time for a customer survey. All that can reasonably be done in a week is to summarize what you already know about the business and where it is headed and to create some forecasts around that information.

A business-plan-in-a-week may not be a bad thing if the boss just needs something to float across the bow of a potential backer. But remember this: Once in print, a business plan inherits an authority that may be out of proportion to the effort put into it. Once those forecasts are set out on paper, they become ingrained in the backer's brain—and it may take much time, analysis, and persuasion to shift those perceptions at a later stage.

Worse still is when a business plan is rushed out, pdf-ed, and delivered by e-mail to the prospective backer. Once in cyberspace, that plan could theoretically (notwithstanding any nondisclosure agreement) make its way to any financier, customer, supplier, or worst, competitor, anywhere in the world—at the click of a mouse.

By all means, rattle off a business-plan-in-a-week, but superimpose every page with the words DRAFT PRELIMINARY (in huge letters). Also, place a disclaimer footnote on every page and only let your would-be backer have one hard copy, with an understanding that it may not be photocopied.

A robust business plan takes at least a month to prepare. Sure, strategy consultants can be engaged, albeit expensively, and they can do the job expertly in two or three weeks. However, if you are to do it in-house, it will take some time. If you and your colleagues have never prepared a thorough business plan before, allow for six to eight weeks and expect many iterations as the draft circulates among the management team.

THE TOOLS. There is some clever software available these days from leading banks or independent providers like Business Plan Pro. These programs provide a business plan structure and ensure that your income statement, balance sheet, and cash flow forecasts (see Chapter 7) are in harmony with each other. Try an Internet search on *business plan software* and see what catches your eye.

The authors have every respect for these software entrepreneurs and hope they do well. But we are assuming that by reading this book you would prefer to follow a written guide, rather than a preprogrammed (and often expensive) electronic process.

Above all, we suspect there is no software available on writing a business plan that offers this book's perspective on addressing the needs of a backer— nor would any such software include the innovative forecasting and risk assessment tools introduced in Chapters 3, 7, and 8 of this book.

The only tools you need to write your essential business plan are off-the-shelf word processing and spreadsheet applications, such as Microsoft Word and Excel, and possibly a presentation application, such as PowerPoint. And this book.

THE CONTENTS. We have seen guides on business planning that suggest that the contents of a plan should be tailored to the specific nature of the business.

This is not so. The contents should be tailored to the needs of the backer. Period.

The backer wants your business and its market context, along with all pertinent risks and opportunities, to be assessed in an orderly, logical, and comprehensive way, as follows:

- *Market demand.* What is driving demand for the buyers of a product (or service) such as yours?

- *Competition.* Is industry competition between you and fellow suppliers of this product intense, and will it intensify?

- *Your strategy.* How well positioned is your company, and what is your strategy for improving that position?

- *Your resources.* What resources will you deploy in implementing that strategy?

- *Your financials and forecasts.* Do your forecasts realistically reflect both external market trends and internal competitiveness?

- *Risk and sensitivity.* What are the main risks and opportunities around the forecasts, and the likelihood and impact of each, and how sensitive are the financial forecasts to adverse circumstance?

It's as simple as that. That is what your backer needs to know. All else is unnecessary detail.

These six areas of analysis form the bedrock of a business plan and are covered in Chapters 3 to 8. These elements of the business plan are flanked by an executive summary (the plan's Chapter 1), an introductory backgrounder on the business (Chapter 2), and a brief conclusion (Chapter 9).

Here, then, are what should be the contents of any business plan. You'll notice that after Chapter 1, all chapter names and numbers are arranged to be identical to the contents of this book:

Business Plan Contents

1. Executive Summary

2. The Business

3. Market Demand

4. Competition

5. Strategy

6. Resources

7. Financials and Forecasts

8. Risk, Opportunity, and Sensitivity

9. Conclusion

10. Appendices

Most plans do not have a chapter on competition. Often there's just a token two-paragraph section, placed in the chapter on the market, that mentions competition. That should make the backer highly suspicious, especially when the financial forecasts show exponentially rising operating margin with no competitive response.

Some plans discuss the company's strategy and resources before the market and competition. This is dangerous thinking. A company exists to serve a market, not the other way round.

Other plans have separate chapters on manufacturing facilities, sales and marketing, IT, employees, management, and so on, rather than just one chapter devoted to resources. This tends to bulk up the plan with data. Again, this is dangerous. Backers need to know if the story line is worth backing. They don't want to get lost in wads of information and data. Details on resources are best relocated to the appendices.

We repeat: This book suggests a business plan tailored for a backer. One of the authors has spent 25 years advising backers on whether they should back business plans. The information recommended in this book is what they need.

THE APPENDICES. Hurrah for appendices! This is where the heavy stuff can be moved, without swamping the reader of the main report with too much information. All the detail needed to justify the conclusions of the main report can be gathered and placed at the end of the document in the appendices: product descriptions and photographs, data on market size and growth by segment, details on competitors' sales, employees, and strategic focus, the nitty-gritty of your company's facilities (along with photographs and site layouts), operations, employees, management biographies, organization structure, sales and marketing teams, advertising campaigns, and so on.

But do not load the appendices with superfluous junk. Only stick in the extra detail if it is going to lend further evidence for your business case and extend further comfort to your backer.

The appendices don't have to be read. Your backers need only dip into those bits as needed when they seek further detail. Everything contained in the appendices will be summarized in the main report.

THE LENGTH. The main document should be 25 to 30 pages (letter size, also known as American Quarto), 35 pages maximum. The main chapters on market demand, competition, and strategy should be three to four pages each; chapters on resources and forecasts can be perhaps a bit longer at four to six pages each. The remaining chapters, including the one on risk, should be just two pages each. The conclusion, however, should be a concisely written and upbeat half a page.

The appendices can be the same number of pages, depending on what further information or evidence you feel is necessary to include to convince your backer.

An alternative to the standard business plan printed as an 8.5 × 11 document is the PowerPoint presentation. The overwhelming advantage of PowerPoint, when done properly, is that it forces the writer to be concise and adhere to a visible story line. The main disadvantage is that many entrepreneurs and SMB managers may not be sufficiently familiar with either business plans or PowerPoint to present a convincing case in that format to the backer.

If you were to hire strategy consultants, PowerPoint would be their format of choice. But they've had decades of experience crafting these presentations; it's what they do for a living!

Our advice is to stick to what you and your backers are accustomed to—and if your business plan is to be presented to a banker, it had better be in portrait, letter size.

THE DRAFTING PROCESS. Beware the perils of drafting your plan as a team. You have just spent a morning adding the final touches to the chapter on forecasts and you receive an e-mail from your colleague with detailed amendments to an earlier draft of that same chapter! Your mood darkens at the thought of having to re-input all those changes onto the latest draft.

This scenario can be avoided by having the team leader retain control of the master draft and by using a rigorous file naming system. Each draft issued by the team leader should have a number and a date—since there could be two or three drafts of the same chapter made on one day. Each draft reviewed by a team member should be initialled.

Example: A typical chapter draft issued by the team leader could be bizplan.ch7.v4.18apr14, which could be subsequently reviewed by his team member, Joe Bloggs, in bizplan.ch7.v4.18apr14.jb.

A touch bureaucratic, perhaps, but a naming system helps to avoid drafting mix-ups, which can be infuriating as the deadline looms.

By now, you've done your essential research. You've sorted out the organizational aspects of the process. You're well prepared. Earlier you established what the purpose of writing your plan was and you learned what the result ought to look like. You understand that your business plan is, first and foremost, written for your backer and that both structure and content need to be drawn up bearing in mind your backer's needs at all times. It's time to begin working on the plan itself.

▫ ▫ ▫ ▫ ▫ **THINKING OUT OF THE BOX** ▫ ▫ ▫ ▫ ▫

Creating Wealth

You are never given a wish without also the power to make it come true. —Richard Bach

There are many strategies for generating sales, profitability, and wealth in every economy. Throughout most of human history, the only way to achieve wealth was to take it away from someone else, to steal it from someone who had already produced the wealth. This desire to expropriate wealth explains almost all the wars of history.

In the last 200 years, the idea of wealth creation, or "making money," has largely replaced the idea of expropriating or seizing wealth in most of the civilized world.

Your ability as an entrepreneur to create wealth where no wealth existed before is the key to your success, and the success of your business. Your business plan should stress your ability to create wealth.

According to the Pareto principle, in every industry 20 percent of businesses earn 80 percent of the profits. Some businesses, selling a similar product in the same market as their competitors, earn ten or twenty times as much as other companies. Your business plan should reflect how you will try to do the same.

Let's look at nine key factors in creating wealth, which should be taken into account when preparing your business plan.

1. Wealth creation occurs when you produce a product or service that people want and need and are willing to pay for, at a price that is in excess of your total cost of producing that product or service.

- The key to business success has always been the same: "Find a need and fill it."
- We all earn our livings by serving other people in some way.
- Your business goal is to find out what people really want and need, and then to give it to them better and faster than anyone else.

2. Hundreds of companies have been studied to discover the secrets of market leadership. What is it? The findings have revealed three basic answers:

- Operational excellence. The company has developed the ability to produce its products and services at a cost substantially lower than its competitors.
- Customer intimacy. The company develops a close relationship with its customers based on excellent knowledge of the customer's business.
- Technological superiority. The company offers a product or service that is technically superior to that of its competitor.

3. There are several strategies that you can follow to create additional value for your customers and additional wealth for yourself:

- Improve your product or service in some way so that it is better than that of your competitors, at the same or at a lower price.

- Produce or deliver your product or service to your customer faster than your competitor.
- Produce your product or service cheaper than your competitor while maintaining or increasing your level of quality.
- Offer better follow-up and support services than your competitors to go along with your product or service.
- Give guarantees and warranties of satisfaction that are more extensive than your competitors.
- Make your product easier to acquire and more readily available than your competitors.
- Make your prices and terms more attractive and convenient than your competitors.
- Include additional products and services with your offerings, at the same price.

4. The most valuable part of your business is your reputation with your customers:

- Your reputation in the marketplace determines how much you can sell, and the prices you can charge.
- The friendliness of your staff and the ease of doing business with you is a key part of your reputation.
- Your credibility with your customers, the degree to which they see you as trustworthy and dependable, is a key value to your customers.

5. When selling your products or services to businesses, remember that business customers are only concerned with how it will affect their sales and profits:

- Businesses think in terms of saving time or money (or gaining time or money) by using your product or service.
- Businesses see your product as a solution to a problem that they have. What is it?
- Know the answer to this question: How quickly does your product pay for itself in increased efficiencies?

6. Selling to individual customers requires that you focus on the improvement that your product/service makes in their lives:

- What does your product achieve for your customer?
- What does your product help your customer to avoid?
- What does your product help your customer to preserve?

➤ How does your product help your customer to get better results in his life?

7. The most important question you need to ask and answer each day is, "What can I do to increase the value of my services to my customers today?"

➤ The value of a business is determined by its ability to improve the life or work of its customers.

➤ The value of an individual is his or her ability to make a valuable contribution to the company, organization, or business.

8. The key to wealth creation has always been the same. It is to "add value."

➤ In what ways can you add value to your customers today?

➤ In what ways can you add value to your company today?

➤ One good idea to add value to your customers, or to add new customers, can be enough to move you into the top 20 percent of companies in your industry.

9. The role of the entrepreneur is to seek out profit-making opportunities.

➤ Profit comes from adding value in some way, before your competitors do it.

➤ The number of ways that you can add value to your product or service, and to your customers, is limited only by your imagination.

What one action are you going to take immediately to create wealth as the result of what you have learned here?

◻ ◻ ◻ ◻ ◻ ◻ ◻ ◻ ◻ ◻ ◻ ◻ ◻ ◻ ◻ ◻ ◻ ◻ ◻ ◻

THE BUSINESS

Vision is not enough; it must be combined with venture. It is not enough to stare up the steps, we must step up the stairs. —Václav Havel

THE PLAN STARTS here. In this chapter you set the scene. You brief your backer on the bare essentials of the business: what it does, for whom, why, where, with whom, with what, and how it got to where it is.

If yours is an established business, you'll also set out briefly how well the business has done so far. If yours is a startup, you'll briefly set out why the business is poised to enjoy a sustainable competitive advantage.

The rest of Chapter 2 of your business plan will be about segmentation. You'll introduce your backer to the product/market segments that matter in your business. Each segment will be analyzed in some depth in subsequent chapters, so it is important to get the segmentation right at the very start.

This chapter will have more detail on the background to your business than you will have set out in your executive summary, but it won't have too much detail. Your plan should be a short, sharp, punchy document aimed at hooking your backer.

There is no place to waffle, whether on background, history, or whatever.

Background

This is where the backer is introduced to the business, where you set out clearly and concisely what makes the business tick. The background section has five headings:

- The opener

- Goals and objectives

- Strategy

- Resources

- Basic financials

THE OPENER

Here, in one paragraph, should be the essence of your business or your business proposition, if yours is a startup.

The opener forms the first paragraph of Chapter 2 of your plan, but your backer will have seen it before. It will be reproduced, word for word, as the first paragraph of the executive summary in Chapter 1 of your plan. All the essential bits of information will be in that paragraph, including:

- Who you are—the name (or code name) of your company

- What products or services your company focuses on

- Which main customer groups the company is aimed at

- Where the company is based, where else it has operations, and where it sells its products or services

- What successes you've achieved, in terms of revenues and operating margin (operating profit divided by sales), and when

Let's look again at the opening summary paragraphs of the executive summary for The Gorge Inn and Oriental Spa:

The Gorge Inn and Oriental Spa ("The Gorge") is a destination with a difference. It is set overlooking the stunning Columbia River Gorge in the Pacific Northwest of the United States and yet offers visitors a touch of the Orient in its room decor, cuisine, and spa. It has 17 rooms for rent, most with views over the canyon, with spa and restaurant facilities offering a menu of Western and Oriental selections to both overnight and day visitors.

It turned over $513,000 in 2013, having grown by 36 percent a year since 2011, and operating margin is expected to top 20 percent in 2014. Further investment of $1.05 million in a 16-room extension and swimming pool is forecast to double sales by 2018 and boost operating margin to 34 percent. Opportunities to exploit a proven concept outshine risks of cost overrun or slower buildup of occupancy.

That's all you need at this stage, an elevator-speech-type introduction to the business and the plan—but with all the main facts tucked into it.

Next, you set out briefly how the business has evolved over time in terms of its goals and objectives, strategy, resources, and financials. There is no need for a separate section on history, but rather all these sections should track key historical developments inasmuch as they are relevant to the company's situation today.

> **TOP TIP:** *Your backer is looking for smart goals and SMART objectives.*

GOALS AND OBJECTIVES

A goal is something your business aims to be, as described in words. An objective is a target that helps to measure whether that goal has been achieved and is typically set out in numbers.

One of your goals may be for your business to be the most customer-centric supplier of your services in the Southeast. Objectives to back up that goal could be the achievement of a "highly satisfied" rating of 30 percent from your annual customer survey by 2014, then 35 percent by 2016 and 80 percent "satisfied" or better by 2016.

Or you may aim for your business to be the Canadian market leader in a key segment, with measurable supporting objectives being 40 percent market share by 2014 and 45 percent by 2016, up from today's 33 percent.

Goals are directional; objectives are specific. You may have come across the useful acronym SMART for setting objectives, which stands for specific, measurable, attainable, relevant, and time-limited. The best objectives are indeed SMART—as exemplified in the previous example:

Specific—There's a market share target in a key segment.

Measurable—Market research to which you subscribe will reveal whether your target of 40 percent is met.

Attainable—You are at 33 percent now and your new product range has been well received.

Relevant—Market share is a good indicator of corporate progress.

Time-limited—Your objectives are stated for 2014 and 2016.

What were the goals and objectives of your business when it started? Were they met? How have they evolved over time to what they are today? This is what you must describe, briefly, particularly if the goals and objectives are still relevant to the issues in the business plan of today.

If your business is a startup, what are your goals? What SMART objectives have you set toward the achievement of those goals?

Goals and objectives are essential for your plan. But you may also choose to delve deeper into the essence of the business by setting out its vision, purpose, and mission—see Thinking Out of the Box (the section that follows) on planning for success.

▫ ▫ ▫ ▫ ▫ **THINKING OUT OF THE BOX** ▫ ▫ ▫ ▫ ▫

Planning for Success

If you don't know where you're going, any road will take you there.
                              —*The Mad Hatter in Lewis Carroll's* Alice in Wonderland

There are a lot of Mad Hatters, living in a kind of Wonderland, who are trying to build successful businesses. Be sure that you are NOT one of them.

Your ability to decide what you want to accomplish in every area of your business and personal life will dramatically increase your results and rewards. When you make clear, written plans with measurable standards and schedules, you increase your probabilities of success many times over the person who is vague or unsure.

The purpose of your business life is to enable you to enjoy your personal life. Fully 85 percent of your happiness will come from your relationships with other people; only 15 percent will come from external achievement.

You need to decide what you really want in life:

What are your personal values? What are your business values?

Personal Values?	Business Values?
1. _____	1. _____
2. _____	2. _____
3. _____	3. _____

What are your three most important goals in life, right now?

1. _____
2. _____
3. _____

What would you do immediately if you learned today that you had just won $20 million?

1. _____
2. _____
3. _____

What would you do, and how would you spend your time, if you learned today that you only had six months to live?

1. _____
2. _____
3. _____

What have you always wanted to do but been afraid to attempt?

1. _____
2. _____
3. _____

What sort of activities give you the greatest sense of fulfillment, satisfaction, and self-esteem?

1. _____
2. _____
3. _____

What one great thing would you dare to do if you knew you could not fail?

_____

_____

In addition, you need to decide what you really want to do with your business by examining a similar series of questions:

Vision—If your business was perfect sometime in the future, how would you describe it?

1. _____
2. _____
3. _____

Purpose—Why have you decided to get into this particular business?

1. _____
2. _____
3. _____

Mission Statement—Describe what kind of a company you plan to be in the future, based on serving and satisfying other people in some way. Start with the words "Our mission is to . . ."

_____

_____

What one action on planning for success are you going to take immediately as the result of what you have learned here?

_____

_____

□　□　□　□　□　□　□　□　□　□　□　□　□　□　□　□　□　□

STRATEGY

This is where you set out your company's competitive advantage and the strategy you are deploying to sustain and enhance it. We'll go into strategy and its definitions in more detail in Chapter 5, but for the time being, just begin by describing, in summary, how the company has maintained its competitiveness over time, including in response to any adverse circumstances.

If yours is a new venture, what is your strategy for creating a sustainable competitive advantage in the marketplace you are targeting?

RESOURCES

You will describe in detail the resources deployed by your company in Chapter 6 of your business plan. Here in the backgrounder, however, in just three or four paragraphs, you will distill the essence.

A timeline chart can be most useful to the reader, showing how resources have developed over time. Your backer may well skip the words in this section and focus just on the timeline chart, which should highlight neatly the main resource-impactful events in the company's history.

Resources covered in the timeline chart could include:

- Location and scale of the business infrastructure (e.g., headquarters, manufacturing facilities, distribution depots, IT centers)

- Notable landmarks (e.g., the hundredth employee hired, Latin American agent engaged, U.K. subsidiary launched, patents applied for or approved)

- Acquisitions of key people and/or companies

If you are starting a new venture, address the basics: Where will it be based? What space and physical assets will you require? How many employees are needed and what kind of systems, and who will manage the venture?

You should include one paragraph on the management team. Investors back people, not businesses. Your backers will want to know what credentials the people heading operations, sales and marketing, and finance possess. They also want to know your credentials, as managing director, and how any changes in management over time have impacted performance in the last few years.

If it is just you in the business at present, as a sole trader, what do you bring to the table in promoting this venture? Will you be contributing transferable experience and capabilities in addition to coming up with the business concept?

Finally, this is where you should add a sentence or two on how the ownership and governance of the business has evolved. A summary is fine for the time being; if ownership and governance are complex, they will be dealt with further in Chapter 6.

BASIC FINANCIALS

In the opening paragraph of Chapter 2 of your plan, you have already set out the turnover and operating margin of the business for the latest financial year.

Here is your chance to summarize recent financial history, showing the financial impact of key developments at the company or in its markets over time.

Again, at this stage aggregate numbers from the income statement, preferably just sales and operating margin, are the only level of detail needed. Balance sheet and cash flow data can be left for Chapter 7. One exception is if a significant item of capital expenditure has influenced performance in recent years, you should highlight it here.

If yours is a startup business, you will not have any sales history to explain. But you will surely have incurred some costs, probably self-financed, and this is a good place to summarize them—as well as specify how much time you and your partners have invested thus far.

Business Mix by Segment

What is your business mix? What products or services does your business offer and to which customer groups?

Which customers account for most in your business?

Backers don't like wasting precious time. They want to focus their thoughts on those chunks of your business that are most important. There is little point in them pondering the merits of a product you offer to a customer group that only contributes to one percent of your sales. They want to know about the 80 percent—as in Pareto's *80/20 principle*—which implies that 80 percent of value is created by 20 percent of a business.

> **TOP TIP:** *Focus on the segments most relevant to the backing decision. These are the ones that make the greatest contribution to your operating profit forecasts over the plan period. They are the segments that matter to your backer.*

Businesses seldom offer just one product (or service) to one customer group. Most businesses offer a number of distinct products to a number of distinct customer groups.

A product (or service) tends to be distinctive if the competition differs from one product to another. Some competitors may offer all your services; others may specialize in one or two of them. Others still may offer just the one product (or service) as a spin-off to a largely unrelated business.

A customer group is distinctive if the customers have unique characteristics and are typically reachable through distinct marketing routes. Thus customer groups can be defined by who they are (e.g., leisure or business visitors, young or old, well educated or uninformed), what sector they are in (especially for business-to-business ventures), where they are located (e.g., town or suburbs, region, country), or in other ways where different marketing approaches will be needed to reach them.

Each distinct product (or service) offered to a distinct customer group is a segment that's called, in rather ungainly business-speak, a "product/market segment" or, more simply, a business segment.

If your business offers two products to one customer group, you have two business segments. If you stick with the same two products but develop a new customer group, you'll have four segments. Introduce a third product and sell it to both customer groups and you have six segments.

How many products (or services) does your business offer? How many customer groups do you market to? Multiply the two numbers together and that's how many business segments you serve.

Now, which two, three, or four segments are the most important? Which contribute most to operating profit (or, more simply, sales, if each segment has a similar cost profile)? And will these same segments be the main contributors to operating profit over the next few years?

This is the information that you need to set out succinctly in Chapter 2 of your plan. Yet, in too many plans, this information is not provided. Sometimes, at this stage a plan will include a pie chart of sales by main product (or service) line, or even sales by region or country, but what is typically left out is:

- Sales by product/market segment—that is, sales of a specific product (or service) line to a specific customer group

- That same information over time—say, over the last three years

Let's take a simple example. Your company makes widgets (small, medium, and large), which you sell to three sectors (manufacturing, engineering, and construction) in each of two countries (USA and Canada). You operate in $3 \times 3 \times 2 = 18$ product/market segments.

By far your biggest segment is large widgets sold to U.S. engineering firms, which account for 40 percent of sales. Your next biggest segments are medium widgets for the U.S. engineering sector at 25 percent of sales and large widgets for Canadian manufacturing at 15 percent of sales. Together, these three segments account for 80 percent of sales. The remaining 15 segments account for just 20 percent of sales.

In nine out of ten business plans, what would be set out here would be a pie chart showing a breakdown of sales by widget size, alongside another pie chart showing sales by country. This is useful information and your backer will be thankful to see it.

But what would be *more* useful would be a pie chart showing the real product/market segmentation, as described previously. It would show one segment alone accounting for 40 percent of sales and another segment accounting for 25 percent of sales.

Your backers would recognize that throughout the business plan's 25 to 30 pages, they should be most attentive to the material on market demand, competition, and company strategy trends in one particular segment—large widgets sold to U.S. engineering. Not large widgets in general, not small widgets, not the U.S. market as a whole, not Canada, not North American engineering, not construction, but specifically large widgets going to the U.S. engineering sector.

Engineering customers will have different demand influences than construction customers. The United States may be at a different stage in the economic cycle relative to Canada. Canadian engineering companies may have historically different solutions favoring medium-size widgets over large widgets. Small widget producers may be more numerous and have more flexible, short-run production facilities than large widget producers.

For any or all of these reasons, your backer would benefit from knowing that one product/market segment, large widgets to U.S. engineering, matters most to your business.

And what of the future? Perhaps you are set to launch an extra-large widget tailored to the U.S. aerospace sector, which, if all goes to plan, could account for 20 percent of sales in three years' time.

So let's put a second pie chart alongside the first, showing forecast sales by main product/market segment in three years' time. Your backers will then know that as they read the rest of the plan, they will have to keep an eye open for the argument on why U.S. aerospace would benefit from extra-large widgets.

In summary, what we need in this business background section is a breakdown of what matters most in your business mix, now and in the near future. Which product/market segments will make or break your business?

The Blues: IBM and Business Mix

IBM bestrode the global computer industry in the 1980s. It was virtually a generic name for mainframes, minicomputers, and later, personal computers, much like Hoover is a recognizable name in vacuum cleaners.

Then in the early 1990s, the world caught up with Big Blue. Growth slowed; profits tumbled. Lou Gerstner, a marketer, not a technologist, was brought in to turn things around. "What happened to this company was not an act of God, some mysterious biblical plague sent down from on high," he exhorted his managers. "It's simple. People took our business away."

IBM had become too inward looking, too distant from customer needs, with too many silos. Gerstner transformed the culture—and the strategic direction. In 1990, IBM was essentially a hardware manufacturer; two-thirds of revenues came from hardware, with the remaining one-third split between software and services.

Ten years later, services and software accounted for three-fifths of IBM's revenues. Further rationalization followed—the personal computer business, along with the ThinkPad laptop, was sold to Lenovo, a Chinese producer. Today, services alone account for 55 percent of a $60 billion turnover.

Companies evolve. Business unit profitability changes over time, likewise segments within business units, so good managers redeploy resources accordingly. A small segment today could be a big business tomorrow. Think of Nokia and its cell phones, American Motors and its Jeep Cherokee pioneering the SUV boom, or more recently Apple and its iPad propelling the tablet computer concept. Or IBM and its Global Services division.

Know your business.

YOU MAY ALSO LIKE...

Your First Business Plan: A Simple...
   by Joseph Covello

Start Your Own Business
   by Entrepreneur Press

Business Plan In A Day: Get it done...
   by Rhonda Abrams

Successful Business Plan: Secrets &...
   by Rhonda Abrams

Anatomy of a Business Plan: The...
   by Linda Pinson

Return Policy

With a sales receipt or Barnes & Noble.com packing slip, a full refund in the original form of payment will be issued from any Barnes & Noble Booksellers store for returns of undamaged NOOKs, new and unread books, and unopened and undamaged music CDs, DVDs, and audio books made within 14 days of purchase from a Barnes & Noble Booksellers store or Barnes & Noble.com with the below

Policy on receipt may appear in two sections.

Returns or exchanges will not be permitted (i) after 14 days or without receipt or (ii) for product not carried by Barnes & Noble or Barnes & Noble.com.

...ive and only if defective. NOOKs purchased from other retailers or sellers are returnable only to the retailer or seller from which they are purchased, pursuant to such retailer's or seller's return policy. Magazines, newspapers, eBooks, digital downloads, and used books are not returnable or exchangeable. Defective NOOKs may be exchanged at the store in accordance with the applicable warranty.

Segmentation in a Startup

The need for segmentation applies likewise to a startup. If your plans are to launch just one product (or service) to one group of customers, fine; you won't need to segment any further. But are you sure you'll only have one product? And only one customer group?

Try categorizing your products and your customers. Is further segmentation meaningful? If so, use it. If not, don't waste time just for the sake of seeming serious. Stick to the one product for the one customer group (i.e., one business segment).

But there is one big difference. No matter how you segment, no matter how many customer groups you identify, they are all, at present, gleams in your eye.

Startups have no customers. Yet. And no matter how attractive the product or service sounds, without customers, it will be of no interest to your backer.

Your product must be couched in terms of its benefits to the customer. That is the *business proposition*. Not the way in which your product or service can do this or do that, at this price. But the way in which your product or service can benefit the target customer.

That is the language your backer wants to hear. Who is the target customer? How will the customer benefit from your offering?

And that is just in the one segment. Are there others?

Segmentation may lie at the very heart of your business proposition. It may allow you to unearth a niche where only your offering can yield the customer benefit. And you can then tailor your offering to address that very niche, that customer benefit.

Here is a slightly different way of looking at it. Does your offering address some marketplace need? Does it fill a gap in a target customer's needs? This is one of the secrets to a new venture's success highlighted by William Bridges in his book, *Creating You & Co*. He suggests that an "unmet need" could be uncovered by spotting any of a number of signs, such as a missing piece in a pattern, an unrecognized opportunity, an underused resource, a signal event, an unacknowledged change, a supposedly impossible situation, a nonexistent but needed service, a new or emerging problem, a bottleneck, or an interface.

However you define the customer benefit, whether in terms of unmet needs or in a way more meaningful to your particular offering, your backers will need evidence of its existence. They'll want as close as you can get to proof. They won't get it—no investment is risk-free. But they can reasonably expect you to undertake some basic research to dig up whatever evidence you can find of customer benefit. (We will return to this subject in the next chapter on market demand prospects.)

THE GORGE INN AND ORIENTAL SPA BUSINESS PLAN, 2014: THE BUSINESS

The job of drafting a business plan for The Gorge's Phase II development is delegated to co-owner Rick Jones. As a former management consultant, he should know his way around it. His wife, Kay, will act as reviewer and sense-checker.

Rick takes care with the opening paragraph, since he knows that it will also form the opening paragraph of the executive summary—which will be the last thing he writes in the plan. Happy with his opener (as reproduced at the start of this chapter), Rick moves on to the rest of the background section. Here is his chance to set out in a bit more detail how The Gorge got to where it is today:

◘ Goals and objectives. These have not changed much, he thinks. The overriding goal was and still is to offer visitors a distinctive, memorable, special stay in glorious surroundings, brushed with a hint of the Orient. The objectives were primarily occupancy related at the outset; now visitor return-rate objectives have been added.

◘ Strategy. The early strategy of maximizing occupancy rates at the expense of average room price has given way to demand-related pricing over the last 12 months, as occupancy has reached a healthy level, but it will need to be resumed after the Phase II extension is built and 16 further rooms have to be filled.

◘ Key dates on the resources timeline chart. Rick sets out on the timeline, with some nostalgia, dates such as the hiring of staff, going live with the new reservation system, the spa opening ceremony, first day at 100 percent occupancy, first major group booking (over ten rooms taken), and the day of the burst water pipe in Room 15.

◘ Financials. Rick explains why the major renovation work in 2009–10 turned out 17 percent over budget and how The Gorge's income statement improved steadily and gratifyingly after the tense opening months.

Then there's the business mix, the segmentation. Rick knows he must be careful here. His is a small, young business, and over-elaborate segmentation could be meaningless.

The Gorge operates in three product segments, with this current breakdown of revenues:

◘ Accommodation (64 percent)

- Catering (16 percent)
- Spa (20 percent)

Rick sees this as valid product segmentation—the business faces a different array of competitors in each segment. But market segmentation is not so straightforward. There are various ways of categorizing types of visitors—for example, by purpose (e.g., leisure, health, business), by duration (overnight vs. day), and possibly by nationality (in the last season, The Gorge attracted a large number of European visitors).

If Rick is to choose to segment visitors by purpose, he will then have three product segments times three market segments, or 3 × 3 = 9 product/market segments. If he opts for segmentation by duration or nationality, he will have six product/market segments.

Rick's reservation system gives him whatever data breakdown he needs for any of these visitor segmentation alternatives, but is there any point? wonders Rick. Around 75 percent of visitors come for purposes of leisure, 85 percent of revenues are from overnight visitors, and 90 percent are North American.

Segmentation by product/market segment would therefore seem an unnecessary level of detail for his business. Rick resolves to stick to a simple segmentation by product for the time being, giving The Gorge just the three segments.

Checklist on the Business

Introduce the bare essentials of your business to your backer. Set the scene, under five headings:

- The opener (the first paragraph of your executive summary repeated)
- Goals and objectives (which should be SMART)
- Strategy (your sustainable competitive advantage)
- Resources (with a helpful timeline on resource buildup)
- Basic financials (recent performance in sales and operating margin)

Set out your business mix, now and over the next few years. Disclose to your backers which products or services are selling to which customer groups, in other words which "product/market segments" will make or break your business plan.

3

MARKET DEMAND

The only function of economic forecasting is to make astrology look respectable.
—John Kenneth Galbraith

THE ANALYSIS of market demand must come right up front in your business plan, whether yours is a start-up or an established venture. It is the crux of the plan. Your products or services address a marketplace that's also served by other producers or service providers. That market must be of sufficient size, now and in the future, to support at least your business, not to mention your competitors.

If there aren't enough buyers of the type of products or services you offer, at the right price, you won't meet your plan.

Your backers want to know, before all else, who these buyers are, how much they are buying, how much they are paying, why they are buying, what has been influencing them, how those influences have been changing, and how much they are likely to buy in the future.

And they want to know all this for each of your main business segments.

If you can make the market demand chapter of your business plan convincing, you may have a backer. If not, you won't.

We have seen many business plans where the analysis of market demand is hedged, sidelined, or compressed into a couple of paragraphs and where the material is not really devoted to the market at all, but to the company's oh-so-stellar products, positioning, and sales.

Most of those plans were written for the sale of a company. Potential backers either walked away or made an offer at a marked-down price.

Your backers want the market demand situation laid out as it is, clearly and concisely. They want to know the scale and nature of the market as a whole. If prospects for demand growth are not great, whether they are flat or even mildly declining, tell it like it is. Don't try to obscure the reality.

If your backers have to find out for themselves that the reality differs from what is presented in your business plan, you will have no backers.

Of course, a backer would prefer to invest in a business that addresses a growing market. But fortunes have also been made through backing winners in a declining but consolidating market.

Let's be clear. This chapter considers demand not just for your product or service, but for all providers of products or services with whom you compete. It looks at overall demand in the marketplace.

Any market is made up of demand and supply. When demand and supply are in balance, that's good news for all concerned. When demand outstrips supply, that's good for the suppliers—though usually only for a while, until more supplies and/or more suppliers arrive.

When demand falls and supply exceeds demand, that's bad news for suppliers. You're one of those suppliers.

We are going to apply those fundamentals to the market for your product or services. We'll look at market supply in the next chapter, when addressing competition, but we'll start with market demand in this one. We'll attempt to forecast where market demand is headed over the next few years. Your backers will also want to know about the risks of things turning out worse than forecast. And, conversely, what the opportunities are of things turning out better.

Market Size and Marketcrafting

If your business is called Wal-Mart, you'll subscribe to a market research organization. You'll feed it data at the end of each appropriate period and receive results promptly on the overall size of the U.S. grocery market, its growth since the previous period, and whether your market share has gone up or down from around 25 percent.

And so it is with most large organizations. Yet many medium-size companies enjoy a similar relationship with a niche market research firm or industry association. Even a company with a turnover of just $10 million can sometimes receive good, regular, informative market data from an external, independent research firm serving that company and most of its competitors.

But for smaller companies, this data may be too expensive to acquire, may not be directly relevant, or may not exist.

Tough. You have to make an estimate. Your backer wants to know whether you are a big fish in a small pond, or vice versa. Suppose you are a mega-fish in a tiny pond, but one that can be protected from other waters. Your backers would like to hear that.

And they will want to know how that market size has changed over the last few years. So you'll have to construct a market estimate not only for today, but also for, say, three years ago.

It is not that difficult. There's a bottom-up process for market sizing termed *marketcrafting*. It was developed by coauthor Vaughan Evans and has been used frequently with entrepreneurs or managers of smaller businesses over the years. And, used with care, it works.

It is a doubly useful method, since it gives you the base data needed not just for market demand analysis (Chapter 2 of the business plan) but for industry supply, too (Chapter 3).

There are seven main steps in marketcrafting:

1. Select your main competitors—those you pitch against regularly, those you exhibit alongside at trade shows—and don't forget the foreign competitors, especially those from lower-cost countries.

2. Starting with competitor A, ask a series of questions: Do you think they are selling more or less than you into this market? If less, by how much less, very roughly? Are they selling half as much as you? Three-quarters? If they sell more than you, by how much more, roughly? Ten percent more? A third more? Is there any publicly available information that can guide your assessment? (Competitor A's sales to this market are unlikely to be available if it is a private company, but employment data can be indicative.) What do customers tell you? And suppliers?

3. Taking your current sales level as an index number of 100, assign the appropriate index number to competitor A. If you think they sell less than you in this market, but not that much less (say, 10 percent less), give them an index number of 90; if you think they sell a lot more than you, perhaps an extra half as much again, give them a 150.

4. Repeat steps 2 and 3 for each of the competitors named in step 1.

5. Make an allowance for any other competitors you have not named, for example, those who are small or only appear now and again. This should also be an index number. If you think all these other competitors together sell about half what you sell to the market, give this "Others" category an index number of 50.

6. Add up all the index numbers (including your own 100), divide the total by 100, and multiply by your level of sales—that is your preliminary estimate of market size.

7. Ask your sales director to complete the same exercise. Get her to talk to the guy on the sales team who used to work at competitor A and the woman in R&D whose former boyfriend now works at competitor B. Get their input. Then get input from your operations director and head of R&D. Wherever their views differ from yours, discuss and refine the numbers. You have now built a reasoned estimate of market size.

Marketcrafting is hardly an accurate process, nor can it be guaranteed that the final number will not be way off. But it is better than nothing, much better, because you can use the results to get indicative values of four parameters key to strategy and business planning:

1. *Market size* (highly approximate).

2. *Market share.* Once you "know" market size, you also know your market share (i.e., your sales level divided by estimated market size); you also have an estimate of the market share of each of your competitors.

3. *Market growth*. Repeat the seven-step marketcrafting approach to estimate your market size of three years ago. For example, did competitor A sell more or less than you to this market three years ago, before that new plant came into operation, and by how much? You now have two data points—market size of today and that of three years ago. Punch that data into your calculator and out will come an average compound growth rate over the three years, which serves as an estimate of recent market growth.

4. *Market share change*. Best of all, since you now know your market share three years ago and today, you also have an estimate of your market share gain (or loss), as well as the gain/loss for each of your competitors. These estimates will be most useful in assessing both competitive intensity (next chapter) and competitive position (Chapter 5).

Table 3–1 is an example of the findings that can be deduced from the marketcrafting process, adapted from an engineering company one of the authors worked with recently.

TABLE 3–1. Marketcrafting: An example.

Competitor	Estimated Index Number for Sales (Latest Year)	Implied Market Share (%)
The Company	= 100	17%
Competitor A	120	21%
Competitor B	85	15%
Competitor Group C	125	21%
Competitor Group D	65	11%
Competitor E	30	5%
Competitor F	20	3%
Others	40	7%
Total	**585**	**100%**

The company's turnover in this segment was about $30 million, so the market size could be estimated at 585/100 × 30, or around $175 million. The company's market share emerged at 17 percent (100/585), rather lower than the 25 percent that management had quoted before the marketcrafting exercise.

Likewise, the market share of the Far Eastern competitors (group C), though significant at 21 percent, did not seem to be as high as the one-third quoted rather sensationally in the trade press.

When we repeated the exercise to estimate market size of three years earlier, we found that the market had contracted heavily during the post-credit-crunch recession, falling by one-third, or roughly 10 percent per year. Meanwhile, Far Eastern competitors had grown share greatly from 9 percent to 21 percent, with corresponding share losses by the domestic players, including that of the company, from 20 percent to 17 percent.

These were important findings. The trends were of course known beforehand, but their quantification through the marketcrafting process, though very rough, put some of the wilder assertions into perspective and helped focus attention on the strategic challenge ahead.

Market Growth

This is the big question. Is demand in each of your main business segments going to grow? Will it be bigger in a few years' time, or smaller, or more or less the same?

It's not the only question, of course. Equally important, as we'll see in the next couple of chapters, is the nature of the competition you are going to face and how you are positioned to compete. And it's all a question of odds. You have a better chance of prospering in a market that's growing than one that's shrinking.

As they say in the world of business, "It's better to be in a market with the wind behind you than in your face."

So how do you find out where market demand is headed? Weave your web . . .

THE WEB OF INFORMATION

In the old days, when advising clients on market trends, you used to have to call up trade associations, write to companies active in the market asking for their annual reports, and visit reference libraries to wade through reams of trade magazines, journals, and so forth.

Or you might have to purchase an expensive market research report—one often only of tangential relevance to the market segment you were researching.

Now it's a breeze. All you have to do is switch on your laptop, click on your Internet connection, pop into Google or Yahoo, and type in the name of your market, alongside such words as *market*, *growth*, *forecasts*, and *trends*.

You'll find that Google comes up with hundreds—maybe thousands—of websites to visit. Most of them will be irrelevant. One, two, or more of them will be spot-on, though. You'll begrudge having to waste time trawling through dozens of useless sites—but, hey, think of the hours and hours of effort you are saving compared with the old days. You just need some patience and perseverance to systematically wade through the referred sites. Open up a Word file, and whenever you come across an article on a website that seems useful, copy it and drop it into your document.

You're weaving your own web of information on your market.

You may find that your search directs you to reports produced by specialist market research companies. These sources should be used as a last resort. Some can be quite good, reflecting the direct access they may have had to market participants and observers, but too many turn out bland. And expensive. Better to do your own digging around on the web first.

Try the national or regional news sites, many of which you can access with ease, without having to register or subscribe. You can also find out much about other companies working in your market by tapping into their own websites. Smaller companies tend to use their websites just as product or service showcases, but some may provide snippets of information on where the market is heading, such as a press release summarizing a recent speech by the CEO to a trade conference. Publicly quoted companies will attach their annual reports, in which you'll find the views of the chairman or CEO on market trends.

Another good source of market information is online trade magazines. Typically they will have at least some sections open to the public without having to take out an expensive subscription. If you work in the automotive industry, for example, you could look up www.automotivenews.com. If you are in the wine business—lucky you—how about www.wine-spirit.com? Whatever sector you work in, there is sure to be an online trade magazine.

Stalling: Movie Theaters and Market Demand

In the mid-1940s, the average American went to the movies two or three times a month. The 1940s spectacular *Gone with the Wind* sold 60 million tickets in the United States, equivalent to half of the population at the time. Now Americans go to the movies four times—a year!

In the old days, Americans spent a whopping $0.23 of their total recreational dollar on the movies. These days it is just two cents.

Who would want to be a theater owner in such a declining market? Well, many do. There are roughly 6,000 sites with 40,000 screens covering the length and breadth of the USA. Four theater chains account for more than half of the screens, but there are a hundred or more operators of multiple sites, ranging from just two or three to many hundreds of theaters, and hundreds more operators of single sites.

The industry survives and the explanation is clear: The decline in theater attendance was precipitous but rapid. By the mid-1960s, the catastrophic, game-changing impact of television on the movie industry had worked its way through the system and admissions had begun to stabilize—and then recover.

Theater admissions in the United States and Canada grew from 1.06 billion in 1985 to 1.64 billion by 2002, an average growth rate of 2.6 percent per year. Positive demand drivers, such as population growth (1.1 percent a year in that period), income growth, more multiplex theaters, and more comfortable environments, outweighed negative drivers, such as the advent of the videocassette recorder and video rentals, which themselves were to be displaced by DVDs, further enhancing the audiovisual experience in the living room of the potential theater customer.

It was a good time to be a movie theater operator. The wind was at your back. But things were to change again. New technology-driven demand drivers entered the equation—the Internet, computer games, large flat-screen televisions, and home theater systems. Theater admissions began to contract, with operators becoming ever more reliant on blockbusters featuring Frodo Baggins, Harry Potter, or a Marvel Comics character to make up their numbers. Despite yet another new positive demand driver, 3-D movies, theater admissions fell, on average, 2.7 percent a year to 1.28 billion in 2011.

And what of the future? Movie theaters are clearly something of a roller-coaster industry. Can they rise again? It will be tough. Filmmakers will have to fight to keep quality on a par with television drama series like *Homeland*, where the 12-episodes-per-series format allows for greater development of quirky characters, twists of plot, and viewer empathy than a 100-minute movie.

And theater operators now face heavy competition from video on demand and catch-up TV, where viewers can accumulate such a backlog of must-watch television programs that they can never find the time to view them all—let alone go to the movies.

And, of perhaps greatest concern, there is competition from Internet-streaming providers such as Netflix, coming perilously close to the holy grail of ultimate video on demand—one provider, any show, anytime, on any device, high-definition.

It is a fast-changing industry. Movie theaters have been around for a long time. They will have to continue to duck and dive just to survive. But one thing is for sure—they will not go with the wind.

THE HOOF APPROACH TO DEMAND FORECASTING

Many years ago, coauthor Vaughan Evans developed a four-step process for translating market demand trends and drivers into forecasts. It's called the HOOF approach. (This name was chosen because HDDF, the strict representation of the first letters in each of the four steps, would be an unattractive, unmemorable acronym. With appropriate creative license, however, the circular O was borrowed as a look-alike to the semicircular D!)

There are four distinct steps in the HOOF approach to demand forecasting. Get this process right and all falls logically into place. Fall out of step, and you may end up with a misleading answer. You need to apply these four steps for each of your main business segments:

1. *Historic growth.* Assess how market demand has grown in the past.

2. *Drivers past.* Identify what drove past growth.

3. *Drivers future.* Assess whether there will be any change in influence of these and other drivers in the future.

4. *Forecast growth.* Project market demand growth, based on the influence of future drivers.

Let's look at each of these steps briefly, then at some examples.

HISTORIC GROWTH. To start, get some facts and figures. It's surprising how the most straightforward of searches can reveal recent growth rates in the markets you're looking for. But be careful not to fall into the trap of relying on one recent number. Just because demand for a service jumped by, say, 8 percent last year doesn't mean that growth has trended 8 percent every year in that market. The latest year may have been an aberration. The previous year might have seen a dip in the market, followed by the 8 percent recovery.

You should try to get an average annual growth rate over a number of recent years, preferably at least the last three or four. As long as there haven't been serious ups and downs each year (and there may well have been in your business in the difficult period 2008–12), you can usually get a usable approximation of average annual growth by calculating the overall percentage change in, say, the last four years and then annualizing it. If there have been ups and downs, you should smooth them out with three-year moving averages before calculating the percentage change.

If yours is such a niche market that there is little or no data to be found, that can't be helped. Yet even then, useful information can still be uncovered. You just need to find out whether the market has been growing fast, growing slowly, holding flat, declining slowly, or declining fast. We can define growing slowly to mean moving along at the same pace as the economy as a whole (gross domestic product, in economics-speak), which is roughly 2 percent to 2.5 percent each a year in the long run in the United States and most other large Western economies. That's in "real" terms—in other words, in terms of tangible, wealth-creating growth. On top of that sits inflation, typically around the same 2 percent to 2.5 percent a year these days, although it has been much higher in the past. Slow growth in terms of "money of the day," or in "nominal" terms, can therefore be defined as roughly 5 percent a year in the long run. Actual data on GDP growth can be extracted from government statistics, if that is helpful.

DRIVERS PAST. Once you have uncovered some information on recent market demand growth, you need to find out what has been influencing that trend. Typical factors that influence demand in many markets are:

- Per capita income growth
- Population growth in general

- Population growth specific to a market (e.g., of pensioners or baby boomers, or general population growth in a particular area)

- Some aspect of government policy

- Changing awareness (perhaps from high levels of promotion by competing providers)

- Business structural shifts (such as toward outsourcing)

- Price changes

- Fashion (even a craze)

- Weather (seasonal variations, but maybe even the longer-term effects of climate change)

Not all of these drivers will be relevant for all your business segments. You need to pick those that are the most important. There may also be factors that are purely specific to your market. Industry trends and fads in particular can have a huge effect on some markets.

DRIVERS FUTURE. Now you need to assess how each of these drivers is going to develop over the next few years. Are things going to carry on more or less as before for a particular driver? Or are things going to change significantly for that driver?

For instance, will immigration continue to drive local population growth? Is the government likely to hike up a local tax? Could this market become less fashionable?

Will a new driver come into play, one that had no impact in the past, but could well influence demand in the future?

The most important driver is, of course, the economic cycle. If it seems the economy is poised for a nosedive, that could have a serious impact on demand in your business over the next year or two—assuming your business is relatively sensitive (or "elastic," in economics-speak) to the economic cycle. Or maybe your business is relatively inelastic, like, for example, the food industry? When composing your business plan, you need to think carefully about the timing of the economic cycle and the elasticity of your business.

FORECAST GROWTH. This is the fun bit. You've assembled all the information on past and future trends and drivers. Now you weave it all together, sprinkle it with a large dose of judgment, and you have a forecast of market demand—not without risk, not without uncertainty, but a systematically derived forecast nevertheless.

Let's take a simple example of a business that offers a relatively new service to the elderly.

Step 1. You find that the market has been growing at a rate of 5 percent to 10 percent per year over the last few years.

Step 2. You identify the main drivers as a) per capita income growth, b) growth in the elderly population, and c) growing awareness of the service by elderly people.

Step 3. You believe income growth will continue as before, the elderly population will grow even faster in the future, and that awareness can only get more widespread.

Step 4. You conclude that growth in your market will accelerate and could reach more than 10 percent per year over the next few years.

You may find that the HOOF approach works best using a simple chart (see Table 3–2), where the balance of demand drivers and their changing influence on future demand for this service to the elderly is clearly illustrated.

TABLE 3–2. The HOOF approach to demand forecasting: An example.

Demand Drivers for a New Service to the Elderly	Impact on Demand Growth			Comments
	Recent Past	Now	Next Few Years	
Growth in incomes	-	o	+	• U.S. to resume economic growth in 2012-13, assuming no double-dip
Growth in elderly population	+	+	++	• Proportion of U.S. population aged 65+ forecast to grow from 13% to 18.5% by 2025 (U.S. Census Bureau)
Increased awareness of service	++	++	+++	• Newspaper coverage, national and local, greater all the time
Overall Impact	+	+	++	
Market Growth Rate	5 % to 10%/yr	5% to 10%	Over 10%/yr	

H   O   O   F

Key to Driver Impact
+++ Very strong positive
++ Strong positive
+ Some positive
o None
- Some negative
-- Strong negative
--- Very strong negative

And now let's have an example of how not to do forecast growth. Many years ago, one of the authors was doing some work with a crane manufacturer in New England and came across a draft business plan. In the section on market demand, the plan stated that there was no data on U.S. demand for cranes to be found anywhere. So, for the purposes of the financial forecasts, real growth in the crane market was assessed to be the same as for U.S. engineering output as a whole, forecast by the Organization for Economic Co-operation and Development (OECD) at 2.4 percent a year.

Oops! The mistake here was one of exclusion. Yes, macroeconomic demand was an important driver of demand in the crane market. But there were three or four other drivers of equal importance for which there was, admittedly, no hard and fast data but plenty of anecdotal evidence. They included evidence of destocking, a thriving secondhand market, and, above all, an imminent downturn in high-rise construction activity.

None of these drivers bore any relation to engineering output as a whole, and their combined impact served to translate the business plan's 2.4 percent a year crane market growth forecast into one of steep decline, possibly at 10 percent a year for two or three years.

The moral of the tale is to make sure all drivers are taken into account, irrespective of whether you can find any hard data on them. Use your judgment.

> **TOP TIP:** *The demand forecasting process is simple and rational. How did demand grow in the past? What influenced that growth? Will those influences change? So how will demand grow in the future? Get this process right and you leap over the first hurdle in gaining credibility with your backers.*

App-reciation: Mobile Apps and Market Demand

In the mid-2000s the word *app* was known only to techies. To laypeople, it was as likely to refer to an apprenticeship or appendix as an application. Today, thanks to its extension from web apps to mobile apps, the word is ubiquitous—describing a market worth $25 billion.

The mobile app market has been an electronic gold rush. Not only have big companies piled into the rush, but so too have thousands of little guys. Some of them, like Instagram, have become big and done so fast. But, as in any gold rush, most have foundered and seen little return on their endeavors.

Created by Apple, followed aggressively by Google, and courted by Microsoft, BlackBerry, and Amazon in the United States, the mobile app came from nowhere and originally focused on basic business needs, like e-mail, stock reports, and weather. Piggybacking on smartphones, more bandwidth-intensive apps, such as games and global satellite positioning, are now common.

Market growth has been exponential and remains rapid—more than 60 percent in 2013. But, as in any product life cycle, the app market will surely follow the standard growth path, from the embryonic and growth stages into those of maturity and decline. The trick for the forecaster is to know when and how fast growth will tail off.

Main demand drivers include smartphone penetration; real personal disposable income growth; the number of app stores; the number of app developers; the emergence of high-profile, successful apps; extension to tablets, laptops, and televisions; the relative cost of app maintenance to app development; consumer acceptance of revenue-raising methods, such as advertising, premium service, and packaging with other services; unit advertising costs; and promotional spend on apps. As the relative impact and weight of these drivers change, so too will the market growth rates.

There is plenty of growth yet to come, but it won't be quite as app-oplectic as in the past.

TOP TIP: *If yours is a startup plan, test the market. Pick up the phone or get out and talk to people. Do some primary market research. Amass, digest, and analyze pertinent data. Be armed for the inevitable grilling from your backer.*

Market Demand for a Startup

This chapter of your plan may well be the most difficult of all to write for a startup. Yours may be a new product or service designed to convey a customer benefit not previously realizable. In which case, how do you define the market? What is market demand for a product that has not previously existed? What is its size? What are its growth prospects?

On the other hand, your startup may be in a market that's already well defined—such as The Gorge Inn and Oriental Spa, which will be unique and distinctive, but fits snugly into an already-buoyant market for three- and four-star tourism in the Pacific Northwest.

Or you may be opening a boutique selling designer children's wear on Main Street. Fine. Again, that is a definable, existing market and can be researched in the same way as set out previously.

But what if yours is indeed something that has not existed before? How can you convince your backers that there will be buyers for your product or service, and at that price? You need evidence.

You'll have to do some test marketing. If yours is a business-to-business proposition, get on the phone and set up meetings with prospective corporate buyers. Explain the benefits of your product and why, at that price, they have a bargain.

Keep a record of these meetings and analyze the findings. Write a report, drawing out key conclusions from the discussions, with each point supported by bulleted evidence—whether comments from named customers, comments from third parties quoted in the press, or data that you dug up while doing your web research. Collate your findings into a short and sharp market research report, which will become an appendix of your business plan. It will be the first appendix because it will be the single most important item of evidence your backer will look for.

If yours is a business-to-consumer product or service, test it downtown. Get out your clipboard, stand in a mall or outside a supermarket, and talk to people. If you are offering a product, show them. If a service, explain swiftly but lucidly its benefits.

Again, collate the responses, analyze them, draw firm conclusions, support them with quotes and data, and stick the market research report in an appendix.

Now, based on those responses, make an estimate of your potential market size. Imagine there were many suppliers of your product or service and that the whole country is aware of its existence; what would the market size be? How does that compare with the market size for products or services not a million miles different from what you'll be offering? Does your estimate make sense?

And how about market demand growth? If your startup is serving an existing market, then you can use the same HOOF approach to demand forecasting that an established business would use.

If your startup is for a new market, the HOOF approach will not be the prime consideration of your backers. They will be concerned with the existence of such a market in the first place. Any growth on top of discovering and serving a new market will be icing on the cake.

◻ ◻ ◻ ◻ ◻ **THINKING OUT OF THE BOX** ◻ ◻ ◻ ◻ ◻

Identifying Your Target Customer

Most successful men have not achieved their distinction by having some new talent or opportunity presented to them. They have developed the opportunity that was at hand.
—*Bruce Barton*

The customer is the most important person in a free market economy. It is not what businesses produce or sell, but only what customers will buy that determines all economic activity.

The entrepreneurial business is intensely focused on the prospective customer. The ability to find a customer, sell your product or service to that customer, and satisfy that customer so that he buys from you again is the central focus of all entrepreneurial activity.

The greater clarity you have with regard to your ideal customer, the more focused and effective your marketing efforts will be.

Everyone is in the business of customer satisfaction in some way. The most important activity of entrepreneurs is to clearly identify the very best customers for their product or service, and then to focus all marketing, advertising, and sales efforts on this particular type of customer.

There are many ways in which to determine your target customer:

Define your product or service from the customer's point of view.

a. What does your product do for your ideal customer?

b. What benefits does your customer receive from using your product?

c. What problems does your product solve for your customer?

d. What needs of your customer does your product satisfy?

e. How does your product improve your customer's life or work?

Define the ideal customer for what you sell.

a. What is the customer's age?

b. What is the customer's education level?

c. What is the customer's occupation or business?

d. What is the customer's income or financial situation?

e. What is the customer's situation today, in life or work?

Determine what your customer must be convinced of in order to buy your product or service.

a. What are the specific benefits your customer is seeking in buying your product?

b. Of all the benefits you offer, which are the most important to your ideal customer?

c. What are the most pressing needs that your product or service satisfies?

d. What is your value offering? Define it in five to ten words.

e. Why should your customer buy from you rather than from someone else?

Determine the location of your ideal customer.

a. Where is your customer located geographically?

b. Where does your customer live or work?

c. Where does your customer buy your product or service?

d. Where is your customer located in a business or organization?

Determine exactly when your ideal customer buys your product or service.

a. What has to happen in the life or work of your customers for them to buy your product?

b. What time of year, season, month, or week do your customers buy?

c. What change in your customers' lives would cause them to buy?

Determine your customer's buying strategy.

a. How does your customer buy your product or service?

b. How has your customer bought similar products or services in the past?

c. How does your customer go about making a buying decision for your product?

Imagine placing an ad in the newspaper for your perfect customer.

a. How would you describe your perfect customer?

b. What prospective customers are the most likely to buy your product or service immediately?

c. What are the most important qualities that your ideal customer would have?

Define and determine the very best customer for your product or service.

    a. How could you find more of these perfect customers for your product?

    b. How could you create new customers for your product?

    c. What is your "unique selling proposition"? Define it and communicate this key benefit in every customer contact.

Most entrepreneurs are not clear about their ideal customer. For this reason, they waste a lot of time and money trying to sell their products to people who are not good potential customers. Your ability to clearly define and then focus in on the customers who can most rapidly buy your product or service can be essential to your business success.

Now, what one action are you going to take immediately on identifying your target customer as the result of what you have learned here?

□ □ □ □ □ □ □ □ □ □ □ □ □ □ □ □ □ □ □

Market Demand Risks and Opportunities

You have now come to a reasonable forecast of what's likely to happen to market demand in your key business segments over the next few years. But your backer needs to know a little more than that. You've assessed what's most likely to happen. But what are the risks of something happening that could make market demand worse than what you are forecasting? What could happen to make things much worse? How likely are these risks to happen?

On the other hand, what could make market demand better than you have forecast? What could make things much better? How likely are these opportunities to happen?

Your backers are going to be very interested in these risks and opportunities. They are going to use your market demand forecasts to help them assess whether your financial forecasts (presented in Chapter 7 of the business plan) are reasonable. Then they'll look at all the risks and opportunities around those forecasts in Chapter 8. And market demand issues will be the first set to be factored in.

Identify the main risks (a half dozen of them) that might affect your market demand forecasts, and then assess them from two perspectives:

   □ How likely are they to take place? Do these risks have a low, medium, or high likelihood?

◘ If they do occur, how big an impact will they have? Would the risks have a low, medium, or large impact?

Now, do the same assessment for the opportunities you identified.

Are any of these risks or opportunities "big" issues? We'll define a "big" risk or opportunity as one where:

◘ Likelihood of occurrence is medium (or high) *and* impact is high.

◘ Likelihood of occurrence is high *and* impact is medium (or high).

Any big issues of market demand need to be set out clearly in your business plan. If it is a big risk, you must explain how you are going to address it and mitigate its impact. If it is a big opportunity, you must elucidate on how you are going to exploit it.

THE GORGE INN AND ORIENTAL SPA BUSINESS PLAN, 2014: MARKET DEMAND

As a former management consultant, Rick Jones knows his first port of call for data on trends in tourism. At the U.S. Travel Association website, he finds some encouraging travel forecasts, dated November 2012:

◘ Following the 9.4 percent slump in U.S. travel expenditure in 2009 and the 2010–12 recovery of 6.8 percent a year, further growth is forecast to 2016 at an average 4.6 percent a year.

◘ International visitors are forecast to increase their share of travel expenditure from 14.6 percent in 2012 to 16.1 percent by 2016.

◘ Domestic person trips, which were more resilient in the recession, dropping by just 3.3 percent in 2009, are forecast to grow at 1.5 percent a year to 2016.

Rick knows that these numbers tell him little of the market for tourism in Oregon, let alone in the Columbia River Gorge. But they do paint a backdrop. And an overall market with unexciting but positive growth will be an initial source of comfort to an investor.

Rick moves on to more regionally relevant research and finds much of interest at www.traveloregon.com, the website of the Oregon Tourism Commission. Most encouragingly, he unearths a biennial Oregon Visitor Study, conducted by Longwoods Travel USA in 2011 and published in March 2013. He finds these statistics:

- Oregon had 28.8 million overnight trips in 2011, a 2 percent share of the U.S. market, plus 44.2 million day trips.

- The number of overnight trips in Oregon was up 4.7 percent from the previous survey in 2009, reflecting average annual growth of 2.3 percent. Longer term, the number was well up on the 19.1 million of overnight trips in 2004, indicating average annual growth over the six years of 7.1 percent.

- Nearly half (48 percent) of these overnight trips were "marketable" (62 percent for day trips), with the balance being business trips or stays with friends or relatives.

- Average spend per person per trip (overnight) was $167 (business visitors $213, leisure visitors $163).

- Of that total spend, $62 was spent on lodging and $40 on restaurants.

- Average length of stay per trip was 3.8 nights, down from the 5.1 nights in 2004 but higher than the U.S. norm of 3.5 nights … of which 2.9 nights were spent in Oregon.

Rick is delighted with this information and embarks straightaway on his write-up of Appendix A on market demand. Just when he is finishing and checking a source, he unearths another report done by the same researchers at the same time—only it's not for Oregon as a whole but for the specific area of Mt. Hood and the Columbia River Gorge! He enthusiastically tweaks his appendix to include these gems:

- 2.5 million overnight trips (9 percent of the Oregon total) included time spent in the Mt. Hood and Gorge area ("the area").

- 50 percent or 1.25 million were "marketable."

- Average spend per marketable trip in the area was $112, of which $45 was spent on lodging; $28 on restaurants (giving a lodging/restaurant spend ratio of 8:5); $13 on retail purchases; $16 on transport at destination; and $10 on recreation, sightseeing, and entertainment, of which an unspecified share would have been on spa services.

- Average length of stay per trip was 4.4 nights, above the state average . . . of which 2.2 nights were spent in the area.

- The main purpose of overnight marketable trips was outdoors (39 percent), followed by touring, special events, and resorts, with 44 percent of visitors originating from Oregon (38 percent from Portland alone), 20 percent from Washington, and 8 percent from California.

- 75 percent of visitors came in their own cars or trucks and 14 percent in a rented car.

- 54 percent stayed in a hotel or motel, 10 percent in a resort hotel, and 12 percent in a country inn or B&B; 24 percent stayed in a campsite or trailer park.

- For activities, 41 percent visited a national or state park, 32 percent a landmark or historical site, 25 percent went shopping, 28 percent went to the "beach or waterfront" (presumably including the river or falls!), 39 percent went hiking, and 24 percent enjoyed fine dining.

- Just 2 percent visited a spa, well below the 5 percent for Oregon as a whole (and the national average).

- The modal income groups were $25K to $50K (25 percent) and $50K to $75K (24 percent), followed, curiously, by $100K to $150K (18 percent)—visitors from this group presumably headed for the luxury resorts—then the under-$25K income category (12 percent).

- Visitors were mainly married (or with a partner), college graduates, and white (91 percent).

There's plenty of information here to assess market size and trend growth, Rick thinks, but then he remembers that Oregon has a state lodging tax—payable at one percent on room revenues alone for all "dwelling units that provide temporary accommodation" for at least 30 days in a year. If he can get data on tax paid, he reasons that should give him the market for room revenues for each time period. True enough, and Rick discovers a comprehensive report by the Oregon Department of Revenue that gives him room revenues by quarter and area (and even county) from 2004 to 2011. Table 3–3 represents Rick's eureka moment.

TABLE 3–3. Oregon taxable lodging sales, 2006–11.

	2006	2007	2008	2009	2010	2011	Growth (%/year)
Providers	2482	2590	2663	2670	2697	2664	1.4%
Sales ($m)	1118	1221	1227	1098	1158	1207	1.5%
Change (%)	18.2%	9.2%	0.5%	10.5%	5.5%	4.2%	n/a
Providers	104	119	128	129	133*	136	5.5%
Sales ($m)	38.6	43.1	44.8	41.9	44.9	47.5	4.2%
Change (%)	21.8%	11.7%	3.7%	-6.5%	7.2%	5.8%	n/a*

* The 133rd lodging provider may well have been the just opened The Gorge Inn!

Rick has found so much useful information on the characteristics of market demand that his problem now becomes keeping his appendix to a manageable three or four pages!

Now all he needs is more data on spa tourism, but that is hard to find. One problem lies in the definition of a spa—which can range from a facility offering a sauna adjacent to a fitness suite to the full works of multiple pools and treatment rooms. There are some research reports available on the national market, but Rick is not convinced that the steep expense will be worth it.

Rick is ready for his Chapter 3 conclusions:

- The addressed travel market in the Mt. Hood and Gorge area can be taken as $52 million for lodging (the $47.5 million of 2011, grown at 4.2 percent a year) plus $33 million on restaurants (using the 8:5 ratio from the Longwoods visitor survey) plus, say, $1 million on spa services, to total $86 million in 2013.

- Trend market growth seems to lie at around 4 percent/year—an estimate that's reinforced by recorded Oregon overnight visitor growth from 2009–11 of 2.3 percent a year and the U.S. Travel Association forecast of national travel expenditure growth, 2012–16, of 4.6 percent a year.

- Rick's addressed market in 2017 can therefore be forecast at $101 million.

- Main long-term drivers have been per capita income growth; the growing propensity of Americans to take multiple short breaks; the steadily improving range of visitor facilities and attractions in the area, as exemplified by investment in scenic road and off-road cycling routes; and the targeted marketing carried out jointly by Travel Oregon and industry players.

- The main short-term driver was the 2009 recession induced by the financial crisis, from which U.S. travel as a whole managed to recover strongly in 2010–12 at 6.8 percent a year.

- Larger and higher-star-rated hotels can be expected to fare better than the average during the economic recovery as visitors reverse their trading down behavior.

- Hotels offering special premium facilities such as spas should likewise fare well.

- The main risk facing Oregon hoteliers is a double-dip recession, which could be sufficiently severe to contract the travel market, as in 2009, but Rick deems this risk to be of low likelihood.

Given how market demand for travel, at national, regional, and local levels, has shown such resilience during four very difficult years for the U.S. economy, Rick feels a backer will not have too many concerns over this chapter. But what of The Gorge's competition for this potential hundred-million-dollar market? That's for the next chapter . . .

Checklist on Market Demand

Set out for each of your main business segments, succinctly but convincingly, your assessments of the following:

- *Market size.* Find a source or perhaps craft it yourself.

- *Market demand forecasts.* Use the HOOF approach.

- *Historic demand growth.* Again, find a source or craft it yourself.

- *Demand drivers past.* What has shaped growth in the past?

- *Demand drivers future.* What is likely to shape growth in the future?

- *Forecast demand.* The forecast is the logical output of "hoofing" it.

- *Market demand risks and opportunities.* Describe what can go wrong or right.

Your market demand assessment should be limited to three to four pages. Supporting data—for example, tables showing market size by segment for each of the last three years and/or composition or trend data on key drivers—should be saved and loaded into an appendix of your business plan.

If your business is a startup in a new market niche, you will concentrate on the rationale for the very existence of that niche. The market research you have conducted to underpin that rationale will be a vital appendix.

COMPETITION

Competition's a bitch—but that's what gives us puppies.   —Unattributed

IT'S A SHAME about competition. If your business were the only provider of your product or service, customers would be queuing round the block and you could charge them what you like, within reason.

But life isn't like that. There is always competition. And the more successful your business, the more likely it is that competitors will be eyeing your niche.

So why is competition frequently dismissed, almost as an irrelevance, in so many business plans? In eight out of ten plans seen by the authors, the analysis has been unconvincing. In half of those cases, the analysis has been so cursory, so derisory, so contemptuous of the reader as to be misleading.

Why are managers and/or entrepreneurs so blindfolded in setting out their plans? Do they really believe that prospective backers will believe them when competitors are ignored or brushed aside?

And think of what happens if your backer, undertaking the most simple of due diligence tasks, picks up the phone and speaks to a customer who tells her that, sure, your firm is good, but such and such a competitor provides as good a product at a more competitive price? Hang on! Could this be the very same competitor that was dismissed in the business plan as producing poorly specified, unreliable product at ridiculously discounted pricing—and few sane customers would take on the risk of buying their product?

Your backers will walk away. End of story. If they lose faith in your perceived commercial awareness, you will have no backers.

Tell it like it is. And at some length. Don't make the section on competition just one or two paragraphs squirreled away in a chapter on your firm's strategy. Give it respect. Make it a separate chapter. Face up to it. You know you're going to have to face the competition head-on. Let your backers know how you plan to do it.

> **TOP TIP:** *Respect the competition. Give competitors the space they merit in your plan. Dismiss them and your backer may dismiss you.*

Your Competitors

With whom do you compete? A straightforward question, but not necessarily one with a straightforward answer.

There can be two areas of complexity in identifying your competitors: variation by segment and indirect competition.

You should expect competition to differ in some of your main business segments. If you recall the analysis you performed in Chapter 2 of the business plan, the "product" part of a product/market segment is itself typically defined by a product, or group of products, having a distinct set of competitors.

Think of Wal-Mart and its lineup of competitors. In clothing it takes on the likes of Kohl's, which sells no food. In CDs and DVDs it used to compete against chains such as Tower Records, Circuit City, and Virgin Megastore, but they have fallen by the wayside. In food, Wal-Mart competes not just with Kmart and Kroger, but with the local grocer, butcher, and fishmonger. In ready-cooked food, Wal-Mart competes with local restaurants.

Then there is indirect competition. These are competitors not directly in your space but infringing on your space by offering an alternative solution to the customer. They are competing for your customer's money. You could argue that the local grocer is an indirect competitor of Wal-Mart since he offers a different service that's more personal, hands-on, quality assured, returns-friendly, neighborly, open all hours, with home delivery—though the latter two services are these days offered by supermarket chains, too. An example of a truly indirect competitor would be iTunes, whose download solution for music reduces demand for CDs sold by Wal-Mart and its competitors.

Now you need to find out all you can about your competitors. You should prepare summary profiles of them for an appendix to your plan, to be summarized here in Chapter 4. These competitor profiles should include:

◘ Sales data—preferably sales by main segment. If the only data you can find are group sales or divisional sales encompassing a number of segments, only some of which you address, make a record of those actual sales but also attempt to estimate sales in each key segment, because you're going to need those estimates for your market share calculations.

◘ Sales growth over the last three years.

◘ Operating and/or net profit margin—if available (which is unlikely if your competitor is a private company).

◘ Ownership—and an assessment of financial depth and backing.

◘ Segments addressed (now and future plans), new products in the pipeline, and new markets/customer groups being targeted.

◘ Location of facilities and sales/service teams.

◘ Physical assets deployed (e.g., numbers and type of machinery).

◘ Strategy—including main focus, recent investments, and growth plans. This information can be derived from, for example, press or trade show clippings, or even customer anecdotes.

◘ Positioning in market—such as the competitor's unique sales pitch and pricing policy.

Only key extracts and conclusions from this appendix analysis should go into Chapter 4 of your plan. Which competitors play in which segments? What's their market share? How have they been performing? Have they been gaining or losing share? Why? What are they up to? What new products or new markets are they planning?

And let's have a couple of pie charts in this chapter. Show us each main competitor's pie slice of market share in your main business segments. If illuminating, include a chart comparing today's positions to market shares of, say, three years ago. If you've been the one who has gained share in this period, this is a must!

This is all background stuff. Important, necessary, but perhaps not very interesting. Much more interesting to your backers, and left out entirely in the vast majority of business plans, is a discussion of competitive intensity and how it has been evolving.

Who Said Mature? Groceries and Industry Competition

Grocers have been around for centuries. When the Pilgrim Fathers boarded the *Mayflower* for the New World in 1620, they left behind a Shakespearean England that boasted a whole variety of market traders and shops, including grocers. Indeed, Napoleon was later to deride England as a "nation of shopkeepers."

A mature industry, therefore, one might think. Yes and no. Yes, in that the main functions of buying, transporting, stocking, displaying, and selling foods remain the same as ever. No, in that differentiated customer propositions have enabled some companies to beat the market, a few with spectacular success.

Sam Walton pursued a "crusade for the customer," and his original 1962 five-and-dime business in Rogers, Arkansas, has grown from a first year turnover of $100,000 to one of more than $450 billion. Wal-Mart has sustained its "low prices, always" positioning throughout the years.

John Mackey took the opposite tack. Like Walton, he started out with a single store, this time in Austin, Texas, in 1978, selling healthy, natural foods. He lived above the store and termed it SaferWay, a crafty spoof on the supermarket giant. He expanded both organically, with identical store growth averaging annual increases of 7 percent in the ten years leading to 2011, and through acquisition, most contro- versially buying Wild Oats Markets in 2008. Whole Foods Market now turns over around $12 billion.

Mackey rejects any comparison with Wal-Mart: "We're selling the highest-quality foods in the world," he has said. "It's like comparing a Hyundai to a Lexus. Their focus is on getting the cheapest stuff in; we're focused on getting the best stuff." (A Wal-Mart for the Granola Crowd [2005, July 30], *The Economist*, 60–66).

But there is an intriguing comparison. Both companies ventured into a mature industry with a differentiated proposition, albeit from opposite ends of the spectrum, and both rammed home that initial competitive edge, rapidly and ruthlessly.

Competitive Intensity

What your backers want to know is how intense competition is within your main business segment, and whether it is going to intensify. And why.

They want to get a sense of what is likely to happen to pricing in your market. Future pricing is critical in financial forecasting, more important even than market share gain, since every penny of a price rise falls straight to the bottom line.

Likewise, every penny of a price reduction directly impacts the bottom line. Your backer needs to know.

There's no better tool for assessing the competitiveness of an industry than Michael Porter's five forces model. It first appeared in his book, *Competitive Strategy: Techniques for Analyzing Industries and Competitors*. Porter identified five main sets of forces that shape competitive intensity, as shown in Figure 4–1. Here's a quick word on each of them.

INTERNAL RIVALRY

Internal rivalry is shaped by three main sub-forces: the number of players, market demand growth relative to supply, and external pressures.

THE NUMBER OF PLAYERS. The more numerous the players, the tougher typically the competition.

Are there many players in your marketplace?

FIGURE 4–1. Five forces shaping competition.

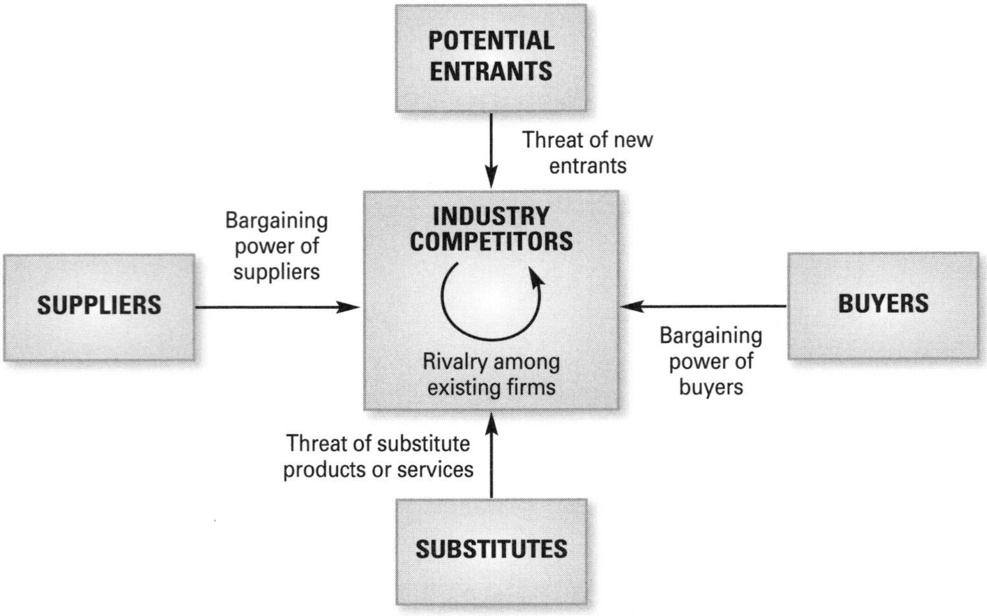

Source: Reprinted with the permission of Simon & Schuster Publishing Group from the Free Press edition of *Competitive Strategy: Techniques for Analyzing Industries and Competitors* by Michael E. Porter. Copyright © 1980, 1998 by The Free Press, a Division of Simon & Schuster, Inc. All rights reserved.

MARKET DEMAND GROWTH. The slower growing the market, the tougher typically the competition. But what of supply? Does your industry have a reasonable balance between demand and supply? If so, then internal rivalry may well be moderate.

If, however, your industry has indications of oversupply—where supply exceeds demand—that will increase internal rivalry. And place a dampener on prices. You and your competitors will have to fight more fiercely for customers, and any planned price increases to meet rising costs may have to be put on hold.

Do your customers have too many suppliers they can choose from? Has this situation worsened in recent times? Are you and your fellow providers underutilized? Is industry pricing being squeezed? These are all signs of supply exceeding demand.

If, conversely, the industry is one of undersupply (or excess demand), where customers compete for relatively scarce supplies, that's good news for you. Internal rivalry will be modest and you and your competitors may be able to nudge up pricing above inflation.

When you analyzed market demand in Chapter 3 of the business plan, how fast did you find your market growing? And how is the market demand-supply balance?

EXTERNAL PRESSURES. External bodies, in particular government and trade unions, have great power to influence the nature of competition in many industries. Government regulation, taxation, and subsidies can skew both market demand and the competitive landscape. Trade unions can influence competition in a number of ways—for example, through restrictive practices that serve to raise barriers to entry.

There are other factors influencing internal rivalry that may be relevant in your industry. One is high barriers to exit, where providers have little choice but to stay on competing when they should be withdrawing (e.g., a restaurant with many employees, hence potentially high redundancy costs, or a service business with a long lease on office space that is difficult to offload). Another is seasonal or irregular overcapacity due to fluctuating levels of demand (e.g., the fruit-picking or ice-cream industries).

Are there many providers in your marketplace? How fast is the market for your services growing (Chapter 3)? What about the other factors? Put all these together to determine the level of internal rivalry in your marketplace. Is it high, low, or medium today? And what about in a few years' time? Why?

THREAT OF NEW ENTRANTS

The lower the barriers to entry to a market, the tougher typically the competition. Barriers to entry can be technology, operations, people, or cost related, where a new entrant has to:

- Develop or acquire a certain technology

- Develop or acquire a certain operational process

- Train or engage scarce personnel

- Invest heavily in either capital assets or marketing to become a credible provider

When barriers are higher, the higher are the costs to the customer of switching from one supplier to another. A beverage manufacturer may shift from one sugar supplier to another with relative ease but may require reconfiguration of its bottling plant in switching from one labeling solution to another.

How high are the entry barriers in your industry? How serious is the threat of new entrants? High, low, medium? Is the threat going to get more serious over the next few years, less serious, or stay more or less the same? Why?

EASE OF SUBSTITUTION

The easier it is for customers to use a substitute product or service, the tougher typically the competition.

Think again of the impact of the likes of iTunes in the music industry. It was a substitute solution to the sale of CDs in the shopping mall and a contributing factor, along with e-commerce and supercenters, in the demise of specialist entertainment retailers such as Tower Records and Circuit City. In this case, the threat of substitution would be classified as high.

How big is the threat of you and your competitors losing share to substitutes? High, low, medium? Is the threat going to grow over time? Why?

CUSTOMER POWER

The more bargaining power your customers have over you, the tougher typically the competition. Ask any supplier to the large supermarket chains. Or to automotive manufacturers.

Often this is no more than a reflection of the number of providers in a marketplace, compared with the number of customers. The more choice of provider the customer has, the tougher the competition.

Customer power is also influenced by switching costs. If it is easy and relatively painless to switch suppliers, competition is tougher. If switching costs are high, competition eases.

How much bargaining power do customers in your industry have over providers? High, low, medium? What about in the future? Why?

SUPPLIER POWER

The more bargaining power suppliers have over the service providers, the tougher typically the competition.

Again it can often be just a function of numbers. There are, for example, numerous steel or aluminium converters, but few (and increasingly fewer) metal producers (e.g., steel mills, which smelt the iron ore and blend it with alloys to make steel blooms, ingots, slabs, and sheet). When these metal converters sell components to automotive manufacturers, they can find themselves in a viselike squeeze, with huge steel or aluminium suppliers at one end and auto giant customers at the other. But the best of them learn how to duck, dive, and survive.

How much bargaining power do your suppliers have over providers of your kind of service? High, low, medium? And in the future? Why?

> **TOP TIP:** *Beware concluding that competitive intensity will ease off over the plan period. It may, but you had better have a watertight argument. Your backers will be wary of such a claim—especially if they are bankers.*

HOW COMPETITIVE IS YOUR INDUSTRY?

These, then, are the five main forces shaping the degree of competition in a marketplace. Put them all together, and you'll have a measure of how competitive your industry is.

How tough is internal rivalry? The threat of new entrants or substitutes? How much power do customers and suppliers have on you and your competitors?

In short, how intense is competition in your industry? High, low, medium?

And what of the future? Is industry competition set to intensify? Because however tough competition is at the moment, it results in you and your competitors getting an average, industrywide operating margin of a certain percentage.

What your backer wants to know is whether competitive forces will conspire to threaten that margin over the next few years. Or whether the industry competition of the past few years is unsustainable and likely to ease off in the future.

In other words, what will be the effect of competitive dynamics on pricing in your industry over the next few years? Your backer needs to know. If competition intensifies, it would put pressure on prices. If it stays more or less as is, then pricing will move as it has been doing in recent times. If competition eases off, players may be able to nudge up pricing over the next few years.

You should address this issue directly in this chapter of your business plan, or your backers may assume the worst.

Block-Busted: Movie Rentals and Industry Competition

There are times when all of Porter's five forces seem to conspire against an industry sector. Just ask Blockbuster.

At its peak in the mid-2000s, Blockbuster had more than 4,000 video/DVD/game rental shops throughout the United States, employing over 60,000 people. It was also the largest such chain in Canada and the United Kingdom and had operations in 17 countries. By the time it filed for Chapter 11 in September 2010, only 700 stores were still trading in the United States. What had gone wrong?

The industry had moved on. As for its main competitor, Movie Gallery Inc. (with Hollywood Video and Game Crazy), which preceded Blockbuster by three years into bankruptcy, the five forces were arraigned against them:

- Industry rivalry had intensified owing to dampened demand.

- Diminished demand was caused by new entrants that focused on alternative, consumer-friendly distribution methods, in particular mail service (Netflix, which had less demanding return requirements) and kiosk-based pickup service (Redbox).

- Availability of substitute products, especially streaming video on demand service over the Internet (Netflix again, far ahead of Blockbuster's own streaming offering), further diminished demand.

- Meanwhile, consumers have become savvier and are able to select from a wider variety of competing offerings for movies, television programs, and games, thereby putting pressure on pricing.

- Suppliers also became more demanding as the bargaining power of brick-and-mortar movie and game rental chains waned.

Blockbuster was bought at auction by Dish Network, the satellite television service provider. Dish resolved to deploy the Blockbuster brand to compete directly with Netflix and keep 90 percent of stores open. These plans seemed highly optimistic and were indeed soon scaled back to retaining only the most profitable branches. Two years on, however, it was with a sense of inevitability, given the malalignment of the five forces against it, that Dish announced the closure of all remaining Blockbuster stores. Progress was blocked, the chain busted.

Competition in a Startup

Too many startup business plans are based on the premise that theirs is a new concept. Competition is nonexistent or irrelevant. In the vast majority of cases, this is at best only partially true.

There is always competition. Whatever your solution to the perceived needs of the customer, someone else somewhere else has another solution. Or will have. If others don't have a solution now, they may well come up with one after they have examined yours.

So, let's look at three aspects of competition in a startup: 1) direct competition, 2) indirect competition, and 3) competitive response.

DIRECT COMPETITION

If your new venture is a business with a clearly defined existing marketplace, then your Chapter 4 analysis will be no different from that of an established business.

You'll identify marketplace competitors (soon to be augmented by one new player—namely, you) and assess competitive intensity, perhaps to be intensified by your firm's entry.

An example would be a startup boutique specializing in designer clothes for children that's opening on Main Street. Your competitors would include other such boutiques; any boutiques focusing on adult clothes but also offering a selection for children; children's wear chain stores; the children's wear departments of department stores; and all variants of the same using different routes to market, for example, catalog shopping businesses or online retailers.

You will be entering a highly competitive market—retail can be an unforgiving competitive arena—but hopefully with a distinctive edge, which you will set out forcefully in Chapter 5 of your business plan (on your strategy).

INDIRECT COMPETITION

What if your idea is a new concept? Who are your competitors?

They are whoever was providing an alternative solution to the customer before your business existed, competing for a similar share of the customer's wallet as you are.

Suppose you invented an ingenious wooden roller-ball back-massaging device that released aromatherapeutic oils as you massaged. It's new, it's unique, it's brilliant, it works!

But it has competition. The customer's need is relief from back tension or pain. Customers are prepared to dip into their pockets to relieve that pain. They have a range of alternative solutions: They can buy other wooden roller-ball devices, plastic and metal versions, or powered massage devices and massage chairs. They can go to a masseur, even an aromatherapist. They can purchase the oils and self-administer. They can take pills.

All these are competitors, even if only indirect ones. Yours will occupy a particular price positioning—above basic roller-ball devices, below power-driven ones—but the customer has the option to trade up or down.

In Chapter 5 of your business plan, you'll set out the pros of alternative solutions from your competitors' perspective and the cons from yours. You'll make your case. But it's a case in relation to the alternative providers—and these competitors need to be identified first, in this chapter, and competitive intensity assessed.

COMPETITIVE RESPONSE

Also frequently absent in business plans is the reaction of competitors if your venture turns out to be a success.

You cannot assume that they will stand idly by and cheer you on. Your backers won't. They will assume that your competitors will respond.

If your new concept is patent protected, that is great. Your backers will need to know full details. But there are ways for a competitor to negotiate a path around a patent, and do it legally. Offering a slight variant on the theme can often be enough.

How will you respond when (not if) your competitors respond to your market entry? Here is the place in your plan to say how.

Suppose your children's wear boutique is successful. How will the department store down the road respond? Perhaps by cordoning off its children's wear department, refitting the design, and engaging a clown every Saturday afternoon. How would you respond to that response?

Suppose your oil-infused roller-ball massaging device is successful? How will producers of basic devices respond? Will they copy the device if unpatented? If patented, could they offer their devices along with freestanding oils for self-administering at 15 percent below your price? How would you respond to that?

Assume competitive response. And prepare your return response.

◻   ◻   ◻   ◻   ◻   **THINKING OUT OF THE BOX**   ◻   ◻   ◻   ◻   ◻

Competing Strategically

The man who knows both himself and his enemy will be victorious in a hundred battles.
                                                                                   —Sun Tzu

The element of competition exists as the primary fact of all entrepreneurial business in a market society. To succeed, you must be able to position and sell your product or service against your competitors.

Your ability to clearly define your competitors, to determine their strengths and weaknesses, and to produce and sell your product or service against your competitors in an open market is the key skill of entrepreneurship.

Effective competitive strategy requires intelligence, judgment, creativity, flexibility, and continuous experimentation. These are all skills that you can learn with practice. The qualities that are required for success as an entrepreneur are the same qualities that are required for success in any competitive sport. You must be continually seeking ways to be smarter, better, and faster than your competition.

You must always remember that your competitors are looking for ways to put you out of business as quickly as they possibly can, by taking away your customers, cash flow, and profits. You must therefore find ways to develop and maintain a superior position in your market and put them out of business before they do it to you.

Here are some key aspects of competing strategically:

Customers want the most for the least amount of money. They will therefore buy from the company that they feel offers them the best choice and greatest benefit. To succeed in any business:

  a. You must develop and maintain a competitive advantage in your market.

  b. You must determine what makes your product or service superior to anything else available.

  c. You must decide on the area of excellence you are going to develop and maintain.

  d. You must be absolutely clear about your "unique selling proposition."

Entrepreneurship is an unending struggle and battle where you must compete vigorously with other companies to win customers over to your product or service.

To succeed:

    a. Be determined to be the best in your market.

    b. Set a goal to be either number one or number two with your product or service.

    c. Continually look for ways to improve your product or service offering relative to your competitors.

Your choice of the companies, businesses, or products that you are going to compete against determines the entire strategy of your business.

    a. Your competitor is anyone who sells a similar product or service that gives customers a similar benefit to what you offer.

    b. Your competitor is any alternate use of the same money that your product costs.

    c. Your competitor may be the fact that your customer does not know that your product or service is available.

Your customer always has three choices in any market:

    a. To buy from you.

    b. To buy from your competitor.

    c. To buy from neither of you and do something else with the same money.

Make a list of all the competitors who can take business or sales away from you.

    a. Why do your customers buy from your competitors?

    b. What benefits or advantages does your customer see in buying from your competitor?

    c. In what ways is your competitor superior to you and your products?

    d. What are the major strengths of your competitor?

    e. What are the major weaknesses or vulnerabilities of your competitor?

Choose your competitor carefully. Be very clear about who you are going to take business and sales away from.

    a. What do you have to do to win customers away from your competitors?

    b. What must your customer be convinced of in order to buy from you rather than from your competitor?

    c. Why should your customer switch from your competitor to buy from you?

    d. What value does your customer seek that your product or service offers, and does so better than your competitors?

    e. Where is your competitor most vulnerable?

To develop competitive advantage in any new market, your product or service must be better than your competitor's offering in one or more of the following ways:

    a. It must sell at a lower cost but at the same or higher level of quality.

    b. It must be of higher quality but at the same or lower price.

    c. It must offer features and benefits that your competitor does not offer.

    d. It must be easier to buy and use than your competitor's product.

    e. It must include delivery and service that's faster than your competitor.

    f. It must have better guarantees and warranties than your competitor.

    g. It must come with superior service after the sale, as compared with your competitor's product.

When entering a new market, be absolutely clear about the competitive advantages you need to develop to succeed.

    a. Be prepared, because it is extremely hard to get a customer to switch from buying from your competitor to buying from you.

    b. Determine how much it will cost for you to develop a product and enter a new market.

    c. Determine how long it will take for you to become successful selling against your competitors.

    d. Consider the possibility of entering a different market, where there is less competition for your product.

Your goal is to develop a product or service that is excellent in one or more ways.

    a. If your product or service were the best in the business, what would people say about it?

    b. What would you have to include in your product or service to get people to say that you were the best in the business?

    In selling against competition, you can always lower your price, offer something different, or sell your product or service in a different market. You must also continually look for weaknesses or vulnerabilities in the products and services of your competitors while continually seeking ways to develop strengths and areas of superiority in the products and services you offer.

Your ability to sell effectively in competitive markets is the key to success as an entrepreneur. What one action are you going to take immediately to compete strategically as the result of what you have learned here?

◻ ◻ ◻ ◻ ◻ ◻ ◻ ◻ ◻ ◻ ◻ ◻ ◻ ◻ ◻ ◻ ◻ ◻ ◻

Industry Competition Risks and Opportunities

You have assessed competitive intensity in your industry, both now and over the next few years. What are the risks to that assessment? What could happen to intensify competition further?

What could happen to internal rivalry, to customer bargaining power, or to other forces to intensify competition? What is the likelihood of those risks occurring? And what would be the impact if they did?

Especially, what are the "big risks," those that are (as defined in Chapter 3) reasonably likely and with reasonable impact? How will you mitigate these big risks should they occur?

Conversely, what are the big opportunities to perhaps balance these risks? And how will you exploit them should they occur?

Chapter 4 of your business plan requires just one or two paragraphs on big competitive risks and opportunities. But your backer will appreciate your candor in addressing and tackling them upfront.

THE GORGE INN AND ORIENTAL SPA BUSINESS PLAN, 2014: INDUSTRY COMPETITION

In the last chapter, Rick Jones identified market demand for lodging, restaurants, and spa services in the Mt. Hood and Columbia River Gorge area as $86 million in 2012, forecast to grow to $101 million by 2017. Now he needs to assess how much competition there is among suppliers to meet that demand in general, and more specifically in his addressed market niche of three- to four-star accommodation with spa facilities.

First port of call again is the website of the Oregon Tourism Commission, where Rick is delighted to find a quarterly publication titled the "Oregon Tourism and Hospitality Indicators Report," commissioned from Smith Travel Research Inc. This report was discontinued in 2010, but Rick extracts some highly useful indicators from the Winter 2009 and earlier editions:

◻ Average hotel occupancy in Oregon in 2009 was 53.9 percent, down 7.7 percent from the 61.6 percent of 2008—which compares with 55.1 percent nationwide, down 8.7 percent.

- Occupancy rates in the Mt. Hood and Gorge area were 56.1 percent, which was down 6.1 percent on the 62.2 percent of 2008—somewhat higher than for the state as a whole.

- Occupancy rates in the area are seasonal, with average rates ranging from 40 percent in December (48 percent in 2008) to 73 percent in August (81 percent in 2008).

- Average room rate for 2009 in the area was $79, compared with $86 for the state and $98 nationwide.

- Revpar (revenue per available room) in the area was $44 in 2009.

This information, plus a Google search to get updated headlines on hotel occupancy, will enable Rick to compare data on his own hotel's performance with local, regional, and national trends in the next chapter of the business plan. It also gives an indication of the supply/demand balance. Average occupancy in the Mt. Hood and Gorge area seems little different from that of all of Oregon or, indeed, the United States as a whole. If there is no indication of localized excess supply (i.e., demand and supply appear to be as balanced as elsewhere), Rick's backer should not be overly concerned with pricing prospects at The Gorge.

Rick now focuses on direct competitors, those playing in the niche of three- to four-star accommodations and/or with spa facilities. In the four years he has been studying, planning, developing, and operating in this market, he has recognized this lineup:

- Three top-of-the-range resorts, with golf courses, swimming and plunge pools, and luxurious spa facilities, operate up in the hills above the gorge, two on the Washington side of the gorge and one on the Oregon side nestled in the foothills of Mt. Hood. There is another such resort with a high-profile spa located in the Willamette Valley.

- One business-style hotel, owned by a chain, is located at Cascade Locks and offers a fitness suite and good basic spa facilities.

- Two first-class hotels, in Hood River and Crown Point, are offering the option of limited spa services such as massage.

- A unique manor-style hotel-cum-hostel destination, featuring spa facilities as well as golf, pools, and craft and theater, is located in Troutdale, close to the Portland airport.

- Five first-rate B&Bs are in the vicinity—one with a magnificent view over the gorge on the Oregon side, another similarly sited on the Washington side, two located on the outskirts of towns (Portland and Hood River), and one near Troutdale—although none of them offers spa services.

◘ Half a dozen first-class spas/wellness centers are located in Portland, two in particular with an Oriental influence.

Rick has met a number of the owners and managers of these businesses, mainly through the Columbia River Gorge Visitors Association and the Oregon Restaurant and Lodging Association, and has a good idea of how they have been faring during the post-credit-crunch recession and tackling the issues that face them all.

Rick assesses competitive intensity in his niche as medium to high:

◘ Internal rivalry is medium, with many players, not just in the Columbia River Gorge, but elsewhere in the state, but there's above-average demand growth in this niche.

◘ Barriers to entry are low, with some establishments setting up a simple treatment room and calling it a spa, but barriers are higher for full facility spas, because of the capital costs of setup and the operating costs of running the dedicated space. Nevertheless, there remains the risk that a directly competitive inn-cum-spa operation, in The Gorge mold, could be launched over the next five years. This situation could be seen both as a threat to The Gorge occupancy rates and an opportunity, with the new competitor helping to spread the word about spa vacationing in the Columbia River Gorge.

◘ The threat of substitutes always looms large—spa holidays have emerged as a substitute for other health-conscious holidays, such as bathing, hiking, or cycling breaks. The Gorge will remain vulnerable to an extent to the advent of the "next big thing."

◘ The bargaining power of customers is high—they have plenty of options on where to allocate their health-holiday spend.

◘ The bargaining power of suppliers is low—for example, there are a number of hot tub suppliers, and labor is plentiful in Oregon.

Rick doesn't envision any significant competitive intensification over the next three years. The main risks remain those of a new entrant or, conversely, that the spa goes the way of a fad. In either scenario, the fallback position is that The Gorge would still remain an attractive destination for the discerning visitor.

That brings the discussion neatly to the competitive positioning of The Gorge, but that strategy is for Chapter 5 of the business plan.

Checklist on Competition

Your plan will stand apart from most others by dedicating a whole chapter to your competitors and competitive intensity. You'll show that you are unafraid of facing up to and tackling any beasts out there in the wild.

Put the details on the size, location, and number of employees of your competitors elsewhere (in an appendix to your plan), but summarize the most illuminating findings in this chapter. Assess how competitively intense your industry is right now and whether competition is likely to intensify by considering the following:

- *The forces of internal rivalry*. Examine the size and number of players, demand growth, external pressures, and barriers to exit.

- *The threat of new entrants*. How sturdy are the barriers to entry?

- *The threat of substitute products or services*. Is there a disruptive technology out there?

- *The bargaining power of customers*. This factor is often dependent on the relative number and scale of providers and customers.

- *The bargaining power of suppliers*. Likewise, this factor is often a function of numbers and scale, but here you are the customer.

Assess, too, what is likely to happen to industry pricing should competition intensify. Finally, point out the main risks and opportunities around industry competition over the next few years.

If yours is a business startup with a new concept, identify competitors providing alternative solutions and analyze the industry accordingly. Consider how competitors may respond to your entry and how you in turn will respond to that.

Your assessment should be done in two to three pages. Any supporting data or evidence on industry competition should be placed in an appendix.

5

STRATEGY

One of the things that is most important for a company is to be very clear about its strategy, so investors get to self-select as to whether or not that's the right strategy for them.

—Jeff Bezos

YOU HAVE already set out the microeconomic backdrop to your business. In Chapter 3 you assessed prospects for market demand and, in Chapter 4, for industry competition. Now it's time to slot your business into that context.

How competitive is your business in each of its main segments? What is your strategy for strengthening competitiveness in key segments? Or boosting the balance of your overall portfolio of segments? What risks might you face and what opportunities can you exploit? That's for this chapter. Then, in the next chapter, we'll look at what resources you'll need to deploy to put your strategy into effect.

And your conclusions based on this chapter will form an essential component of the justification of your sales and operating profit forecasts, which will be covered in Chapter 7.

One caveat: As with Chapters 3 and 4, this chapter will set out conclusions from the extensive research and analysis you'll undertake before writing your plan, in this instance, on your competitive position and strategy. Very little of the detailed analysis that we'll explain will find its way into your plan, however. You would lose or bore your backer in no time. Only the conclusions go into the plan. Any further detail can be laid out in an appendix to your plan on competitive position.

But it would be hugely beneficial if you can convince your backer that your assertions aren't pulled out of thin air but are built from a foundation of solid research and analysis. Your assertions should have depth, balance, and relevance. In so many business plans, the writer waxes lyrical on the company's strengths—for example, how a product has a feature that is unique or by far the best in the market. That may have a bit of truth, but let's have some perspective. Do customers perceive a *significant difference* between your product and that of the closest competitor? Do they care? How important is that feature in an assessment of overall competitive position? Will customers pay extra for that feature? Without the rigorous analysis, the reader may remain unconvinced.

In describing your strategy, you must not overexaggerate your strong points or their importance to the buying decision, or gloss over your weak points. You must place your firm's strengths and weaknesses in the context of both the customer's buying decision and the capabilities of the competition. Imagine if a competitor stumbled across a stray copy of your business plan, left lying on a table at a conference. (It does happen.) Would your one-sided hyperbole produce sidesplitting laughter?

Your assertions must be sufficiently robust to withstand the forensic examination of your backers. If they are not, your backers will pull out of any deal, having wasted your time and theirs.

> **TOP TIP:** You can always find something nice to say about somebody's character, appearance, and skills, even though in reality you may think that person is a rude, scruffy layabout. So too with companies. If you trumpet only your firm's strengths, without putting them in context, you invite your backer to be skeptical of your conclusions about your firm's competitiveness.

Competitive Position

First you need to be clear about how your business stacks up against the competition. In each of your main business segments, how well placed are you? And how is your position likely to change over the next few years?

To answer that, you should ideally go through three stages, for each of your main segments:

1. Identify and weight customer purchasing criteria (CPCs)—in other words, in each segment, identify what customers need from their suppliers, which would be you and your competitors.

2. Identify and weight key success factors (KSFs)—that is, what you and your competitors need to do to satisfy those customer needs and run a successful business.

3. Assess your competitive position—by rating yourself against those key success factors relative to your competitors.

Appendix A to this book shows you how to develop a systematic assessment of where your firm is placed relative to your main competitors and how this competitive position is likely to develop over the next few years.

We strongly recommend that you follow the approach of Appendix A. It is comprehensive, rigorous, and it can be revelatory. It is not, however, necessary for your business plan. Indeed, it won't be part of your business plan as delivered to your backer but, rather, will be provided as background, forming a solid bedrock of research and analysis to underpin your financial forecasts (Chapter 7), ready to draw upon to counter any clever cross-questioning from your backer.

The alternative, a shortcut, is to set out your firm's strengths and weaknesses, as recommended in most business plan guides. We have three problems with this approach:

1. Stating strengths and weaknesses without weighting and rating them and deriving a reasoned, balanced conclusion (preferably a weighted average assessment of competitive position) can be misleading.

2. This exercise is seldom done for each main business segment, where, virtually by definition of being a different segment, both the

weighting and rating, and indeed the overall competitive position, will differ.

3. Too often the alternative becomes a SWOT exercise (strengths, weaknesses, opportunities, threats), which is a dreadful construct. SWOT typically shows just a jumble of items, ungraded for importance, relevance, probability, or impact. It muddles up business opportunities with market opportunities, business risks with market risks, and comes to no conclusion whatsoever. It is a mess.

By all means have a go at assessing strengths and weaknesses, if you would prefer not to go through the rigor (and, yes, time) of deriving your competitive position using weighted CPCs and KSFs, as outlined in Appendix A. If so, please observe these tips:

- Give your backer some impression of the relevance of each main strength or weakness in assessing your firm's competitiveness.

- Explain to what extent this relevance is more important in some segments than others.

- Explain your performance *relative to the competition*. Sure, your customer retention rates are high, but are they higher than those of the market leader? If not, how do you plan to raise them to be the best in the business?

- Do not mix opportunities and threats with this assessment of your firm's strengths and weaknesses. Market opportunities and threats have already been discussed in Chapters 3 and 4; business opportunities and threats will be assessed in a separate section here in Chapter 5, on strategy, and again later in the section on strategic risk.

Once you have set out your firm's competitive position in its main business segments (following the recommended approach of Appendix A in this book), or else taken a shortcut and listed your firm's strengths and weaknesses (observing the tips just described), it is time to describe your plans for proactively strengthening your firm's competitiveness position. That is, it is time to present a strategy.

Tasty: Samuel Adams' Differentiation Strategy

Charles Koch was a fifth-generation brewer. Koch beers had been brewed in St. Louis, Missouri, since the mid-nineteenth century, except for a hiccup during the Prohibition era. But it looked like his son Jim would be anything but a brewer, with the Harvard graduate pursuing a career in management consulting. However, beer was in his blood and he kept one eye on what was happening in the industry.

Jim noted that the U.S. beer industry of the early 1980s offered virtually no variety. The likes of Budweiser, Busch, Schaefer, Schlitz, Miller, Michelob, Coors, and Molson were all pale lagers, manufactured by large, mass-market breweries. Pale lagers, derided as insipid by Europeans accustomed to a fruitier taste, were clearly the preference of most Americans. But if they wanted a beer with a bit more flavor, they had to drink an imported Heineken or Beck's—or indeed, at the other extreme, a British ale.

Jim believed that the American consumer wanted more choice, to try something different. He dusted off a recipe from his great-great-grandfather's records and tried brewing it in his Boston kitchen. Father Charles thought he was crazy, especially when Jim quit his consulting group to take on the venture full-time. But Jim pressed on. He named his beer inspirationally after the Bostonian revolutionary, Samuel Adams, who was himself a brewer, and carted his sample bottles around to the bars and restaurants of Boston.

Samuel Adams Boston Lager made its debut in around 25 Boston venues in April 1985, produced by a company with no office, no computers, no distributors, and just two employees, Jim and his partner. By the end of the year, sales had reached 500 barrels and word was spreading. In 1988, a small brewery was built and 36,000 barrels were sold.

Sam Adams is a classic example of differentiation strategy. All the big guys were producing pale lagers, with differences, yes, in packaging, advertising, price positioning, and, slightly, flavor. But each was essentially a pale lager. Sam Adams was a "better," malt-flavored beer.

The differentiation strategy worked. Many new lines followed the original Sam Adams, and distribution became both nationwide and international. Parent company Boston Beer was to pioneer a microbrewery explosion throughout America. It now has sales of more than $500 million and, following the $52 billion takeover of Anheuser-Busch by the Belgian/Brazilian InBev in 2008, Boston Beer is now, remarkably, the largest American-owned brewer. Not bad for a niche business!

What Is Your Strategy?

There are myriad definitions of strategy, starting with the lasting words of General Sun Tzu ("know your opponent") in the sixth century B.C. to the rather more recent interpretation from Professor Kenichi Ohmae ("in a word, competitive advantage").

One of the authors is an economist, so he believes that we should bring the word *resources* into the definition. Just as economics can be defined as the optimal allocation of a nation's scarce resources, so a company's strategy can be defined thus:

Strategy is how a company deploys its scarce resources to gain a sustainable advantage over the competition.

What your backer needs to know is how you plan to allocate your company's resources over the business plan period to meet your goals. These resources are essentially your assets—your people, physical assets (e.g., buildings, equipment, inventory), and cash (and borrowing capacity). How will you allocate—or invest—these resources to optimal effect?

More precisely, your backer needs to be convinced that your strategy will enhance your firm's competitive position in key business segments.

So far, you have already set out your firm's competitive position and even had a go at examining how that position may change over time. Now, you must show how you can proactively improve that position through deployment of a winning business strategy. That is how you will provide a commercial underpinning to your financial forecasts in Chapter 7 of your plan. That is how you will convince your backers to back you.

What is your company's strategy? How will you deploy your scarce resources to gain a sustainable competitive advantage?

First, let's look at the generic strategies.

GENERIC STRATEGIES

There are again many definitions of generic strategies, with many different business gurus seeming to come up with their own. But in essence, and in the vast majority of cases, a company needs to choose between two very different and easy-to-grasp generic strategies: 1) low-cost or 2) differentiation.

Either strategy can yield a sustainable competitive advantage. Either the company supplies a product at lower cost to its competitors or it supplies one that is sufficiently differentiated from its competitors that customers are prepared to pay a premium price—where the incremental price charged adequately covers the incremental costs of supplying the differentiated product.

For a ready example of a successful low-cost strategy, think of Southwest Airlines or the Canadian airline WestJet. Relentless maximization of load factor enables them to offer seats at scarcely credible prices and still produce a profit. Or think of IKEA's stylish but highly price-competitive furniture.

A classic example of the differentiation strategy would be Apple, which is never the cheapest, whether in PCs, laptops, smartphones, or tablets, but always stylistically distinctive and feature-intensive. Or Nike, known for its state-of-the-art R&D into sports shoe design and body impact. Or Lady Gaga with her outrageous flamboyance—a contemporary variant on Josephine Baker and her brazen banana costume.

One variant on these two generic strategies worth highlighting is the *focus strategy*, developed prominently by Professor Michael Porter. While a firm can typically prosper in its industry by following either a low-cost or differentiation strategy, an alternative is to not address the whole industry but narrow the scope and focus on a slice of it, a single product (or customer) group. Under these circumstances, a firm can achieve market leadership through focus and exceptional differentiation, thereby leading simultaneously to scale-driven low unit costs.

A classic example of a successful focus strategy would be Honda motorcycles, whose differentiated focus on product reliability over decades has yielded the global scale to enable its quality products to remain cost competitive.

STRENGTHENING COMPETITIVE POSITION

Having clarified which generic strategy underpins your business, how are you planning to improve your competitive position over the plan period? How will you reinforce your competitive advantage?

The answer should lie in the analysis you have already done when assessing your competitive position vs. your competitors.

Against which key success factors do you rate less favorably than a key competitor? Is this an important, highly weighted KSF? Will it remain so in the future? Could it become even more important over time? Should this relative weakness be addressed? Should you take action to strengthen your performance against this KSF?

Or should you instead be building on your strengths, widening an already-existing gap between you and competitors in a particular KSF? It is inadvisable to generalize, but in theory investment in building on strengths should offer a more favorable risk/reward profile than investing to address weaknesses.

If your generic strategy is to provide a product or service at low cost, what investments or programs are you planning to reduce costs even further to stay ahead of the competition? What major investments in plant, equipment, premises, staff, systems, training, and/or partnering are you planning? What performance improvement programs are underway or planned?

If your generic strategy is one of differentiation, what investments or programs are you planning to reinforce that differentiation and make you stand out even more from your competitors? What major investments in plant, equipment, premises, staff, systems, training, marketing, and/or partnering are you planning? What strategic marketing programs are underway or planned?

If your generic strategy is one of focus, what investments or programs are you planning to reduce costs and/or reinforce your differentiation? What major investments, performance improvement, or strategic marketing programs are underway or planned?

How will these investments or programs impact your competitive position in key business segments? Your backer needs to know.

> **TOP TIP:** Whatever your firm's competitive position in a key business segment today, it probably won't be the same in three years' time. Markets evolve; competitors adapt. Your firm needs to take control over its future. Convince your backer that your firm is proactively advancing its competitiveness.

BOOSTING STRATEGIC POSITION

So far our analysis has been premised on the strengthening of your competitive position in your key product/market segments over the next few years.

But suppose you don't have the resources, whether in cash, time, or manpower, to do all you would like to do. How should you prioritize between the segments? Which investments or programs should you do first? Which should be dropped, possibly forever? Which segments should you exit?

You may benefit from undertaking a portfolio analysis. This analysis will identify how competitive you are in markets ranked by order of attractiveness. You should invest ideally in segments where you are strongest and/or that are the most attractive. And you should consider withdrawal from segments where you are weaker and/or that are less attractive.

And, finally, should you be looking to enter another business segment (or segments) with more attractive markets than the ones you currently address? If so, do you have grounds for believing that you would be at least reasonably placed in this new segment? Or that you could readily become reasonably placed?

This analysis will identify your *strategic position*. This is not to be confused with your competitive position, which relates to how competitive your company is in a particular product/market segment. Your strategic position relates to your balance of competitiveness across all segments of varying degrees of attractiveness.

First, let's be clear what we mean by an "attractive" market. The degree of market attractiveness should be measured as a blend of four factors:

1. Market size

2. Market demand growth

3. Competitive intensity

4. Market risk

The larger the market and faster it is growing, the more attractive the market is (other things being equal). But be careful with the other two factors, where the converse applies. The greater the competitive intensity in a market and the greater its risk, the less attractive it is.

You will have to use your own judgment on the weighting you apply to each of these factors. Simplest would be to give each of the four an equal weighting, so a rating for overall attractiveness would be the simple average of the ratings for each factor.

You may, however, be risk averse and give a higher importance to the market risk factor. In this case, you would need to derive a weighted average of each of the four ratings.

An example may help. Suppose your company is in four product/market segments and you are contemplating getting into a fifth. You draw up a strategic position chart, where each segment is represented by a circle.

The segment's position in the chart will reflect both its competitive position (along the x-axis) and its market attractiveness (along the y-axis). The size of each bubble should be roughly proportional to the scale of revenues currently derived from the segment.

The closer your segment is positioned toward the top right-hand corner, the better placed it is. Above the top right dotted diagonal, you should be thinking of investing further in that segment. Should the segment sink toward the bottom left dotted diagonal, however, you should consider exiting.

The strategic position shown in Figure 5–1 is sound. It shows favorable strength in the biggest and reasonably attractive segment C and an excellent position in the somewhat less attractive segment A. Segment D is highly promising and demands more attention, given the currently low level of revenues.

FIGURE 5–1. Strategic position: An example.

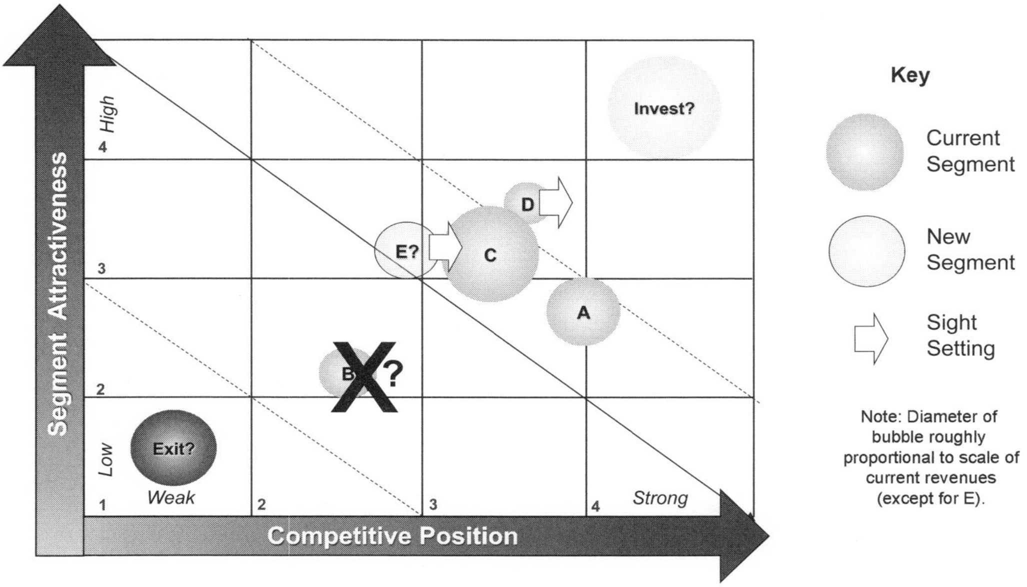

Segment B should perhaps be exited. It's a rather unattractive segment, and you are not that well placed. The new segment E seems promising.

In developing a strategy for this example, you may consider the following actions worth pursuing:

- Continued development in segments A and C

- Investment in segment D (with the arrow showing the resultant improvement in competitive position)

- Entry to segment E (with competitive position improving over time as market share develops)

- Exit from segment B (crossed out in Figure 5–1)

What is your strategic position?

Hopefully your main segments, from which you derive most revenues, are positioned above the main diagonal. Which segments are so important that you would derive greatest benefit from improving your competitive position? Where should you concentrate your efforts? Do you have any new segments in mind? How attractive are they? How well placed would you be? Are there any segments you should be thinking of getting out of?

One final word on strategic position. The example cited here showed the strategic position of a small company involved in five product/market segments. Exactly the same analysis can and should be undertaken for a larger company involved in, say, five businesses—or strategic business units (SBUs, in management-speak). Each SBU can be plotted against both competitive position (itself a weighted average of that SBU's competitive position in each of its addressed product/market segments) and market attractiveness (again a weighted average).

And the same conclusions can be drawn (i.e., invest in one SBU, hold another for cash, exit a third, and so on).

If you have plans for improving your strategic position, they should be in your business plan. Your backer needs to know.

Cheap and Cheerful:
Southwest Airlines' Low-Cost Strategy

The Southwest story is well known, but it remains the quintessential example of Porter's generic low-cost strategy. It is among the elite American companies in history that have turned an industry's rules of the game upside down, not just in the United States, but throughout the world.

What Southwest strived to do from the outset is what it has consistently and profitably achieved. Its goal was "to meet customers' short-haul travel needs at fares competitive with the cost of automobile travel."

A low-cost strategy both requires and creates high utilization. In the case of airlines, utilization is measured as load factor—the proportion of paid-for seats on the average flight. From the start, Southwest packed in the passengers, primarily by offering extraordinary fares, like the renowned Pleasure Class $13 flight from Dallas to Houston, but also through engendering a "fun-LUVing attitude" among its employees and customers.

But that was just the top line. To turn a profit, Southwest also had to keep costs as low as conceivable at every stage of the value chain. As examples:

◻ Southwest provides point-to-point flights. It does not use hub-and-spoke services, thereby speeding up turnaround times, maximizing average flying hours per day, and improving punctuality.

◻ New aircraft minimize downtime and improve punctuality again.

◻ It operates a single type of aircraft, the Boeing 737, thereby minimizing costs of spares, storage, mechanic and pilot training, and repairs and maintenance, and achieving purchasing economies.

◻ Secondary city airports, like Chicago Midway, are favored.

◻ There are no frills—no seat allocation, no boarding preference for frequent fliers or higher-fare passengers (until recently), just basic, standard, single-class seating and no meals (only refreshments for purchase on board), which facilitates intraflight cleaning and improves flight turnaround times.

◻ There's nontraditional union representation, with specific Southwest unions for pilots and flight attendants formed to represent their interests.

◻ Since the late 1990s, most booking and checking-in are done over the web.

◻ Southwest maintains a lean, well-compensated management structure.

◻ The airline is known for its careful hedging of fuel prices.

From its origins as an intrastate Texan Airbus operator, Southwest became not just the most highly capitalized airline in the United States, but also a role model to budget carriers throughout the Americas, Europe, and Asia—from JetBlue to EasyJet, Azul Brazilian to AirAsia.

Strategy in a Startup

The process described in this chapter is not that different for a startup, whether serving an existing market or creating a new one. You need to assess your likely competitive position in the main segments where you intend to compete and develop a strategy to enhance that competitiveness over time.

There are three main differences, however:

1. Your competitive position is in the future rather than the present tense.

2. It will be affected adversely from the outset by a low rating against all key success factors pertaining to experience.

3. Your backer will want to know whether it is defensible once achieved.

Your competitive position in a new venture is a judgment on the future. For an established business, the debate revolves as much around the present and recent past as it does the future—around the weighting of KSFs and/or your ratings against specific KSFs, as justified by evidence from customer, supplier, and other interviews, each of which will be based as much on fact and performance track record as judgment.

But for a startup, the debate will be part conjecture, especially if your venture is in a new market. So your arguments must be stronger. And you must seek evidence from any potential source.

There is nothing you can do about your new venture's rating against those KSFs that demand experience. Your rating against market share will be low at the outset, and so too perhaps against some cost-related factors, especially those pertaining to scale.

Likewise your rating against some differentiation factors may be low. Your lack of track record may count against you in the areas of consistency of product quality, delivery, customer service, and sales and marketing.

In that case, how will your firm compete? The answer is that it's not easy being a new entrant in an existing market. Your competitive position may well indeed be low relative to the leaders at the outset. But if you are addressing a growing market and/or you can substantially differentiate your product or service, things should improve. Your competitive position in three to five years' time should have improved measurably—your market share rating should be up, your unit costs down, and your service performance improved.

But this analysis further highlights what we discussed in Chapters 2 and 3 about segmentation. If your new venture does not serve an existing market but creates its own, then everything changes. The analysis of competition will be undertaken not for the market as a whole but for your addressed product/market segment. And if that is a new segment, created by your new venture, you effectively have no direct competition.

But there are two caveats:

1. You will have indirect competition, as discussed in Chapter 4.

2. You will in due course face competition from new entrants, if your new market is worthy of pursuit.

Which brings us to the third of the main differences between strategy for a startup and that for an established business: its defensibility.

Remember the definition we used for strategy: "Strategy is how a company deploys its scarce resources to gain a sustainable advantage over the competition." The all-important word for a startup in a new market is *sustainable*.

If your new venture succeeds, you will be targeted. Competitors will eye your newly carved space with envy. They will come after you. And soon.

How will you protect yourself against that competitive response? Your backers need to know. If they are venture capitalists, they'll be looking for an exit after five or seven years. In that time, could your competitors have started taking chunks out of your market share? If so, VCs might find it hard to sell out, or only at a discounted price. If there's a chance of that scenario from the outset, they will be wary of backing you.

There are a number of ways you can try to sustain your competitive advantage in a startup:

- Patent protection of key products

- Sustained innovation (i.e., staying one step ahead in product development)

- Sustained process improvement (i.e., staying one step ahead in cost-competitiveness, efficiency, and service)

- Investment in branding (i.e., identifying in the mind of the customer the particular benefit brought by your offering with its name)

- Investment, for business-to-business ventures, in customer relationships

Set out here how you are not only going to achieve a competitive advantage in this newly created market, but also how you will sustain it. However you aim to do so, this strategy must form a key component of your business plan.

□ □ □ □ □ **THINKING OUT OF THE BOX** □ □ □ □ □

Pumping Up Profit

There is no prosperity, trade, art, city, or great material wealth of any kind, but if you trace it home, you will find it rooted in a thought of some individual man.

—Ralph Waldo Emerson

No matter what your business, you must be continually focused on profits and the bottom line at all times. Like driving down a winding road, if you ever take your eyes off the road in front of you, you will quickly go into the ditch or off the edge.

There are only two ways that you can increase your profits: First, you can increase your revenues while holding your costs constant. Second, you can lower your costs while keeping your revenues constant. The very best solution is for you to look for ways to do both of them at all times.

Step 1: Market More Effectively
Because 80 percent of your potential market is still untapped, you must:

- *Specialize*. The key to successful marketing is to develop a narrow focus on the products and services you offer, the customers you serve, and the markets you enter.

- *Differentiate*. Find ways to differentiate your product or service from those of anyone else competing with you in your marketplace. It is the key to business success.

- *Segment*. Select your target market so that you can identify the very best customers for your area of specialization and differentiation.

◻ *Concentrate*. Focus and concentrate all of your energies, efforts, and expenditures on selling to those few customers who can and will appreciate your offerings the most.

Step 2: Analyze Your Marketing Mix

These are the key factors that determine the success or failure of your marketing efforts. You must be continually thinking about changing one or more of them as markets and competition change.

◻ *Product/service*. Define your product or service in terms of what it "does" for your customer vs. what it "is." Is your product or service, as you are offering it today, ideally suited for your current market and customers?

◻ *Price*. Is your price the right price for what you are selling? Should you change your price in some way? Should you increase it, decrease it, combine your price with other items, add items to your price, change your terms, or change your value offering?

◻ *Promotion*. How are you currently promoting and selling your product? Should you change your methods of advertising, marketing, selling, or acquiring customers in any way?

◻ *Place*. Where exactly do you sell your product? Do you sell locally, statewide, nationally, or internationally? Do you sell in stores or by direct selling or direct mail? Should you change the places where you offer your products?

◻ *Positioning*. What is your position in the hearts and minds of your potential customers? What are the words that people use to describe your company and your offerings? How do customers talk about you and think about you when you are not there? The answers to these questions determine everything that happens to you in the business world.

Step 3: Promote Your Product Aggressively

The key to business success is for you to have a good product or service and then to vigorously, aggressively, and continuously offer and promote it every reasonable way possible. Should you change your advertising or your offerings? Should you advertise on radio? Television? Newspapers? Other media?

Especially, should you upgrade and improve your direct selling presentation and capabilities? Usually, this step is key to business success.

Step 4: Differentiation

There are three considerations in differentiating your product or service from those of your competitors:

1. *Your area of excellence*. What is it that you do better than 90 percent or more of your competitors?

2. *Your area of superiority.* What specific ways is your product or service superior to that of any other similar product or service on the market today?

3. *Your unique selling proposition.* What is it that you and only you offer to your customers that makes your product or service unique, special, and different from anything else offered?

The answers to these questions are essential for determining every part of your marketing strategy, your sales efforts and presentations, your advertising, and for identifying your customers.

Step 5: Determine Your Driving Force

Every company has a single driving force, around which all of the other driving forces combine to achieve business success. Your business may be:

- *Product driven.* Your product is fixed and your driving force is to sell more of your product to more people in every way possible.

- *Market driven.* You are committed to serving a particular market with whatever products or services that market needs or demands.

- *Distribution channel driven.* What you sell is determined by the way that you get your product or service to the customer, either by direct sales, multilevel marketing (MLM), pipeline, telemarketing, Internet, or some other channel.

- *Method of sale driven.* The strategic emphasis in your company is determined by how you sell your product or service, either directly or indirectly, by mail or by retail or wholesale.

- *Technology driven.* Your unique and special technology determines the strategic focus of your business, whether computers, an Internet service, or another high-tech product.

- *Return/profit driven.* The most important consideration in determining your strategy is the amount of profit you can earn on the sale of a particular product or service, whatever it is.

- *Size/growth driven.* Your strategy is determined by your goal of dominating your market, of being the biggest, even if it requires that you give up short-term profits in exchange for size.

Step 6: Analyze Your Profits

This process requires that you continually analyze your business so that you know exactly the profitability of every product and service you sell in comparison with every other product or service you sell.

- Determine the exact sales revenues from a product or service. Make all deductions so that you are crystal clear about the exact amount left over.

- Determine your exact costs, including your direct, indirect, variable, semi-variable, and fixed costs as they are related to a specific product that you sell. Be accurate.

- Include all advertising, promotion, marketing costs, labor costs, time costs, and your own time investment, based on your hourly rate.

- Rank all your products or services from the most profitable to the least profitable. Write your rankings on a list.
  a. What is your most profitable product, after you have deducted all your possible costs?
  b. Evoke the 80/20 rule: What are the 20 percent of products or services that account for 80 percent of your revenues and profits?
  c. Usually, you'll observe that there is little relationship between the amount of time and money you spend creating and selling a product and the amount of profit you earn.

Step 7: Practice Zero-Based Thinking

Ask this question: "Is there anything that I am doing that, knowing what I now know, I wouldn't start again today, if I had to do it over?"

- Is there any product or service that you would not bring to the market, offer, or sell if you had to do it over again starting today?

- Is there any person in your personal or business life that you would not hire, assign, or become associated with if you had to do it over again today?

- Is there any supplier, banker, or vendor that you are dealing with that, knowing what you now know, you wouldn't get involved with again today, if you had to do it over?

- Is there any customer that you are selling or servicing that, knowing what you now know, you wouldn't take on as a customer?

- Is there any expenditure in your business, any process, procedure, or activity that, knowing what you now know, you wouldn't start up again?

- Is there any advertising, marketing, or selling methodology or expense that, knowing what you now know, you wouldn't start up again?

- What is your "citadel strategy"? That is, if you had to withdraw to a single product or service in the face of business adversity, what one product or service would you retain while letting all the others go?

Step 8: Apply the Seven Rs of Business Management

1. *Reevaluate*. Look again at every part of your business, especially where you meet resistance, frustration, or failure of any kind.

2. *Reorganize*. Keep moving people and resources around to ensure the highest level of output per unit of input.

3. *Reengineer*. Continually look for ways to simplify the process of working. Delegate, outsource, and eliminate every possible task. Consolidate, compress, and expand responsibilities of various people to simplify the work process.

4. *Restructure*. Move people and resources to higher-value, revenue-producing activities and away from activities that generate no income for the company.

5. *Reinvent*. Imagine reinventing yourself and your business every six months. If your business burned to the ground and you had to start over, what would you start up and what would you not start again?

6. *Refocus*. With the information coming from these questions, what one activity, task, product, or service should you focus all your efforts on selling more of? Refocus your energies as well on your most valuable tasks, which are the tasks that only you can do that can make a real difference. Think on this: If you could only do one thing all day long, what one task or activity would contribute the greatest value to your business and to your life?

7. *Retake control*. Take control of your business and your life by deciding what you are going to do and then taking vigorous action immediately.

Step 9: Apply the Theory of Constraints
There is always something holding you back from achieving your most important goals. What is it?

- Start by becoming absolutely clear about your goal. Is it sales? Income? Profitability? Define it.

- Why aren't you at your goal already?

- What sets the speed at which you achieve your goal? What is the bottleneck or choke point?

- What is holding you back from achieving your goal?

- What are the internal constraints, within yourself or your company, that are holding you back?

- What are the external constraints, the outside factors that determine the speed at which you achieve your goal?

Always remember, most of the reasons you are not achieving your goals are within yourself and the result of your own qualities, behaviors, or activities. Search there first.

Step 10: Attract Perfect Customers
There are four levels of customer service:

1. Meet expectations.

2. Exceed expectations.

3. Delight your customers.

4. Amaze your customers!

Always look for ways to delight and amaze your customers if you want to grow in sales and profitability.

- Describe a perfect customer as if you were going to run an ad in the newspaper for this type of customer. What kind of person would the customer be? What kind of qualities would this person have?

- Describe the "ultimate customer experience." What would have to happen for your customer to be ecstatic about working with and dealing with you?

- Describe how you would treat customers if you loved them. If your customers were the most important people in your world, how would you treat them, from the first contact and throughout your relationship with them?

- What would you have to do to deserve perfect customers for your business? What changes would you have to make? What would you have to do more of, less of, start or stop?

- Complete this sentence: "I deserve to have perfect customers because I always . . ." How would you finish this sentence?

There are always great opportunities for great people. You have within yourself, right now, the ability to sell more, better, and faster to those 80 percent of customers that you have not yet contacted, or who may not even be aware that you exist.

Review these guidelines regularly. Based on the ten steps outlined, look for one thing that you can do differently every single day to create and keep better customers, increase your sales and revenues, cut your costs, and boost your profits.

What one action are you going to take immediately to pump up your profits based on what you have learned here?

- - - - - - - - - - - - - - - - - -

Strategic Risks and Opportunities

In Chapters 3 and 4, you pulled out the main market demand and industry competition risks and opportunities in your line of business. Now you can add those risks and opportunities that relate to your competitive position and strategy over the next few years.

So far, in this chapter, you have assessed your competitive position (or prospective position if your venture is a startup) in key segments. You have set out your strategy for strengthening your position in each key segment, as well as your overall strategic position. That is what you believe to be the most likely scenario.

Now, what are the risks that your competitive positioning could turn out to be worse than that? Suppose, for example, a competitor were to steal a major customer from you? How likely is that to happen, and what sort of impact would it have? What could happen to make your positioning even worse than that?

Conversely, what could happen to significantly improve your competitive prospects? Could a major competitor exit from the market, for example? How likely, and with what impact?

What are the big risks, those that are reasonably likely and with reasonable impact (as defined in Chapter 3)? What steps can you take to mitigate them? What are the big opportunities? How can you exploit them?

You will return to these big risks and opportunities in Chapter 8 and learn a unique way to view them from two perspectives.

THE GORGE INN AND ORIENTAL SPA
BUSINESS PLAN, 2014: STRATEGY

Rick Jones has found that competition in the three- to four-star hotel/spa business in the Columbia River Gorge is of medium intensity (Chapter 4), with the main risk being that the spa goes the way of a fad. But what of The Gorge's competitive standing in this market, and how might it be improved if Rick achieves the funding needed for his proposed Phase II development?

Rick is a former management consultant and appreciates that his findings must be rooted in competitive research and analysis, as set out in Appendix A of this book. He rolls up his sleeves. He scans the web, talks to fellow members of the International Spa Association (ISPA), reviews notes and literature from the last couple of ISPA October conferences he has attended, and examines recent reports by the Professional Beauty Association on the spa/salon industry.

He compares this research with his own experience at The Gorge over the last three years and concludes that the main purchasing criteria for customers of spa services are the effectiveness of the treatment (customers must feel that the treatment has done them good), the standard of the premises (preferably clean, hygienic, spacious, with a relaxing ambience), and, of course, price.

He finds that as customers start to consider the range of facilities provided important, from hot tubs to swimming pools, saunas to Jacuzzis, and as they become more savvy, they will place greater emphasis on the range of treatments provided—as shown in Table 5–1.

TABLE 5–1. Customer purchasing criteria from spa services.

Spa Customer Purchasing Criteria		Importance	Change
Effectiveness	• Therapist capabilities • Understanding of benefits • Confidence in process	*High* *Low/Med* *Med*	→ → →
Efficiency	• Effort • Timeliness	*Low/Med* *Low*	→ →
Relationship	• Rapport • Enthusiasm	*Med* *Med/High*	↑ →
Range	• Facilities • Treatments	*Med/High* *Low/Med*	→ ↑↑
Premises	• Cleanliness, hygiene • Space, decor	*High*	↑
Price		*Med/High*	↑

He then translates these customer purchasing criteria (CPCs) into key success factors (KSFs), as shown in Table 5–2. He finds that the winning provider of spa services will have highly skilled and experienced therapists, quality premises, a positive, upbeat culture, and tight control of costs.

TABLE 5–2. Key success factors in spa services.

Spa Customer Purchasing Criteria		Importance	Change	Associated Key Success Factors
Effectiveness	• Therapist capabilities • Understanding of benefits • Confidence in process	*High* *Low/Med* *Med*	→ → →	• **Therapist skills** • **Qualification** • **Track record**
Efficiency	• Effort • Timeliness	*Low/Med* *Low*	→ →	• **Availability** • **Work ethic** • **Delivery**
Relationship	• Rapport • Enthusiasm	*Med* *Med/High*	↑ →	• **People skills (communication)** • **Positive, upbeat culture**
Range	• Facilities • Treatments	*Med/High* *Low/Med*	→ ↑↑	• **Range of facilities** • **Range of treatments**
Premises	• Cleanliness, hygiene • Space, decor	*High*	↑	• **Spa quality premises**
Price		*Med/High*	↑	• **Cost-competitiveness**

Finally, he allows for the two incremental KSFs of market share and management factors and computes the weighting to each. Rick is now ready to rate his offering at The Gorge against these KSFs. He is mildly surprised but proud to find that The Gorge's overall competitive position in spa services in the Columbia River Gorge area is favorable, a 3.3 on a scale of 0 to 5. Table 5–3 shows the results for The Gorge, while Appendix A explains the methodology for how ratings are calculated.

TABLE 5–3. The Gorge Inn competitive position in spa services.

Key Success Factors	Weighting	The Gorge Inn	Belmont	Best American	Reina's	The Gorge Phase II
Market Share	15%	1.5	4	2	2.5	2.5
Cost Factors: Overhead control, Scale economies	25%	3.5	2	3	3	4
Management Factors: Marketing	10%	1.5	4	5	3	2
Differentiation Factors: Effectiveness—Standard of therapists	10%	5	4.5	3	4	5
Efficiency—Work ethic, Delivery	5%	5	4.5	3	4	5
Relationship—Communication, Attitude	10%	5	4	3	5	5
Range—Facilities, Treatments	10%	2	5	2	4	3.5
Premises—Hygiene, Décor, Space	15%	4	5	4	4	4.5
Competitive Position	*100%*	3.3	3.8	3.1	3.5	3.9

Key to Rating: 1 = Weak, 2 = Tenable, 3 = Favorable, 4 = Strong, 5 = Very strong

Selected Competitors: The Gorge Inn & Oriental Spa; Belmont Hot Springs Resort & Spa, Mt. Hood; Best American Cascade Hotel, Cascade Locks; Reina's Spa, Troutdale

The fabulous Belmont, with 250 rooms and its state-of-the-art spa and aquatic facilities, set among the contrasting greens of fairways, pine trees, and mountains, emerges on top, of course, but by not that much. Rick believes that his team of therapists is more skilled and more enthusiastic than at Belmont, thanks to the personal care and attention given to their recruitment, training, and motivation by Rick's wife, Kay. He also believes that the sense of personal space and relaxation at The Gorge is at least on a par with the gloriously luxurious, if slightly less personal, feel at Belmont.

In contrast, Rick does not view the spa services offered at the Cascade Hotel, part of the Best American franchise, the nearest alternative offering to The Gorge, as serious competition. The service is what one would expect from a business hotel, competent but less personal, an add-on service for overnight business folk, as opposed to an attraction in its own right.

On the other hand, Reina's is a genuine player, as are half a dozen other specialist spa houses in nearby Portland, but with a distinctive twist. Sited within a quirky resort, combining a hotel with a hostel, sports with arts, Reina's offers a broad range of services and good facilities, all touched with its owner's irrepressible and lovable personality.

Rick knows that little of this analysis, and certainly none of these figures, will find their way into his business plan (we'll review, later on, what will go in). But what the exercise has given him is analysis in depth, thinking in depth, and findings rooted in research. And balance.

Rick has shown to himself that The Gorge is a credible player in the spa services business, with its strong points not overexaggerated and its weak points not glossed over. This perspective must shine through in the business plan.

Even more important, this analysis has provided a construct for framing the project at the heart of his business plan, the proposed Phase II development of 16 additional rooms, plus a swimming pool. The final column of Table 5–3 shows that the project could render The Gorge the leading spa operator in the Columbia River Gorge, thanks to:

◻ Increased market share (hence spreading the message)

◻ Greater contribution to overheads (hence lower unit costs)

◻ Broader range of facilities (not far behind what's offered by Reina's Spa)

Rick now reproduces this analysis for The Gorge's other two main business segments, accommodation and catering. For the purposes of this book, we need not go into similar detail, but suffice it to say that Rick's conclusions are similarly encouraging.

Rick can now put into words, wrapped up in just three to four pages, what his analysis of competitive position has concluded, namely:

◻ The Gorge has come from nowhere to be a credible player in its niche.

◻ It has done so, on the one hand, by:

– Offering the overnight visitor an experience somewhat out of the ordinary—clean, crisp, comfortable accommodation spiced with a hint of the Orient, with stunning views over the Columbia River Gorge

– Offering the diner the choice of traditional American fare or home-cooked, delicately spiced Oriental cuisine, with the same lovely views

– Creating a spacious, relaxing environment, a high quality of therapy, and a culture of service and enthusiasm in its spa services, factors that counterbalance the limited range of facilities offered compared with leading local competitors

◻ And, on the other hand, it has succeeded by keeping a tight control over overheads.

◻ The Gorge's occupancy rates provide evidence: Average room occupancy by Year 3 of operations is 71 percent, well above the average of 62 percent for Columbia River Gorge hotels in pre-crash 2008 (see Chapter 4).

◻ Completion of the two-phase strategy could make The Gorge one of the leading providers of spa services in the Columbia River Gorge area, not in terms of scale or market share, but competitive position, hence profitability.

◘ Strategic risks are low. In Phase II, The Gorge will offer more of the same successful formula of Phase I, and it seems unlikely that this concept, so successful so far, will become dated and of lesser appeal over the next five years.

Rick will now proceed to assess the resource implications of this strategy in the next chapter of his business plan. Before that, however, he cannot resist comparing what he has written in Chapter 5 with what he would have written four years earlier when starting up the venture. For Phase I, he had used a mortgage plus the proceeds from the sale of the family home in Boston as finance—and he never got around to writing a business plan for himself as the backer (though it might well have been a useful exercise).

He finds that much of what he has written in 2014 would have been the same as in 2009. He had researched then the spa services market in depth, so his findings on CPCs and KSFs would not have changed much in the interim—only perhaps in the weighting attached to, for example, range of treatments offered.

The main difference would have been in the use of tense. In 2009, his plan for the new venture would throughout have been in the future tense. His main bullet points would be virtually identical four years earlier, except that they would reflect aspirations for the future, not the factual present. Thus the first two bullet items would have read:

◘ The Gorge should become a credible competitor in its niche by 2013.

◘ It will do so, on the one hand, by offering the overnight visitor an experience somewhat out of the ordinary—clean, crisp, accommodation spiced with a hint of the Orient, with stunning views over the Columbia River Gorge . . . and so on.

Things have worked out pretty much as planned, which gives Rick a feeling of great satisfaction and indeed optimism that Phase II will be worthy of securing a backer.

Checklist on Strategy

Your chapter on strategy will stand out from 90 percent of other business plans because of its underpinning in research and analysis. Your backer will appreciate this thoroughness.

Very little of the research you undertake when following the guidelines in Appendix A of this book will find its way directly into your business plan's strategy chapter. But it will be there indirectly. This chapter will be just three or four pages long, but it will radiate latent power. The impression will be conveyed to your backer that each statement is rooted in either fact or rigorously supported judgment.

Derive your firm's competitive position coherently:

- Demonstrate your understanding of customer purchasing criteria in key business segments. Make cursory but pertinent reference to research you have done on this point, with further detail, as appropriate, available in an appendix to your plan.

- Likewise, demonstrate your understanding of key success factors.

- Explain your firm's competitive position. Lay out the source of your firm's competitive advantage in key segments.

Next, demonstrate how your firm's strategy will improve performance over the next few years. Tell your backers:

- Which of the generic strategies you will deploy

- What steps will be taken to strengthen competitive position in key segments, by building on strengths and/or working on weaknesses

- How your firm will boost its strategic position by optimizing its portfolio of business segments

If yours is a new venture in an existing market, explain why you have a sufficiently distinctive angle to survive in the early stages. If you are creating a new product or service, convince the reader that you will find ready buyers, in the right quantities and at the right price.

Finally, alert your backer to the key strategic risks your firm may face and how you intend to mitigate them. And, conversely, highlight the strategic opportunities that may be there for the taking, which will represent upside to your plan's forecasts.

RESOURCES

It's not the size of the dog in the fight, it's the size of the fight in the dog. —Mark Twain

IN THE LAST chapter you set out your firm's strategy over the next few years. You explained how you plan to strengthen your competitive position in strategically selected product/market segments—whether by building on your strengths against key success factors (KSFs) or by working on weaknesses.

In short, you explained what your firm planned to do to achieve the goals identified in Chapter 2. In this chapter, you will set out how you will deploy the firm's scarce resources to implement that strategy.

One caveat: If yours is a medium-size business or bigger, you may be tempted to delegate each of the sections of this chapter to the respective department heads—the marketing director, the chief information officer, or whomever. That's fine, but make sure you edit these sections in the style of the rest of the document. This business plan must flow with one style only. Your department heads are capable of writing a 25-page report on their pet function alone, but you need to restrict them to three or four pages, summarize their main findings in half a page or so, and put their reports into the appropriate appendix.

All resources must be competently deployed for your business plan to be successful. But some resources are more critical than others.

In our experience, having reviewed hundreds of business plans on behalf of investors or lenders, the backer's pecking order of priority goes like this:

1. Management

2. Marketing

3. Operations

Many investors say they back people, not products or services. That's not the whole story—as we'll explain later—but it's a hefty chunk of it.

And investors know that it's no good having the best widget on the market if customers are unaware of how good it is. So they are always keen to learn in detail a firm's marketing plans.

They also realize that management and marketing must permeate every link in the value chain in a successful organization (see Figure 6–1). Managerial capability must be as evident in the inbound logistics as in the service ends of the business. A culture of marketing should ensure that product development, indeed the full R&D program, will be driven by the needs of the customer.

FIGURE 6–1. The value chain as seen by your backer.

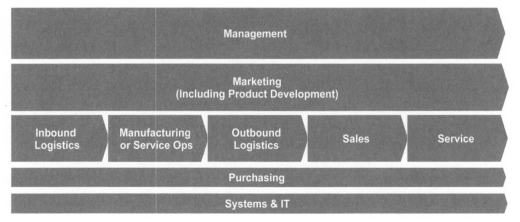

Then there's the rest of the value chain. Each link is important; no link can be broken. But each link can be strengthened relatively painlessly if there is a weakness. Getting the supply chain right, streamlining the manufacturing process, outsourcing the logistics function, or installing new enterprise resource or customer relations management software can arguably be undertaken as a fix—whether with the firm's existing resources, through targeted recruitment, or with the appropriate guidance from external consultants.

This is not necessarily the case with management. If a manager is not up to the job—and this is seldom a black-and-white issue—it can take time to fully appreciate the implications, whereupon finding the right replacement manager at the right time can be hit or miss.

Likewise, with marketing, it can be difficult to change the culture of an organization that believes in "the way we have always done it here," or "the kind of product we have always made here," so screw the customer. Your backer needs to know that your firm is market-led, not product- or production-led.

So you'll start Chapter 6 of your business plan with how your management resources are up to the task of delivering your plan, move on to your marketing resources, and then address the rest of the value chain.

Management

In this section, you'll explain why you have the right management team to ensure delivery of the plan. But be aware that your backers will be looking for a different balance of capabilities in an established business compared with a startup.

AN ESTABLISHED BUSINESS

There are two schools of thought on management in an established business. There are some private equity players who say that, as in a startup, management is the most important of all considerations in deciding whether to invest in a business. To back up that belief, they will offer management teams extremely generous, ratcheted equity packages conditional upon delivery of the plan.

At the other extreme are private equity players who regard management effectively as units of production. They should do their job, be rewarded very well if they deliver, and be replaced, ruthlessly, if they don't. These players will undertake detailed due diligence on the market, finances, and legal issues but give little attention to the management. No need—management is replaceable.

Most private equity players lie somewhere in between. They conduct detailed management due diligence before investing. They would rather not have the hassle of replacing a manager during the plan period. It's better to weed the team before investing and stick with those managers they back.

Wherever they lie on the management dispensability spectrum, all private equity players will agree on one thing: They are looking for managers who can deliver against the plan and who can implement the strategy. They want managers who can not only identify where the firm needs to strengthen its performance against one or another KSF, but also execute that performance improvement.

There are implications, then, for what should go into your business plan, for each key manager:

- For an appendix to your plan, include a one-page curriculum vitae for each manager, specifying roles held, with which firm and for how long, and highlighting major achievements against specific objectives within those roles.

- For this section of Chapter 6, include a one-paragraph summary, with a sentence or two on relevant experience, including length of service at the firm and selecting one example of how the manager delivered in a relevant role or against a relevant project.

After reading through six paragraphs on six key managers, your backer will be left with one overriding impression: These guys are doers, your backer will think. They look like they can deliver this plan.

So, who should these six key managers be? It depends on the size and nature of the business, but it should certainly include those managers in charge of your firm's strategy (probably the managing director in a small firm), sales and marketing (one person may handle both functions in a small firm), finance, and operations. In a larger firm, it may well include the heads of technology, human resources, and IT, as well as the heads of the most important business units.

Your backer will also want to know about organization and governance in your firm. Here may be the place to include an organization chart, kept simple and showing in particular who reports to whom in the top management team.

One paragraph on governance should suffice, unless your situation is out of the ordinary. A list of who is on the board of directors may be useful, especially if one or two board members play an important guiding role in the firm's strategic direction, functional performance, or networking.

A STARTUP BUSINESS

There is no debate that management is a more important factor in a startup than in an established business. It is crucial. You will not find any venture capitalist dismissing management as dispensable, as you may find in some buyout houses.

Typically, the earlier the stage in the investment cycle, the more crucial management is. The right managers are more important to the backer in seed capital (for the very early "proof of concept" stages of a business) than venture capital (for the early, high-risk, high-growth years of a business), and more important in venture capital than development capital (for growth businesses with an established track record).

Many venture capitalists say that they back the person, rather than the product or service, in a startup. If entrepreneurs have the right spirit, passion, and dedication to their cause, they are well on the way to obtaining backing.

But this is a great oversimplification. As has been pointed out in earlier chapters, first and foremost is the business proposition. The offering must have a sustainable competitive advantage. There must be customers prepared to pay the right price for the product or service. If those boxes are checked, and the entrepreneur is the right person, then the venture capitalist will get excited.

Note the use of the word *entrepreneur*, not *manager*. That is because backers are looking for someone quite different in a startup. They are not looking for a solid, steady, nine-to-fiver with a proven track record of delivering to plan. They are looking for a visionary, a leader, a person who believes wholly in the product or service, who will inspire and motivate though passion, energy, and darned hard work.

Think Bezos, Branson, or Buffett. On a smaller scale, as yet, think Simon Cowell: Love him or loathe him, he has created a global media empire from scratch. But these are exceptional people and surely your backers can't expect you to be like that?

Yes, they can, and they will. The authors have worked over the years with managers in the least glamorous businesses you can imagine—from sewage pumping companies to makers of stair lifts for the elderly and infirm—and we have found leaders who genuinely convey passion to their employees, customers, and other stakeholders. If they can do it, so can you. So must you.

If you are starting up a new business, you must feel and convey that passion. You may even possess the Celtic *hwyl*—the passion, spirit, fervor that can lift you to extremes of success. (For further reading, try Vaughan Evans, *Backing U! A Business-Oriented Guide to Backing Your Passion and Achieving Career Success*, Business & Careers Press, 2009.)

But passion won't be everything. As we saw for an established business, you must also be able to deliver. And in this section of your business plan, you must explain, succinctly, how you have delivered in the past and how you met the objectives set, whether by you or your boss.

As for the passion, don't leave that for the presentation. You may not get that far. The passion should shine through on every page of the plan. And when you do get to that presentation, let it rip.

> **TOP TIP:** Let your backer be infused with your passion.

Marketing

Once again, your backers will be looking for somewhat different capabilities in an established business compared with a startup.

AN ESTABLISHED BUSINESS

Your backer needs to know that yours is a market-driven firm. You make products or supply services to customers that fill an identified and researched customer need, and that convey a definable benefit to the customer. And your backer needs to know that you will deploy a coherent array of marketing tools to ensure that customers are sufficiently aware of these benefits that they will purchase your product or service in sufficient quantities and at the right prices for you to make your plan.

Don't make the mistake of confusing marketing with advertising. The latter is just one component of the former. Marketing is much bigger. It is a mindset. It is about the orientation of a firm toward serving the customer.

In his classic text, *Basic Marketing: A Managerial Approach* (Irwin, 1960), which has been elaborated on since but not markedly improved, Jerome McCarthy set out four components of the marketing mix known as the four Ps: product, place, promotion, and pricing. This categorization should more than suffice for this section of your business plan. It should contain one to three paragraphs on each, as follows:

◘ *Product*. If your firm follows a differentiation as opposed to a low-cost generic strategy (see Chapter 5), show how it is the satisfaction of identified customer needs that has shaped your products (or services). Show, too, how product development, and also research, is oriented to meeting future customer needs and does not exist in an ivory tower, presided over by experts with little knowledge of and interest in the needs of the marketplace.

◘ *Place*. Show which distribution channels are of greatest importance to your firm, now and over the next few years. Do you focus on direct sales or indirect sales using agents, wholesalers, or distributors? Why? How cost-effective is your direct sales force? What channels does the competition use? How does your ratio of sales to number of salespeople compare with that of the market leader? How have your online sales developed in recent years? To what extent have they cannibalized offline sales or brought in new business? What are the prospects for the future?

◘ *Price*. What is your firm's price position relative to the competition? Is it broadly in line with the average, at a discount, at a premium? Why? How is this pricing aligned with strategy? How elastic are volumes sold in your business to price? What are the prospects for raising prices in line with inflation over the plan period? What are your assumptions?

◘ *Promotion*. What are the main ways you have been promoting your products in recent years? Do you rely on advertising (through which media—print, screen, radio, Internet?), trade promotions, public relations, sponsorships, exhibitions, trade shows, seminars/conferences? Why? How will this promotional mix change over the plan period?

Finally, you should include here a word or two on the results of all this marketing. How satisfied are your customers with your product or service, and with your performance? If you have undertaken any satisfaction surveys, here is the place to include the headline results. You may even include a one-page synopsis as an appendix to your plan, along with other marketing data you think might be useful evidence to your backer (for example, a breakdown of your marketing budget over the last three years).

To what extent is this customer satisfaction expressed in repeat business? This is the lifeblood of every business. The cost of winning a new customer greatly exceeds the cost of winning repeat business. If you have some good statistics on repeat business, set them out here. And emphasize how much better your ratio is than that of your competitors (assuming that's the case).

□ □ □ □ □   **THINKING OUT OF THE BOX** □ □ □ □ □

Magical Marketing

Success is a journey, not a destination. The doing is often more important than the outcome.
—Arthur Ashe

Peter Drucker, the management guru, once said, "The purpose of a business is to create and keep a customer. Therefore, the basic management functions are innovation and marketing, because only they are capable of generating sales, revenue, and cash flow."

The most important skill of the entrepreneur is the ability to market the product or service. This skill involves determining exactly what is to be produced and sold, how it is to be produced and sold, and how the product or service is to be positioned in the marketplace.

Fortunately, marketing is a systematic process that you can learn through repeated practice. Marketing is the process of determining what is to be produced and sold. Selling is the process of determining how the product or service is to be sold in a competitive market. Marketing and sales go together, but marketing comes first.

Here are the fundamentals of "magical marketing" for a product or service (henceforth referred to simply as "product"):

□ The key questions in marketing and business success are: *What* exactly is to be sold, and *to whom* is it going to be sold, and *by whom*, and *how* is it to be sold and paid for, and how is the product to be produced, delivered, and serviced?

Each of these questions must be asked and answered over and over again, especially in the development of a new product. Most ideas for new products fail because one of these questions was not adequately or accurately answered.

□ The key to business success is simple: The product is well suited to the current market, priced appropriately, and aggressively marketed and sold. In addition, there are a few rules for success:

a. The customer is always right.

b. If the product is not selling in sufficient quantities, it must be improved or removed from the market.

c. It is not what companies produce, but what customers want, that determines market demand.

◘ Any new product must be better than the competitor's product in at least three ways to break into a competitive market. For example:

a. The product is clearly superior in some way to any existing products available.

b. The product is cheaper than competitive products.

c. The product is easier to use than competitive products.

d. The product is more convenient to buy or more readily available.

e. The product is more attractive.

f. The product offers additional features or benefits.

g. The product is of a higher quality and achieves the value offering better than anything else.

h. The product satisfies the customer's deepest needs better than its competitors, in some way.

i. The product may be similar to competitive offerings, but the service in which it is wrapped is superior.

◘ There are four keys to strategic marketing: 1) specialization, 2) differentiation, 3) segmentation, and 4) concentration. The application of these strategic principles determines business success or failure.

◘ Specialization means providing a clear, specific benefit to a particular customer group. A company may specialize in:

a. Servicing a particular market

b. Providing a particular benefit

c. Providing a particular service

d. Offering a particular technology

e. Servicing a specific type of customer

f. Servicing a particular location or geographical area

◘ Differentiation is the most important element in strategic marketing and the critical determinant of business success. A company can differentiate itself through:

a. Competitive advantage, whereby the company's offering is superior to the competition in one or more ways

b. Area of excellence, with the product being clearly excellent in at least one way relative to its competition

c. Unique selling proposition, where the product has at least one feature or benefit that makes it superior in terms of satisfying customer needs and that no other competitor offers

◻ Segmentation means the company does careful market analysis to identify its ideal customers for a particular product or service. The company identifies:

a. The exact type of customer who can most benefit from the superior features of the product. This person is your target market.

b. The precise location of the ideal customers for this product.

c. The ideal method of sale that can be used to approach this particular customer.

d. The ideal marketing channel through which it can sell to the ideal customer for its product.

◻ Concentration means the company focuses time, attention, and money on selling more of its products to its very best potential customers. The 80/20 rule applies here:

a. 20 percent of prospects will generate 80 percent of sales.

b. 20 percent of customers will account for 80 percent of sales volume.

c. 20 percent of customers will account for 80 percent of company profitability.

d. In addition, the company concentrates its best people and resources on selling its best products to its best prospective customers.

e. All advertising and promotion is focused and concentrated on those customers who can buy the most and contribute the greatest revenues to the company.

◻ The ability of the entrepreneur to continually innovate and create better, faster, cheaper ways to service its customers is essential for business success.

a. Continually seek out or develop new products for the highest-profit customers of the company.

b. Continually seek to improve existing products for the most important customers.

c. Continually seek out better ways to market, sell, promote, and distribute the product to the customer.

◻ The process of marketing and innovation requires that the entrepreneur continually identify customers who are not yet being served.

a. What additional customers exist for the products of the company?

b. What additional products could the company develop for its existing customers?

c. How could we improve our existing products to make them more attractive to our existing and future customers?

Marketing is the process of continually seeking new and better ways to create and keep customers. Profitability in a business is the result of finding and serving customers with more and more of what they want at prices that enable the company to make a profit. The more dynamic and creative the marketing function in a company, the greater will be the sales and the higher will be the level of profitability in the organization.

What one action related to magical marketing are you going to take immediately as the result of what you have learned here?

□ □ □ □ □ □ □ □ □ □ □ □ □ □ □ □ □ □ □ □

Bullish: Red Bull's Marketing Resources

In Southeast Asia there lives a massive black bison-type creature with a prominent curved ridge on its back, drooped shoulders, and ferocious curved horns. This endangered bovine is a gaur, and it proved an inspirational name for the energy drink created by Chaleo Yoovidhya, a Thai pharmaceutical businessman. His concoction was a concentration of ingredients, such as sugar, caffeine, taurine, and vitamins, and it soon developed a reputation for keeping the body alert and awake, becoming particularly popular with Thai truck drivers. *Krating daeng* (red gaur) was pitched squarely at the common man, and launch promotion included sponsorship of Thai boxing tournaments.

An Austrian marketer, Dietrich Mateschitz, came across this drink on a business trip to Thailand, liked it, and linked up with Chaleo to take the brand into international markets. He launched Red Bull in his home country on April 1, 1987, with the rather cumbersome tagline "Red Bull: so awesome that the polka dots will literally fly off your tie"! But within a year Red Bull had found its marketing sweet spot, sponsoring the Dolomitenmann, a marathon endurance event combining mountain running, paragliding, kayaking, and mountain biking through the Dolomites range in northeastern Italy.

Soon Red Bull was to sponsor Flugtag (fly day) in Vienna, a wacky event where teams compete to launch homemade, human-powered, creative, and/or flashy flying machines (an event later to be rolled out in more than 40 countries). The die was cast, as was the tagline: "Red Bull gives you wings."

Red Bull's market positioning has been ruthlessly consistent. If an extreme or endurance sport exists, especially if it relates to flight, or at least speed, the company will sponsor either the event or a team (or individual). Thus, Red Bull started its own Formula 1 team in 2005 and was rewarded with three successive victories for both driver Sebastian Vettel and constructors in 2010–12 (although its venture into NASCAR racing proved less successful, resulting in team withdrawal in 2011).

If an extreme sport didn't exist, Red Bull invented it. Thus the Red Bull Crashed Ice in Stockholm (racing on hockey skates down an ice track with obstacles and jumps), the Red Bull X-Fighters in Valencia, Spain (motocross-cum-bullfighting), or the Red Bull X-Alps, where masochistic athletes hike and/or paraglide over an extraordinary 1,200-mile journey from Austria to Monaco!

The company has also moved from old to new. In 1999, Red Bull sponsored BASE jumper Felix Baumgartner when he leaped off the world's then tallest building, Petronas Towers in Kuala Lumpur, where he broke the then record for longest free fall (eight seconds) and fastest speed achieved (105 mph). Thirteen years later, Red Bull sponsored the same daredevil's leap from the edge of space, 128,000 feet aboveground. This time, 8 million people watched live on YouTube (with another 30 million views later) as Baumgartner became the first individual to travel at supersonic speed, namely, 833.9 mph!

As an example of sustained market positioning, Red Bull is hard to beat. The message "Red Bull gives you wings" is persistently reinforced and backed up by targeted sponsorship of events that purport to do just that. That message has powered sales reaching almost 5 billion cans in 2012. What's next for the company? Red bulls jumping over the moon, while the dish runs away with the spoon?

STARTUP BUSINESS

The questions on marketing are all the same in a startup. But the answers differ in two respects. They are in the future tense. And they aren't just important; they're critical.

Marketing is the lifeblood of a startup. If customers don't know you exist, you'll have no customers. You'll be one of the thousands of companies that start up and disappear each year without a trace.

In Chapter 3 of your business plan, you identified promising market demand prospects. In Chapter 4 you concluded that the competitive environment was favorable. In Chapter 5 you set out why your offering enjoyed a distinctive competitive edge.

Here, in this section of Chapter 6, you'll tell your backers how customers are going to be put in touch with your offering. This information is crucial. It will require you to set out a detailed marketing plan in your appendix and summarize it here, convincingly.

You'll show how each component of the plan will reinforce the other, how the customer will be bombarded with the same message, from different angles and different people, until they are eager to purchase your offering.

You'll write this section of the plan with passion, even with some marketing hype thrown in. But your marketing plan must be sensible, rational, and doable, too. It must convince.

> **TOP TIP:** If no one knows you're there, you sure won't get your share.

Operations and Capital Expenditure

This is the section for your chief operating officer, if you have one. Or for you again, if you don't. Here you need to cover the main issues affecting your firm through the value chain, from the sourcing of supplies through to customer service. Remember that your backers don't need to know the detail. They want the helicopter view in general and the ground-level view only when an issue arises that could have a material impact on your business plan.

In this section, you'll consider the implications of your firm's strategy over the next few years on these aspects of operations:

- Supplies

- Purchasing

- Manufacture or service provision

- Research and development

- Distribution, storage, logistics

- Customer service and technical support

- Systems and IT

- Quality and financial control

- Regulatory compliance

Under each link in the value chain, you'll consider what resources are required to meet the plan. And, of particular relevance for the next chapter on financial forecasts, you must explain what key items of capital expenditure are needed to support the plan today and beyond. State your case in no more detail than is needed, but convincingly, for the major items of capital expenditure. Include the following information:

- The nature of the capital project

- Why it is needed

- The alternatives considered and rejected

- How much it will cost

- How long will it take to be implemented

- What impact it will have on future revenues or costs

- The risks associated with the investment

Again, your backers don't need to know about every item of capital expenditure, just the main ones—the value-impacting ones.

SUPPLIES

Supply of raw materials can be a critical issue. If your company manufactures aluminium car parts or wear-resistant cobalt cutting tools, your backer needs to know that the metal inputs to the production process will be available as and when you need them. And when the metal price goes up, as indeed it will, as for any commodity raw material, to what extent will you be able to preserve your margins through the pricing mechanism?

Metal converters are an extreme case. Few manufacturing companies, and no service companies, are as sensitive to raw material supply and pricing as a metal converter. But think of producers of plastics, glass, or folding cartons: All are highly sensitive to the availability and price of their key raw materials, respectively, polypropylene (itself extremely sensitive to the price of crude oil), silica, and cartonboard (which is highly sensitive to supplies of recycled and virgin pulp).

Think of an automotive manufacturer. An automaker is sensitive to the price of galvanized, low carbon steel for chassis, but has a whole range of other suppliers for seats, plastic fuel tanks, or tires, which tends to spread the risk and limit exposure to the availability or price of steel.

The higher the proportion of cost from a single raw material in your business, the more your backer will need to know the detail. If you run a metal converting business, you should devote a page or two in your appendix to the pricing cycle of that metal over the last few years, highlighting the drivers behind each major upswing or downswing.

How dependent is your firm on the provision of supplies not just of one commodity but of one supplier? If that supplier fails to deliver, or exploits its bargaining power to dramatically raise prices, what options do you have for shifting to another supplier? And what are the switching costs?

If yours is a service business, don't think this section doesn't apply to you. It is likely that your main supplies will be people. But how easy is it to find people of the right background, qualifications, and experience to replace employees who move on?

And even service businesses can be reliant on goods. A dental practice needs regular supplies of equipment, products, and materials, not just hygienists. How reliant has an insurance broker become on its main software supplier? Can your building firm find sufficiently well-qualified, competent, and enthusiastic plumbers?

Most businesses will have a reasonable choice of suppliers and relative predictability in the cost of the supplies. But not all. Your backer needs to know where your business lies.

PURCHASING

Supplies and purchasing used to come under the same heading in the old days. A manufacturer would purchase the supplies, convert them to some product, ship them out, sell them, and provide service support.

Then along came outsourcing. Now every stage in the value chain can be outsourced. Manufactured modules can be "bought in" from external providers (or the whole manufacturing process may be outsourced), transport operators contracted, distributors engaged, agents hired, and service companies instructed.

And it's not just in manufacturing. It's the same with service companies. Insurance companies now outsource chunks of claims management. Banks outsource software development and payment processing. Prisons outsource prisoner transfer.

Whatever the sector, whether in manufacturing or services, activities such as cleaning, maintenance, IT services, and catering are often outsourced. Likewise customer service and technical support are outsourced, often to offshore providers.

Today's firm can often be seen as an aggregator of products and services, overlaid with design, management, and marketing value added. At every stage in the value chain, the firm can be a purchaser. Not just in supplies, but in operations, logistics, sales, service.

How sharp is your purchasing capability? Do you consider purchasing to be a key success factor? If not, why? How well trained is your team in negotiation?

Do your competitors buy their raw materials cheaper than you do, even if their quantities purchased are of similar scale to yours? What about the bought-in products used in manufacturing? Are they competitively priced? And logistics? Technical support? Customer service? Are you getting consistently good deals in your purchasing, relative to your competitors?

This section could run from one paragraph to a page, again depending on whether your firm's purchasing capabilities may be an issue to your backer.

Confronting China: Rodon's Production Resources

A 2013 report by the Economic Policy Institute found that the United States lost over 5 million jobs in manufacturing between 2001 and 2011. More than one-third of these jobs went to China. Manufacturing of higher-value, high-tech goods, such as semiconductors and electronics, was hit hardest, with lower-value, bulky, or time-critical goods more likely to avoid trans-Pacific migration.

Offshoring of production transitioned from being a profit enhancer to a survival necessity for many U.S. companies during this period. To compete with the ever-improving quality yet much lower prices of Far Eastern manufactured goods landing in U.S. ports, U.S. manufacturers had little choice but to lower production costs. For manufacturing workers, however, they lost out either way—either their employers could not compete and shed jobs or went under, or the employers could only compete if manufacturing jobs were relocated offshore.

But things are changing. China's growth has been so rapid that its cost base has been rising. Real wages have quintupled in China in ten years, while oil prices have tripled and transport costs have also inflated. Mexico has become a more attractive alternative for many companies, including BlackBerry.

Meanwhile some U.S. companies are fighting back. The family-owned Rodon Group is a small plastics parts producer, founded by Irving Glickman in 1956, operating out of Hatfield, Pennsylvania, and a sister business of toy company K'NEX. At the age of 100, Glickman took the fight to the offshore producers in 2012 with an award-winning "Cheaper than China" marketing campaign.

And this is not just wishful thinking. Rodon demonstrates to its clients the hidden costs of offshore sourcing and the benefits of onshore sourcing, claiming that Rodon beats China pricing once customers take certain factors into consideration:

- *Product quality risks.* Rodon has a state-of-the-art plastic injection molding facility, with ISO 9001 certification and a tooling lifetime guarantee.

- *Supply chain risks.* Rodon supplies just-in-time, versus 45 days on the water.

- *Payment risks.* Rodon deals in U.S. dollars.

□ *Communication risks.* Rodon speaks the customer's language, in or close to the customer's time zone.

Rodon's "Cheaper than China" marketing campaign raised its profile stratospherically, earning its managers numerous network TV appearances. The company even received a visit from President Obama. As Buddy Holly might have said, rave on, Rodon!

MANUFACTURE OR SERVICE PROVISION

Succinctly explain how you make your product or deliver your service.

If you are a manufacturer, where are your facilities? How large are they? How long have you been in operation? What scope is there for expansion, and what constraints need to be overcome (e.g., in relation to planning permits)? What are the options if you have to move to another site? How do your facilities compare with those of the competition?

What are your main items of capital equipment? How have they changed in recent years? Where do they sit on the value/quality spectrum—that is, are they the Bentley, the BMW, or the Ford Fusion equivalent in their field? What additional equipment do you need, as replacement or for growth? How does the equipment you deploy compare with that of your competitors?

What are your main manufacturing processes? How have they developed in recent years? Do you ask the "make or buy" question at each stage of the manufacturing process? Which components or processes have you outsourced in recent years? What plans do you have for future outsourcing? What do your competitors do?

If yours is a service company, the same questions generally apply, except that you may be delivering your service from an office or a depot rather than a factory; the equipment deployed may be more computer-related than manufacturing-related (although many service firms, for example, in healthcare, use highly sophisticated equipment); and your processes involve the movement of paperwork (or e-information these days) rather than goods.

Above all, how do the facilities, equipment, and processes you deploy in providing your service compare with those of your competitors? What are you planning to do to stay ahead, keep pace, or catch up?

RESEARCH AND DEVELOPMENT

You will have already discussed product development in your section on marketing resources, earlier in this chapter. But here is the place to tell your backer a bit more about your research and development (R&D) operations. How many staff members do you have, and what have they been working on in the last few years? How long have products taken to come on stream? How successful have the launches been? What impact have new products had on your manufacturing processes and equipment?

What products are currently in R&D? Are these new products or revamped versions of an existing product range? Are they being developed to meet gaps in the market? If so, define the gaps and set out the timeline for launch and the implications for manufacturing and distribution.

Is your product line regarded in the market as being up-to-date, long in the tooth, somewhere in the middle? Or is it varied? What plans do you have to improve that positioning? How extensive is your current product pipeline compared with the recent past?

How do your firm's R&D capabilities compare with the competition? Who is recognized in the industry as the innovator? Are you more of a follower? Are you happy with that positioning?

In short, are there any issues with R&D that your backer needs to know about?

DISTRIBUTION, STORAGE, LOGISTICS

Explain how your goods get out of the factory and into the hands of the customer. What are the various routes to market? Do you sell through a wholesaler or distributor? To an agent? Directly to the customer? A mix of all three? How has distribution changed in recent years? How will it change in the future? Why? What logistics do your competitors deploy? Does that work better or worse? What do you plan to do about it?

Again, only go into detail if there is an issue, good or bad, that your backer needs to know about. For example, you may want to demonstrate a competitive advantage, or you may need to highlight a competitive weakness, albeit one that you are in the process of rectifying. Because such an issue may well have cost implications, your backer needs to know.

CUSTOMER SERVICE AND TECHNICAL SUPPORT

These are areas where again you must be candid and upfront. If you aren't, you will be found out. Remember, your backer will probably insist on speaking to a few customers, and if your customer service or technical support is not up to scratch, your customer will seize the opportunity to tell it like it is.

It is not the end of the world if you don't have the best reputation in customer service, in every place, for every customer, for every product line. It's a trade-off. Customer service is expensive; so, too, is technical support. Often it is the largest player in your industry that has the best service and support, because it can afford to, with its economies of scale.

One of the authors reviewed the business plan of a company that had superb technical support in one region but very limited support in the region it wanted to expand into—a key growth component of the business plan. The company recognized this limitation and was assessing options for strengthening that capability by partnering with a service company in that region. This was an issue for the backer, rightly recognized by the company, and argued credibly in this section of its business plan. How is your customer service and technical support? Is it outsourced? Does it work well? And in relation to the competition and the market leader? How can it be improved? What would be the cost implications?

SYSTEMS AND IT

What are the key systems and IT you use in your manufacturing or service operations? How long have they been in place? What did you use before? How effective have these new systems been? How do they compare with the systems and IT of the competition?

What are the shortcomings of your systems and IT? How can they be improved? What are the cost implications? One of the authors reviewed the plan of a global player in payments. Its systems were an acknowledged weakness and any prospective buyer was made fully aware that a major investment would be needed in updating the systems very soon after taking over the company. The backer needed to know and was told upfront.

Your situation is unlikely to be so drastic; nonetheless, if there are any systems or IT issues that your backer needs to know about, here is the place to lay them out.

QUALITY AND FINANCIAL CONTROL

Control is important to your backers. Even if things work out according to your business plan, and your assessments of market demand, industry competition, and your strategy and plans for improving competitive advantage are solid, can your backers rest assured that you have sufficient control over quality and finances that the whole thing won't crumble?

What controls do you have in place for ensuring quality of output? This question applies as much or more to a service business as to a manufacturer. How do your controls compare with those of competitors? What is best practice?

And if something goes very wrong in quality of output—think Perrier or Toyota—what contingency plans do you have to put it right? At what cost?

What financial controls do you have? How do you ensure that invoices are paid on time? Can you control inventory if there is a dip in sales? How can you detect fraud at an early stage?

Again, if you feel that all is indeed under control when it comes to quality assurance and your financial systems, or that you are at least on par with everyone else in the industry, just mention it here. There should be no need to go into the issue at great length.

REGULATORY COMPLIANCE

Your backers need to know that your firm is on top of all compliance issues, especially in environment, health, and safety.

Taking environmental compliance, as an example, what is your firm's track record over the last few years? How has legislation changed in this period and how have you responded? How does your response compare with that of competitors? How may legislation change further in the future and how will you respond? What are the cost implications?

Address similar questions in all major areas of compliance. If your firm is in financial services, how have you responded to tighter regulation following the financial crash of 2008?

If all is under control in major areas of compliance, say so. If there are issues, explain what they are and how you will address them. If there are major issues, detail them in your appendix and summarize them and their costs here.

Resource Risks and Opportunities

You have already pulled out the main risks and opportunities relating to market demand (Chapter 3), industry competition (Chapter 4), and strategy (Chapter 5). Now it's time to add the major resource risks to your plan, as well as resource opportunities.

These resource risks could relate to management (e.g., a key manager is lured away to a competitor), marketing (an expensive advertising campaign flops), or operations (potential distribution disruptions if the new regional depot's systems fail). What are the resource risks that are reasonably likely to occur and with reasonable impact if they do occur? These are the big risks, as defined in Chapter 3. How can they be mitigated? What are the big opportunities? How can you exploit them?

We will return to these big resource risks and opportunities in Chapter 8.

THE GORGE INN AND ORIENTAL SPA
BUSINESS PLAN, 2014: RESOURCES

Rick Jones has set out his strategy for lifting The Gorge to be a leading provider of spa services in the Columbia River Gorge through completion of the second phase of development. Now, in Chapter 6 of his business plan, he sets out the resource implications, along with their risks and opportunities. Here are his highlights:

▫ *Management.* Having completed Phase I development of The Gorge, management is now proven. Before, neither Rick nor his wife, Kay, had had any experience in hotel or spa management, which could have been a problem in obtaining external funding. Now, with three years' proven experience behind them, with ups and downs, yes, but overall success, management is a strength of this plan, not a weakness. Rick further explains his plans for how he will recruit a manager of the new spa offering, preferably someone with an Oriental heritage to complement the business's positioning.

▫ *Marketing.* The Gorge has developed, to date, through judicious use of local and regional advertising, attendance at regional promotions, competitive pricing off-season, and other special packages, such as during weddings. Rick recognizes that marketing to fill 33 rooms will be a greater challenge than for 17 rooms, but he sees it largely as more of the same, rather than an entirely new tack. One possibility is do more partnering with successful spa hotels elsewhere, giving them a cut on business referrals and offering the customer greater variety in where to stay next time.

▫ *Operations.* Rick doesn't see any likely issues with regard to supplies, purchasing, provision of services, systems (the reservation system has worked very well after the inevitable teething problems), controls, or compliance. The one major issue relates to the planning permit, which, after some to-ing and fro-ing, Rick's architect has now secured from the county.

Rick sums up the major resource risks and opportunities as being the slippage and/or cost inflation in construction work and any upsets in the health of the owners. On the first point, and given his experience in Phase I, Rick has already built in an extra two months and 10 percent contingency into his construction plans. As concerns the latter issue, he and Kay are firm believers that no one is indispensable—if something were to happen to them, others would come in to take their place!

Checklist on Resources

Demonstrate how your firm will deploy its scarce resources to implement its strategy (laid out in Chapter 5) to achieve its goals and objectives (stated in Chapter 2). Set out your plans for deploying resources in three main fields—management, marketing, and operations:

- *Management.* Explain how you will have the right team of managers, with the right experience, qualifications, and skills to implement the strategy.

- *Marketing.* Describe how you will create sufficient awareness of the firm's offering over the plan period.

- *Operations.* Tell your backer how you will deploy your resources to ensure that supplies, purchasing, manufacturing/service provision, R&D, distribution, customer service, systems and IT, control, and compliance are sufficiently aligned to deliver the plan.

Finally, describe the big resource risks and opportunities that may impact the achievability of your business plan.

FINANCIALS AND FORECASTS

In the business world, the rearview mirror is always clearer than the windshield.
—*Warren Buffett*

IN CHAPTER 6 of your plan you set out how you would deploy your firm's scarce resources to achieve the goals of Chapter 2 while following the strategy of Chapter 5. Now you must show how that strategy will translate into results—in terms of both key measurable parameters and money.

And you are going to do it in a way that will convince your backer, using a method that you won't find in other guides to business planning.

Using this method, you will forecast your *sales growth* in a way that is consistent both with the trends in market demand that you identified in Chapter 3 and your growth plans of Chapter 5. You will forecast your *profit margin* development in a way that is consistent with the competitive dynamics assessed in Chapter 4 and your profit improvement plans of Chapter 5. Then you'll translate these forecasts into full financial statements, with the detail that your backers will expect to see in the business plan (though, in reality, they may well have their own financial model to slot your numbers into).

But first we start with the actual numbers—the historic financials.

Historic Financials

Start by setting out your last three years' actual financials, as well as those for the current year's budget.

If your firm has only been going for a couple of years, provide as much financial information you can. If your firm is five to ten years old, don't put down the whole history, just the last three years, unless circumstances suggest otherwise.

Remember, you are trying to give your backers enough information for them to make their backing decision. You don't want to overload them with data and information. If the last three years have been reasonably indicative of what is likely to occur in the future, then three years should be sufficient.

But if your business operates in a highly cyclical industry, or if some extraordinary event occurred in a particular year, like the loss of a major customer or a warehouse fire, you may need to provide four or even five years of historic data.

We won't go into detail here on how to draw up historical accounts. This is a book on planning, not on accounting. If yours is an established business, your accountant has already drawn up the accounts and you hopefully have a reasonable idea of what they mean. But we'll show you how to draw up coherent financial forecasts in a later section of this chapter.

If yours is a business startup, you will have no history. Your financials will all be forecasts, which we'll also address in a later section of this chapter.

For now, you should begin with four major financial statements, for each year, the historic actual years and the budget year, namely:

1. Sales and profit margins by main business segment

2. Income statement (overall, for all segments)

3. Cash flow statement

4. Balance sheet

Then, in one or two pages of narrative, you should describe the highlights that underpin these financials. Start with the basic structure of your firm's current financials:

◘ Remind the reader which business segments *contribute most to sales* (already covered in Chapter 2 of your plan), which business segments contribute most to profit (also in Chapter 2), and *how overall sales have changed* from the previous year and are expected to change in this year's budget.

◘ Describe the major constituents of expense in the income statement—and how gross and operating profits have changed from the previous year and are expected to change in next year's budget.

◘ Describe the major influences in the cash flow and balance sheet.

Then, while addressing each of those items, look for other items of interest in the financials. Look for change from year to year. Look in particular for anomalies, for unexpected or atypical change. Look for what your backer will look for—anything that did not perform to trend or that could not easily have been predicted.

And explain why. What was behind that change? Was it a one-off or could it happen again?

Here are some examples of anomalies that you might need to address:

◘ A dip in sales in one business segment due to loss of a customer. Was this due to a situation change for the customer (e.g., bankruptcy, takeover, change of management) or a plain old dastardly switch to a competitor?

◘ A jump in cost of goods sold. Was this due to costlier raw materials (in which case, explain the extent to which the cost was passed through to the customer), a new supplier, or renegotiation of volume discount terms?

◘ A sharp increase in a particular overhead item, say, rent. Was this due to taking on more square footage, a lease renewal, or relocation of premises?

◘ Counterintuitive trends in working capital, with, for example, inventory rising one year despite flat sales. Was this due to inadequate production or inventory controls?

◘ Ups and downs in annual capital expenditure. What were the big items, and did they come in on time and within budget?

Again, remember, this is not a thesis. Only highlight those items that your backers should know about. But don't overlook anything, whether deliberately or accidentally, that they really must know about. Because when (not if) they find out, you may have to look elsewhere for your backing.

Market-Driven Sales Forecasts

Without sales, you have no business. Sales forecasts matter. But they need to be credible and convincing.

The secret is to lay out your sales forecast in a market context so that you have a market-derived perspective on its achievability. It's a top-down, market-driven approach. The bottom-up approach, where you set out specific initiatives for developing business in each of your segments, can then be added to get total revenues in each segment.

Deriving market-driven sales forecasts is best done by assessing average change over a fixed period of time, typically a three-year but possibly a five-year time frame. You'll relate your forecast sales growth to medium-term trends in the market over that time period. Having completed this process, however, you will still have to set out your sales forecasts, at least the totals, for each intervening year. They will be needed for the yearly income statements and other financial forecasts later in this chapter.

The process is straightforward, as long as you take one step at a time. The flow is an eight-step process, with each step following logically from the previous one. Here it is:

1. *Business segments*. List each main segment, which will be forecast separately.

2. *Revenues*. What revenues were achieved in this segment in the last financial year? If this year is atypical in some way, you should substitute a "normal" level of revenues for the year (from Chapter 2 of your plan).

3. *Market demand prospects*. How do you expect the market to grow (preferably as a percentage) each year over the next few years in this segment (from Chapter 3)?

4. *Competitive position*. How does your firm measure up relative to the competition in this segment, and how may its position change over the next few years (from Chapter 5)?

5. *Likely revenue growth.* Based on your future competitive position, is your firm likely to keep pace with, exceed, or fall short of market demand growth in this segment? What is your likely revenue growth rate?

6. *Top-down revenues.* What are the resultant revenues from the market-driven forecast growth rate?

7. *Bottom-up revenues.* What initiatives are planned to grow sales above (or below) market-driven growth rates in this segment? For example, are you planning the launch (or removal) of new products within the product group? What about entry into (or withdrawal from) new markets within the market group? Will you be taking on (or possibly losing) new customers? Will there be a significant marketing investment in a segment? What are the likely incremental revenues from any such new bottom-up initiatives in three years' time?

8. *Total revenues.* Add up the market-driven and bottom-up revenues to get the total forecast revenues for this segment in three years' time.

The beauty of this process is the transparency. Your backers will see to what extent your revenue forecasts are:

- Consistent with market demand prospects and your firm's competitive position, within each segment

- Dependent on new initiatives in sales and marketing, including new product launches or new market entry, if they are to be achieved

The process is best captured in a table format. Because there are eight entries in the process flow, we take eight columns—as shown in Table 7–1.

The first four columns are easy to fill in—you've already done the work, in chapters 2, 3, and 5. Here you just need to add information to columns 5 to 8.

Column 5 is the clincher. Your likely market-driven revenue growth rate must be consistent with:

- Market demand forecasts, as set out in Chapter 3 of your plan

- Your firm's competitive position, as set out in Chapter 5

- Your firm's track record over the last few years

TABLE 7–1. Drawing up a market-based sales forecast.

Business Segments	Revenues ($000)	Market Demand Growth (%/year)	Company Competitive Position (0–5)	Likely Revenue Growth (%/year)	Top-Down Revenues ($000)	Bottom-Up Revenues ($000)	Total Revenues ($000)
	Latest Year	Next Three Years	Next Three Years	Next Three Years	In Three Years	In Three Years	In Three Years
1	2	3	4	5	6	7	8
Source:	Chapter 2	Chapter 3	Chapter 5	Here in Chapter 7			
A							
B							
C							
Others							
Total							

Here's an example of consistency: If you find that the market in a business segment is set to grow steadily, and you assess your firm as having a favorable competitive position (and a sound track record), then all else being equal, you should be able to grow revenues in pace with the market. If, however, your plan is to grow way faster than that, you will need convincing reasons on how you'll do it.

Your backer won't necessarily be fazed by a high-growth plan, as long as it's consistent. Suppose your competitive position in a business segment has been and should remain strong (rated around 4 on scale from 0 to 5 scale, as used in Appendix A), and is demonstrated by your having outperformed the market in the past. If you are planning to continue to beat the market in the future, then your backer should find the assumptions *consistent*.

But suppose your competitive position in a segment is just tenable (a rating of around 2) and you've underperformed against the market in the past. Suppose, too, that your position isn't expected to show any significant improvement in the future. If your plans for this segment show you beating the market in the future, expect your backer's eyebrows to raise. Your plans are *inconsistent* with both your future position and your previous performance.

Suppose, however, you've underperformed against the market in the past, but you've recently taken steps to improve your competitive position to favorable (around 3). If you are planning to grow with the market in the future, then your story will at least be consistent. All your backer will need to do is confirm that you have indeed sharpened up your act.

Take a look at the example of RandomCo in Table 7–2. Whoever prepared these forecasts was all over the place. Some forecasts seem consistent with market prospects and the firm's positioning, but some are way out of whack. Have a go yourself at filling in the boxes in the final column.

TABLE 7–2. A Test: How consistent are RandomCo's sales forecasts?

Business Segments	Revenues ($000)	Market Demand Growth (%/year)	Company Competitive Position (0–5)	Market-Based Revenue Growth Forecast (%/year)	Market-Based Revenues ($000	How Likely the Growth Forecast? (1. Most likely 2. Likely 3. Unlikely 4. Most unlikely)
	Latest Year	Next Three Years	Next Three Years	Next Three Years	In Three Years	
1	2	3	4	5	6	
Source:	Chapter 2	Chapter 3	Chapter 5	Chapter 7		
A	10	5%	3.0	17%	16	
B	10	5%	3.0	5%	12	
C	10	5%	3.0	0%	10	
D	10	5%	2.0	9%	13	
E	10	5%	3.5 to 4.0	12%	14	
F	10	-2.5%	3.0	14%	15	

Answers: A:3, B:2, C:1, D:3, E:1, F:4

Did you get them all correct?

This is unrealistic, you may think. No one in his right mind would forecast revenue growth as, for example, in segments A or F. Not so. The authors have come across countless examples over the years of good companies with atrocious forecasts. The worst are the so-called hockey stick forecasts, which show a recent or imminent downturn in revenues followed by future exponential growth!

In segment F, market demand is set to decline, thus competition is likely to get tougher. RandomCo is no more than favorably placed in that segment, so other things being equal, it is likely to show sales decline in line with the market. Yet this forecaster is showing strong revenue growth, beating the market by a wide margin, despite having no new initiatives in the pipeline. This wild forecast fully justifies the *most unlikely* answer.

There's one extra flourish you can apply to this chart. Since historical performance is such an important factor in assessing achievability of forecast performance, a couple of extra columns can be added before column 2, setting out revenues for each of the previous two years. Then you can add a column after column 2 for the average annual revenue growth rate per segment over the last three years. Column 3 is then split into two, showing average annual market demand growth in the *last* three years and that of the *next* three years. These extra columns help set the forecasts in a historic context, enabling forecast future performance against the market to be compared with past performance against the market. The downside is that the extra four columns can make the chart unwieldy and hard to read for some.

A final word on these market-driven sales forecasts. You won't find them in most business plans. If you include such a forecast, or something like it—a variant tailored to the circumstances of your business—your plan will be distinctive. It will show you understand and are confident about where you are in the market today and where the market and you are going in the near future. It will impress your backer.

> **TOP TIP:** *In these forecasts your backer is looking for three of the seven Cs: consistency, coherence, and credibility. Your coherent sales forecasts will be consistent with market demand forecasts, your firm's competitive position, and bottom-up sales initiatives. And your coherent margin forecasts will be consistent with industry trends in competitive intensity and bottom-up profit improvement initiatives. They will be credible.*

Competition-Driven Margin Forecasts

You have placed your sales forecasts in a market demand context. Now you need to put your profit margin forecasts in a market supply context—or, in other words, a competition context. Again, this will be distinctive. You will impress.

The process has three parts (current profitability, competitive environment, forecast profit) and flows like this:

1. *Business segments*. Look at one segment at a time.

Current Profitability

2. *Revenues this year*. This information comes from Table 7–1.

3. *Profit margin this year.** What percentage profit margin will you make in this business segment this year?

4. *Profit this year.* Revenue multiplied by profit margin.

Competitive Environment

5. *Recent competitive intensity.* How tough is competition compared with other segments? High, medium, or low (from Chapter 4 of your plan)?

6. *Future competitive intensity.* How tough is competition likely to be over the next few years compared with other segments—high, medium, or low (also from Chapter 4)?

Forecast Profit

7. *Planned profit margin.* What percentage profit margin are you planning to make in this business segment in three years' time?

8. *Forecast profit.* Forecast revenues from Table 7–1 times planned profit margin (as indicated in step 7).

9. *Planned profit improvement measures.* What measures are you planning to improve margins to support your planned profit margin (from Chapter 5)?

Again, this forecasting process works well in a table. There are nine entries in the process flow, so in the example shown in Table 7–3 we have nine columns.

Most of the work needed to fill out this chart you have already done. Columns 2, 3, and 4 are your current margins by segment. In columns 5 and 6, you put in indicators of how intense competition is today and how that is likely to change over the next few years—using your conclusions from Chapter 4.

The meat of column 9, your profit improvement measures, you have already set out in Chapter 5 on resources. Here you just need to flag references to the specific initiatives underway or planned.

Now you need to add the critical column 7, whereupon column 8 falls into place from column 7 (planned profit margin) times the revenue forecast of Table 7–1.

---

* Gross profit is typically used, which is revenues less costs of materials and other direct costs. Better, where data is available, is contribution to fixed overhead, which also takes into account variable overhead costs. In many small businesses, marketing spend can differ greatly by business segment. If that's so in your business, you might choose to define marketing as a direct cost and the pertinent profit margin as revenues less costs of materials, other direct costs, and marketing costs.

TABLE 7–3. Drawing up a competition-based margin forecast.

Business Segments	Revenues ($000)	Profit ($000)	Profit Margin (%)	Competitive Intensity (Low-Med-High)		Planned Profit Margin (%)	Forecast Profit ($000)	Planned Profit Improvement Measures
	Latest Year	Latest Year	Latest Year	Latest Year	In Three Years	In Three Years	In Three Years	
1	2	3	4	5	6	7	8	9
Source:		Chapter 2			Chapter 4		Here in Chapter 7	Chapters 5 and 6
A								
B								
C								
Others								
Total								

There are three main factors that will determine how credible your margin forecasts of column 7 are:

1. Pricing pressures from competitive forces in the marketplace ("top-down," as in columns 5 and 6)

2. Initiatives to improve the cost-effectiveness of your business ("bottom-up," as in column 9)

3. Any initiatives you may have to invest in strengthening an existing line of business or in launching another ("investment," also in column 9)

As in the first stage, your backer is looking for consistency in the profit margin forecasts. If competition is going to get stiffer, pricing is likely to come under pressure, so backers will expect profit margins to be slimmed. If your plans show profit margins moving the other way—actually improving—you'll need some good bottom-up reasons to explain why.

Conversely, if competition is set to ease up and your planned profit margins are expected to stay flat, or even shrink, your backer may think you are being rather conservative—unless there are bottom-up reasons why you feel the need to be adding cost.

Whatever your plans for driving down cost and improving profit margin from the bottom up, they'll need to be consistent and convincing to your backer.

As with the market-driven sales forecasts, however, your competition-driven margin forecasts will be distinctive. Few business plans will present margin plans within such a context. Your backer will find your plan more credible.

Funding the Plan

By now, you have a set of market-driven sales forecasts and competition-driven margin forecasts. You have identified capital expenditure requirements from your analysis of resources in Chapter 6.

Before you proceed to draw up the full suite of forecast accounts, you should pause to think about how your business plan will be funded. If your forecasts are showing serious growth, and certainly if yours is a startup, the business may well need an external cash injection upfront to enable and underpin that growth.

The fact that you are writing a business plan suggests that your business is in need of some financial backing. If your business is throwing out enough cash each year to fund its growth prospects, you may well not need to be writing a business plan—unless instructed to do so by your divisional manager or your board.

Funding for your plan can come in the form of equity or debt, or various rather complex hybrids of the two. We'll keep it black-and-white here and discuss only equity and debt.

The huge advantage of *equity finance* is that it does not require servicing. There is no obligation on the part of directors to pay out dividends to shareholders unless the company can afford to do so, unlike with debt finance.

The problem with equity is that it is expensive. An equity backer expects a rate of return commensurate with the risk taken on. For an established business, that could be in the region of 30 percent to 40 percent per annum. For a startup, an investor may well be looking for double that return.

The return expected will be directly in line with the perceived risk of the venture. The lower the risk, the lower the expected return demanded by the investor. Start-ups are by definition riskier than investments in established businesses. Venture capitalists expect that three or four in ten of their startup investments will go under and around the same number will do all right. But hopefully one or two will be stellar. If your business plan offers just a 10 percent per annum return to the venture capitalist, they will walk away. They are effectively being offered a 10 percent to 20 percent chance of a 10 percent return. Not a great deal.

Debt finance, on the other hand, demands a fixed return, one that is not in line with the performance of the business. It demands a fixed rate of interest or, more typically, a fixed spread over a specified benchmark rate of interest, which has to be paid irrespective of the performance of the business. In both times of plenty and times of scarcity, the interest payments must be made.

And debt finance requires security. In return for accepting fixed, regular, unexciting (with no share of the upside if the business takes off) payments, the bank demands security—generally first call on the assets of the company upon default.

Debt finance is cheaper, but more onerous and less flexible, than equity finance.

In general, the more confident you are in your business plan, the more you should try to obtain debt funding in preference to equity. If you can fund all future growth through debt finance, then once the debt is paid down the residual equity is all yours.

But by maximizing the debt finance, you are raising the risk of financial instability. You raise the risk of having to go cap in hand when times get tough and asking the bank to restructure its loans and covenants. It may do so, but at a punitive cost. Or it may not and elect instead to close down your business.

It is a balance. If you need a significant equity cushion, you should try to argue your case so well that your backer gives you a preferential class of equity, one that gives you incentive to maximize profit growth of the business. Such incentives to owner-managers can include:

- A larger shareholding than the proportion of cash you will inject into the business: Suppose the business needs $1 million to get going. Your equity provider puts in $900,000 and you put in $100,000, but you manage to negotiate from the start a shareholding not of 10 percent but of, say, one-third.

- An equity ratchet: In this case, your level of shareholding reaches a higher level once the company has met certain prespecified performance targets. For instance, you may be given a 20 percent shareholding upfront, which could be ratcheted up to 25 percent, 30 percent, or 35 percent should operating profit reach certain levels by, say, year three.

For the time being, you can assume that the funds needed to drive your plan forward all come in the form of debt finance. All backers will be interested in seeing how the full financial forecasts develop on the assumption of all-debt finance. They will want to stress-test the forecasts to see how sensitive the cash flows are to adverse assumptions and whether an all-debt capital structure can weather such fluctuation and, if not, how much of an equity cushion the business needs to survive hard times.

An assumption of all-debt finance presents a worst-case scenario from the perspective of cash flow in the business. It is a good starting point for discussion and negotiation.

Full Financial Forecasts

You have already forecast the main guts of your business over the next three years. You have set out and *justified in a market context* where sales are going to be. And you have set out and *justified in a competitive context* what contribution these sales will make to the overheads of your business.

You have forecast the capital spending needs of your business in the appropriate sections of Chapter 6 on resources. All that remains to be forecast are the overheads, interest, and tax expenses for your income statement and the working capital needs for the cash flow statement.

Much of the rest of the financial forecasts is padding, or "accountant-ese." But it needs to be done nonetheless, if only because your backer expects it.

The frustrating thing is that if your backers come from a finance firm as opposed to, say, your board of directors, they will have their own financial models to slot your sales and margin numbers into—which means that all the effort you'll put into creating a full set of projected accounts will be in vain!

But that's life—it's part of the price you pay to get the backing.

The intent here is to show you the financial forecasts you need. You must set out the current year's budget numbers plus three-year forecasts for three interlinked sets of accounts:

1. Income statement, including overheads

2. Cash flow, including capital expenditure

3. Balance sheet

We'll take them one at a time.

INCOME STATEMENT

You have already done the top line of the income statement. That's the sales forecast—by far the most difficult and critical line in any financial forecast.

You have also forecast (in a previous section) the gross profit line, or possibly the contribution line, or even a hybrid of the contribution line defined as gross profit less marketing expense.

Now you can fill in the bits in between, specifically, the various items of direct cost, such as cost of goods sold, ensuring that the margins emerge as already forecast.

That just leaves overheads to be forecast before you get to operating profit—and overheads are the easiest of the cost items to forecast.

So we are almost there. Even before we seem to have started, you basically have your income statement! Let's remind ourselves exactly what items need to be forecast in an income statement, using Table 7–4.

TABLE 7–4. Forecasting the income statement.

ITEM	NOTES
Sales	Already done!
less Direct Costs	To be consistent with gross profit forecast—see Note 1
Gross Profit	Already done!
Gross Margin (%)	= *Gross profit divided by sales*
less Depreciation	The main noncash provision—see Note 2
less Other Overheads	Forecast each main item separately—see Note 3
Operating Profit	= Gross profit less depreciation and overheads
Operating Margin (%)	= *Operating profit divided by sales*
plus Other Income	Typically investment income—see Note 4
EBIT	= Earnings Before Interest and Tax—see Note 5
less Interest	That's net interest—see Note 6
PBT	= Profit (or Earnings) Before Tax
less Tax	Easier said than done—see Note 7
PAT	= Profit After Tax, aka Net Profit, the "bottom line"
Net Margin (%)	= *PAT divided by sales*

Notes

1. You have already determined that gross margins are going to be a certain percentage in three years' time. Now you need to project the various items of direct cost, such as raw materials and direct labor, to ensure that the gross margin emerging in year three is as you have forecast. Does your gross margin forecast still ring true?

2. Depreciation is not a cash expense—it is a provision for future capital expense. Capital expenditure is by definition a lumpy, one-off investment designed to spread benefits over more than 1 year, sometimes 5 years (like some IT investments), 7 (a vehicle), 10 (equipment), or 20 (a building). You won't need to spend on that item again the following year, but you will at some stage in the future. You need to provide for that circumstance, and the tax authorities will allow you to offset that provision against tax. Your annual depreciation provision on an asset equals the capital expenditure divided by its anticipated length of useful life. Amortization is usually added in here, too, and represents capital expenditure on an acquired intangible asset (like brand value), again divided by the anticipated useful length of life of the asset.

3. Overheads are easy to forecast, but do not make the mistake of leaving them as is. ("Oh, we have loads of office space and plenty of back-room staff to handle a tripling of sales!") Your backer won't believe you. It's true; overheads tend not to rise as fast as sales. Indeed, that is where the source of future profit typically resides. But they do rise. Some overheads (e.g., the sales function) increase at around (very roughly) one-half of the rate of growth of sales, others (e.g., the admin function) a bit slower. Don't forecast them to remain at the same percentage of sales as they are today—that is far too conservative and negates the purpose of growth. But, on the other hand, don't forecast costs to grow so slowly that your operating margin by year three becomes insupportably high.

4. Investment income is the item that differentiates between operating profit and EBIT and relates mainly to the dividend income from minority shareholdings positions in other companies (not subsidiary companies, whose results would be consolidated into the accounts of your firm). This item is typically not a factor for a small and medium-size business, where operating profit and EBIT are often one and the same.

5. EBIT is the parameter you'll often hear associated with the value of a company, as in "company ABC is worth X times EBIT." An alternative valuation parameter, nowadays more commonly used, is EBITDA, which is EBIT plus depreciation and amortization. It is the closest indicator in the income statement to the pretax cash (as opposed to profit) generated by the business. Whether you use EBIT or EBITDA as the basis for valuation, you are assuming an all-equity capital structure; when the appropriate multiple is applied, you derive a value for the enterprise, against which the value of the debt must be deducted to give the value of the equity.

6. Remember that you need to include not only the interest your firm pays on its short- and long-term debt, but also the interest it has earned over the same period from its bank deposits. It is your net interest paid that should represent the difference between EBIT and EBT.

7. Tax calculations are an esoteric art, with their intricate patchwork of allowances and rates comprehensible only to highly paid tax advisers. But for purposes of forecasting, keep it simple. Apply the standard rate of corporation tax to PBT less any accumulated tax losses in your business.

And that's it! Simple enough. Later in this chapter we'll check that you have picked up all the main points by taking a closer look at our fictional case study and how Rick Jones has forecast the income statement of The Gorge Inn and Oriental Spa.

For now, let's do a sense check. What's your net margin today? What have you projected it to be in three years' time? Does it make sense? If it has grown significantly, what are the main factors driving that growth? Are you assuming revenue growth, expense items growing less quickly, cost taken out? Can those assumptions be justified? Robustly?

The Gorge's forecasts show net margin leaping from 15 percent to 24 percent. How? In a high fixed cost business like the hotel trade, profits are highly sensitive to volumes. By adding more rooms and more visitors, The Gorge will have more revenues to spread across the fixed overhead expenses of facilities such as the restaurant, spa, and swimming pool. Logically, it makes sense.

Do your net margin forecasts make sense?

CASH FLOW

These are the forecasts your equity backer is most interested in. Investors want to know how much cash they have to put into the business and how much cash the business will throw off each year to generate a return on that investment.

We start with the end result of the income statement, the profit after tax or "net profit," and make a few adjustments to derive the cash implications of the business activity, as summarized in Table 7–5.

Table 7–5. Forecasting the cash flow statement.

CASH FLOW ITEM	NOTES
Profit After Tax	The bottom line of the income statement
plus Depreciation	Add back depreciation (and amortization)—see Note 1
Operating Cash Flow	= PAT plus depreciation
less Change in Inventory	See Note 2
less Change in A/C Receivable	See Note 3
plus Change in A/C Payable	See Note 4
Cash Flow from Operations	= Operating cash flow after working capital
less Capital Expenditure	See Note 5
Cash Flow Pre-Financing	
plus Finance Provided	See Note 6
Cash Surplus (year)	The cash added to or subtracted from cash reserves after the period of trading (typically a year)
Cash Surplus (cumulative)	The cash retained in the business at the end of the period

Notes

1. Depreciation (and amortization) is a noncash item in the income statement, so it needs to be added back for the cash flow statement. In other words, the cash generated by one year's trading is larger than what is recorded as "profit" due to the often hefty provision for future capital expenditure called depreciation.

2. There are three working capital adjustments, and all are effectively items relating to timing. Inventories bought (or finished goods manufactured) today may not be sold for many weeks. An increase in inventory should be subtracted from operating cash flow, while a decrease in inventory should be added. Excel makes working capital forecasts easy. If your inventory levels today are, say, the equivalent of 45 days' worth of revenues, you take the change in revenues in one year and multiply by 45/365 to get the increase in inventory holding. You then replicate the formula across the years.

3. A sale may be made today, but payment as registered by cash in your hand or bank account may not be received until 10, 30, even 60 days hence. An increase in accounts receivable (what your customers owe you) should be subtracted from operating cash flow, a decrease added—the same as for inventory.

4. Supplies may be received today, but your payment to that supplier may be 10, 30, even 60 days later. An increase in accounts payable (what you owe your suppliers) should be added to operating cash flow, a decrease subtracted—the opposite of inventory and accounts receivable. It can represent in effect an extra source of funding for your business.

5. Capital expenditure is defined as spending designed to produce a benefit to the business that should last beyond the 12 months of the accounting period. It is allowable against tax only in the form of a depreciation charge spread over the useful life of the asset. In Chapter 6 of your business plan on resources, you set out your plans for capital expenditure for each of the next three years on buildings and works, equipment, and vehicles. Here you should enter the total capital spending for the year.

6. Net long-term finance provided to the firm over the previous 12 months should include both loans raised and/or equity injected, less loans repaid in part or full. In many years, this item may be a blank, since the cash required to grow the business will be raised from cash generated from within the business and there will be no need for the addition of funds from external sources.

The end result of this flow of cash, including all inflows and outflows over the 12-month period, will be an increase or decrease of the accumulated cash surplus of the company. In cash flow forecasts, these are best assumed to be retained within the company and, for the sake of clarity, not distributed to shareholders as dividends in the forecast period. In reality, of course, dividends may well be paid and unnecessarily high reserves of cash taken out of the company. But for the purposes of financial forecasting, it is instructive to see how the cash surplus accumulates on the cash flow statement and how the cash reserves build up on the balance sheet.

This leads us to the final financial statement you need to prepare, the balance sheet.

BALANCE SHEET

While the previous two statements represent a flow over a 12-month period— profit in the case of the income statement, cash in the case of the cash flow statement—the balance sheet represents a snapshot in time. If your firm's financial year ends on March 31, the balance sheet represents a statement of your firm's financial situation as of midnight, March 31. It shows the assets your firm holds and the liabilities it owes at that moment of time.

The balance sheet is the financial statement most beloved by your banker. While your equity investor loves the cash flow statement, the banker, while also admiring the other two statements, likes the balance sheet best. It shows how indebted your firm is. It shows bankers how much security their loan has, and how much equity cushion there is, should things go wrong. It shows them whether they have any cause for concern.

It is fairly straightforward to draw up a balance sheet on Excel from your income and cash flow statement worksheets. They are all interlinked. The changes in the balance sheet from the previous date to the current date will be exactly the same as what you have already computed for the relevant items of the income and cash flow statements.

If you find this DIY prospect a tad daunting, there are plenty of off-the-shelf software packages you can acquire to guide you through it. Take a look at them on the web—like the curiously named Up Your Cash Flow, which ranks high on Google—but check out some review sites before purchasing one of these products. They all have similar functions—this is not rocket science. Go for whichever software is rated the simplest to understand for the end user.

> **TOP TIP:** *If stuck, take a break. When numbers go wonky, walk away. Better, sleep on them. Return afresh and, presto, you'll spot the wrong link or formula in your spreadsheet in an instant!*

Like most of you reading this book, neither of the authors is an accountant. But, acting on behalf of you, a fellow layperson, one of them tried out the recommended process for drawing up a set of balance sheet forecasts from income and cash flow forecasts, using data from The Gorge case study. It wasn't terribly hard, but he did make mistakes. And it did take him longer than he had thought—a whole morning just on the balance sheet forecast and reconciliation. Some readers may well be smarter and faster. Others may struggle even more than he did—in which case you may choose to invest in software. Having undertaken this exercise, however, he is able to give you some firsthand tips on what can go wrong—and how to put it right (see Table 7–6).

TABLE 7–6. Forecasting the balance sheet.

BALANCE SHEET ITEM	NOTES
Current Assets	= Cash and other assets that can be expected to be converted into cash over the next 12 months
Inventory	= Inventory held at start-year plus the change in inventory levels during the year *in the cash flow forecast*
Accounts Receivable	= Accounts receivable at start-year plus the change in such levels during the year *in the cash flow forecast*
Other	= Deposits, prepayments, etc., made by customers at start-year plus the change in such levels during the year *in the cash flow forecast*
Cash	= The figure for cumulative cash surplus in the *cash flow forecast*—see Note 1
Total	
Capital Assets	= Assets that are not easily converted into cash and are usually held for a period in excess of one year
Net Fixed Assets at Start-Year	= Net fixed assets at start-year, namely, the net fixed assets shown at end-year in the previous balance sheet
plus Capital Expenditure	= Capital expenditure during the year *in the cash flow forecast*
less Depreciation	= Depreciation during the year in the *income statement forecast*

Net Fixed Assets at End-Year	This will be the same as fixed assets at cost less cumulative depreciation from the date of asset acquisition to end-year
Other	= The value of investments or intangibles (if any) held at start-year plus the change in such levels during the year *in the cash flow forecast*
Total	
TOTAL ASSETS	= Total current and capital assets
Current Liabilities	= Liabilities that can be expected to be paid in cash to creditors over the following 12 months
Accounts Payable	= Accounts payable at start-year plus the change in such levels during the year *in the cash flow forecast*
Provision for Taxation	= Provision for taxation at start-year plus the change in such levels during the year *in the income statement forecast*
Short-Term Loans	= Loans (specifically, those due within the next 12 months) at start-year plus the change in such loans during the year *in the cash flow forecast*
Total	
Long-Term Liabilities	= Liabilities that are not expected to be paid out in cash over the next 12 months
Long-Term Debt	= Debt, including mortgages on business property, at start-year plus any change (new loans taken out, less those paid back) during the year in the cash flow forecast
Pension Obligations	= Pension obligations (if any) at start-year plus any change during the year *in the cash flow forecast*
Total	
Owner Equity	= Total assets less current and long-term liabilities = residual claim of owners on the assets = "net worth"
Share Capital Paid Up	= Equity investment paid in cash, cumulative to date, at start-year plus any further injection during the year *in the cash flow forecast*
Income Statement Account	= Cumulative net profit at start-year (i.e., the total of all net profits—or losses—in all previous income statements) plus the net profit (or loss) during the year *in the income statement,* less any dividends paid out during the year *in the cash flow forecast*—see Note 2
Total	
TOTAL LIABILITIES	= Current plus long-term liabilities plus owner equity = current liabilities plus "capital employed"—see Note 3

Notes

1. This "cash" figure may of course be spread over a number of places—in the till, a current account, a deposit account—but for the purposes of forecasting it is best to have just the one total number. Then it can be compared directly with the cumulative cash surplus number in the cash flow statement each year. They are one and the same.

2. It is best to assume that no dividends are paid out in the forecast. Then your backer can see clearly how the income statement account (which, together with paid-up share capital, comprises owner equity) builds up over time on the liabilities side of the balance sheet and how this buildup is reflected in the cash item on the asset side of the balance sheet.

3. Total liabilities are, by definition, equal to total assets. It is best to insert in your spreadsheet a check item, a row showing one minus the other. This should at all times and in all cells be zero. But of course it may not be. Mistakes may have crept in while trying to reconcile the balance sheet with the income statement and cash flow. If the check cells don't all show zeros, examine some areas that may have gone wrong. You need to ensure that:

- You have given the right signs to the changes in working capital in your cash flow forecast: An increase in inventory is a cash outflow, as for accounts receivable, but an increase in accounts payable is a cash inflow.

- Your cash row in the balance sheet is identical to the cumulative cash surplus row in the cash flow forecast.

- Your net fixed asset number at end-year picks up both the capital expenditure during the year (from the cash flow forecast) as well as the depreciation provision (from the income statement forecast).

- Any increase in long-term liabilities, whether in debt or equity, is reflected in a corresponding increase in net fixed assets in that year (assuming the finance raised is for such purposes).

- What goes into the income statement account item in the balance sheet is the cumulative, historical income statement, not just the income statement result for that year.

You now have all the financial forecasts you need for your business plan. You have a market-driven sales forecast, a competition-driven profit margin forecast, and a full set of financials.

One final word of advice: Make sure you specify clearly and throughout the bases for each of your forecast assumptions. By their very nature, forecasts are dependent on judgment. One person's reasoning will not be the same as the next person's. Set out your assumptions and justify them. Draw on evidence wherever possible.

These forecasts should represent your base case, which is defined as the most probable outcome. They should not be what you hope will happen, but what is most likely to happen.

In the next chapter you will reexamine these forecasts from different perspectives. What would happen if all goes right? This is the so-called upside case, one that an equity investor will enjoy hearing about.

And what if all goes wrong? This is the downside case, one that your banker also will want to know all about.

Forecasts in a Startup

Market-driven forecasts for a startup are different from those prepared for an established business. There is no track record on which to base one's judgment. There is no past or present, only future.

Nevertheless, it needs to be attempted. In Chapter 3 of your business plan, you identified the market you will be addressing—whether an existing market, a new one, or a variant of the two. In Chapter 5 you assessed what your competitive position will be upon entering this market and how that position may improve over the next three years.

Now you need to try and place some numbers around this picture. Let's assume for now that yours is an existing market, which you are entering with a business proposition with a difference. What is the size of this market? What share of this market are you likely to capture after three years? What revenues does that translate into?

Of course, it's easier said than done. If you are starting up the fourth mobile phone network in a country that already has three, you can readily find data on the size of the market and its growth rate, and you can make various assumptions on your market share development over time. It is most unlikely you will reach a one in four share (25 percent) within three years, unless you are launching something sensationally different or at much lower cost. But you might hope for 8 percent to 10 percent share following an intensive marketing campaign and that will translate into X amount of millions of dollars in three years' time.

Small to medium-size companies typically don't have that sort of data available. But, depending on your market and your circumstances, you should consider giving it a go.

TABLE 7–7. Drawing up a market-based sales forecast for a startup.

Business Segments	Market Size ($000)	Market Demand Growth (%/year)	Forecast Market Size ($000)	Company Competitive Position (0–5)	Likely Market Share (%)	Likely Revenues ($000)
	Latest Year	Next Three Years	In Three Years	Next Three Years	In Three Years	In Three Years
1	2	3	4	5	6	7
Source:		Chapter 3		Chapter 5	Here in Chapter 7	
A						
B						
C						
Others						
Total						

Do you have the kind of data that could fill in Table 7–7? Your backers would love to see your revenue forecasts framed in a format such as this. It will give them a concept of the scale of the gamble they will be making. Are you forecasting to gain 25 percent share of market, from a standing start? Or 5 percent? That's a big difference in the nature of the bet.

And are you forecasting to gain 25 percent of the market with a competitive position of 3.5 (favorable to strong) or 2.5 (tenable to favorable)? Again, a different sort of bet.

Don't worry if your business proposition doesn't lend itself to this form of analysis. In the example of The Gorge Inn and Oriental Spa, we don't use this framework. The data is difficult to come by and market share is so small as to be misleading. Instead, we use benchmark data on room occupancy and rates.

But the important thing is to frame your sales forecasts in a market context. However you choose to do it, you should attempt to provide points of *market reference* for your backer. You will greatly strengthen your case if you can do that.

Likewise with your margin forecasts. If you can set them in a competitive context, that would be most useful to your backer. Try and find out whatever you can about the profitability of competitors, whether competing directly or indirectly. If you know that Competitor X is highly profitable, with an operating margin of 20 percent, say, then your forecast of achieving an operating margin of 15 percent by year three will seem more achievable to your backer than if most competitors are registering margins of just 5 percent to 10 percent.

Even more so than with the sales forecasts, however, a small- to medium-size company is likely to be constrained in its margin forecasts by the availability of data. You probably won't be able to find such data on your competitors-to-be. But you can look for clues. What evidence of prosperity do your competitors display? Are the owners or managers leading new-Mercedes or aged-Chevy lifestyles?

Once you have put your sales and margin forecasts in a market framework, then you need to build up the full financial statements, as set out in the previous sections. The process for drawing up income statement and cash flow forecasts will be the same as for an established business; the only difference in the first balance sheet forecast will be that your start-year assets and liabilities are zero.

Thus the cash surplus entry in your first-year balance sheet will be the same as the cash surplus for the year in your cash flow statement. And the income statement account entry in your balance sheet will be the same as your net profit for the year in your income statement. For subsequent years, all financial forecasts will be as for an established business.

◻ ◻ ◻ ◻ ◻ **THINKING OUT OF THE BOX** ◻ ◻ ◻ ◻ ◻

Basic Budgeting

Nothing is likelier to keep a man within compass than having constantly before his eyes the state of his affairs in a regular course of account.
—*John Locke*

Many entrepreneurs launch a new business without carefully analyzing the financial prospects in advance. They think that they can produce and sell a product at a profit, and that this will be sufficient. All they need to do is sell enough of the product to create a profitable business. But that's seldom the case.

The act of budgeting for your business forces you to think through all the important numbers and to develop a picture of what your business is going to look like in three, six, nine, and 12 months. A budget is a powerful business tool that will help you make better decisions. It allows you to develop and maintain a thorough understanding of the internal financial workings of your business.

One of the most important skills of entrepreneurs is the ability to prepare budgets and accurate financial forecasts for their business. Your ability to set financial goals for sales, expenses, and profits is a true measure of your ability to succeed in business.

The purpose of the budget is to give you a visual description of the expected financial results of your business activities.

- ◻ The budget should cover 12 to 24 months of business operations.
- ◻ You can start with paper spreadsheets that you fill out in pencil.
- ◻ You can use computer programs like Excel that allow you to change numbers quickly.
- ◻ You should work out a complete budget before beginning business operations.
- ◻ Each month you should review, revise, and update your budget for the next 12 months.

A basic business budget contains four major numbers:

1. Projected sales and revenue
2. Projected total costs of achieving that level of sales and revenue
3. The profit or loss from operations based on the previous two numbers
4. The cumulative total of profits and losses on a month-to-month basis

Your sales and revenue projections should be based on experience, market analysis, and research. The first and most important number, however, is the top line—the estimated sales for the month:

- This number will be the result of a complete analysis of your marketing and sales activities.
- Your ability to project this number with accuracy is a key measure of your talent as a businessperson.
- You should have three different numbers for this first line:
  1. High sales estimate
  2. Medium sales estimate
  3. Low sales estimate
- Key rule: Your business should be profitable even if your low sales estimate turns out to be correct.

For the second number in your budget (i.e., projected total costs), you include all the costs of operation involved in producing and delivering the product or service to the customer. Your final number should include 100 percent of all out-of-pocket expenses necessary to achieve your estimated sales revenues. That means adding in:

- All the costs of purchasing or producing the product or service
- All costs related to sales and marketing of the product or service
- All the costs of administration and operation of your business
- All fixed, variable, and semi-variable costs of business operation

The third major number is the total profit or loss from operations for that month:

- There will sometimes be months of the year where your business loses money.
- In a new business startup, the first few months will usually show losses.
- It is the general sales and profit trends that are most important.

The final number is the cumulative profits or losses of the company over a period of months:

- Profits or losses are added together each month to get a running total.
- These totals tell you when your business will break even and begin earning a profit.
- The peak total loss will indicate how much money you will have to borrow or provide to the business before it becomes profitable—in addition to the funding required for fixed and working capital investment.
- This business budget is essential if you want to borrow money from any bank or lending institution.

◻ An accurate business budget tells you, and others, the truth about your business potential.

If you have more than one business within your company, you should create a budget for each one:

◻ Each manager should create a budget for each department or business line.

◻ These budgets should be as accurate as possible and reviewed regularly.

◻ The ability of an entrepreneur or manager to budget accurately is a key measure of talent and effectiveness.

Each major number in your budget should be reviewed each month:

◻ You should compare the actual results in each category against the projected results.

◻ The most important consideration should be the variances from projections.

◻ A large variation from an expected number should be studied carefully.

◻ Both positive and negative variations may indicate a lack of competence.

◻ The act of studying each number each month will improve performance in that area.

Developing operating budgets is a business skill that you can learn quickly and efficiently. It is a valuable skill because:

◻ An accurate business budget will tell you immediately whether or not something is a good investment opportunity.

◻ A proper budget gives you targets to aim for in all your business activities.

◻ The more often you prepare and review your budgets, the better you will become, and the more accurate your projections will be.

◻ The bigger and more successful your business becomes, the more important it will be for you to develop complete budgets.

Many entrepreneurs and businesses invest many hours in the preparation of accurate business budgets and in reviewing actual vs. budgeted numbers and examining the variances and finding out why. As a result, they save enormous amounts of time and money, and often many months and years of wasted effort.

Be sure to do your homework and check the accuracy of every number that goes into your budget. Imagine that a banker was going to ask you for proof of every financial projection. Be sure that you have the documentation ready.

As the result of what you have learned here, what one action are you going to take immediately related to basic budgeting for your business?

◻　◻　◻　◻　◻　◻　◻　◻　◻　◻　◻　◻　◻　◻　◻　◻　◻　◻

Financial Risks and Opportunities

So far, you have identified the main risks and opportunities relating to market demand (Chapter 3), industry competition (Chapter 4), strategy (Chapter 5), and resources (Chapter 6). Now you need to add the final set, those relating to specific financial issues.

The most obvious financial issues that could impact your business plan will be interest rates, exchange rates, and tax rates. Ask yourself to what extent your business plan would be affected if there were a significant change in any of these rates, whether in a favorable or unfavorable direction.

What are the financial risks that are reasonably likely to occur and with reasonable impact if they do occur? These are the big risks, as defined in Chapter 3. How can they be mitigated? What are the big opportunities? How can you exploit them?

All big risks and opportunities, whether financial or related to market, resources, or competition, will be examined together in the next chapter.

THE GORGE INN AND ORIENTAL SPA BUSINESS PLAN, 2014: FINANCIALS AND FORECASTS

Rick Jones has set out his strategy for The Gorge, as well as the resources he will require to implement the strategy. Now for the numbers.

He starts by setting out the financial history of the inn since it opened in late 2010. He lays out the main business parameters in the three major financial statements—income statement, cash flow statement, and balance sheet. (This actual data is presented alongside his financial forecasts, which we'll get to shortly.) He makes explanatory comments only when helpful to the prospective backer. For instance:

◘ Occupancy may seem low in retrospect in 2011, but the 39 percent seemed like a major achievement at the time, and a hugely welcome outperformance on his expected 25 percent to 30 percent.

◘ They have been able to push up the AARR (average achieved room rate) by 7.5 percent per annum since the first year, with budget 2014 showing a further 3 percent increase.

◘ Breakeven at the operating profit level was achieved in early 2012 and at the bottom line toward the end of the year, both ahead of plan.

◘ Marketing expenditure peaked in the first year at more than $25,000 and can be expected to return to that level or beyond with the opening of the Phase II development.

◻ Following the financing at the outset of a mortgage of $500,000 and owner equity of $550,000, the venture has needed no further cash injection and has been operationally cash positive since 2012.

◻ By the end of 2013, the book value of owner equity has reached $431,000 and seems set to exceed the $550,000 invested by 2015; this figure takes no account of the enhancement in the value of the property since purchase and renovation.

Rick then moves on to the forecasts. He has carefully prepared market-based sales forecasts (following the recommendations in this chapter), but he suspects they are not directly appropriate to his plan. After all, he is planning a doubling in-bed capacity over the plan period, so his revenues should grow way faster than the market.

Nevertheless, he has a go, if only because our book says that it will impress a backer. Lo and behold, the exercise is quite useful. The forecast Rick prepares—see Table 7–8—shows the backer that:

◻ The Gorge seems well placed to beat the market even in the absence of the Phase II building program. It can do so in two main ways:

1. Growing accommodation revenues faster than the market, due to a strong competitive position. This growth would be achieved by nudging up room rates, rather than through higher occupancy, since The Gorge already enjoys high occupancy.

2. Deriving a higher share of revenues from spa services, for both overnight and outside guests, even in the absence of the Phase II facilities, as The Gorge's range of services continues to develop and becomes better known.

◻ More than three-fifths of revenues by 2018 would be derived from the existing business, with the balance from the Phase II development.

TABLE 7–8. How achievable are The Gorge Inn's sales forecasts?

Business Segments	Revenues ($000)	Market Demand Growth (%/year)	Company Competitive Position (0–5)	Likely Revenue Growth (%/year)	Top-Down Revenues ($000)	Phase II-Derived Revenues ($000)	Total Revenues ($000)
	2013	2013–18	2013–18	2013–18	2018	2018	2018
1	2	3	4	5	6	7	8
Source:	Chapter 2	Chapter 3	Chapter 5	Here in Chapter 7			
Accommodation	326	3–4%	3.6 to 3.9	5%	416	217	633
Catering	82	2–3%	3.3 to 3.5	3%	95	64	159
Spa	105	4–5%	3.5 to 4.1	7.5%	151	133	284
Total	**513**			**5.2%**	**662**	**414**	**1076**

Rick thinks carefully about drawing up competition-based margin forecasts, but decides there is no benefit in doing so because he envisages no significant competitive intensification over the forecast period. The risk identified in Chapter 4 of a new, directly competitive entrant will be treated separately in Chapter 8.

Rick moves onto the financial forecasts and sets out the three main financial statement forecasts to 2018—see Tables 7–9, 7–10, and 7–11. He sets the forecasts alongside the historic financial statements for 2011–13 and the budget for 2014 to show continuity and consistency to the backer.

For the income statement (Table 7–9), he provides these explanatory comments:

◻ There's an assumed 10 percent drop in average achieved room rate and a 20 percent drop in occupancy rate once the new accommodation capacity comes on stream in 2015. Given how full the inn has been in recent months and the

TABLE 7–9. The Gorge Inn's income statement forecast.

The Gorge Inn & Oriental Spa:	Income Statement Forecast, 2014-18							
	Actual			Budget	Forecast			
	2011	2012	2013	2014	2015	2016	2017	2018
Average number of rooms available	17	17	17	17	17	33	33	33
Average achieved room rate ($/night)	64.1	69.5	73.9	75.5	79	70	72	74
Average room occupancy	39.2%	55.9%	71.4%	75.0%	75%	60%	65%	71%
Revenues	$000	$000	$000	$000	$000	$000	$000	$000
Rooms	155	240	326	354	368	506	564	633
Restaurant and bar	45	65	82	87	87	135	145	159
Spa	76	92	105	109	109	263	273	284
Total Revenue	276	397	513	550	564	904	982	1076
Cost of goods sold	-14	-15	-20	-22	-22	-34	-36	-40
Gross Profit	262	382	493	528	542	870	946	1036
Gross Margin	94.9%	96.2%	96.1%	96.0%	96.1%	96.2%	96.3%	96.3%
Expenses								
Directors' salaries	-100	-100	-100	-100	-100	-100	-100	-100
Wages	-64	-71	-77	-80	-84	-173	-178	-184
Maintenance	-16	-15	-22	-20	-20	-35	-37	-40
Gas, electricity & water	-15	-17	-19	-20	-22	-35	-37	-40
Telecoms & IT	-7	-7	-9	-10	-11	-11	-12	-12
Insurance	-10	-11	-11	-12	-13	-20	-20	-20
Vehicle running	-5	-5	-6	-6	-6	-7	-7	-7
Admin	-7	-7	-8	-8	-9	-12	-12	-12
Marketing (incl. travel)	-25	-18	-22	-20	-30	-30	-25	-20
Property taxes	-10	-11	-11	-12	-13	-20	-22	-25
Miscellaneous	-19	-9	-14	-20	-20	-30	-30	-30
Total Expense	-278	-271	-299	-308	-328	-473	-480	-490
EBITDA	-16	111	194	220	214	397	466	546
Depreciation	-101	-101	-101	-101	-101	-185	-185	-185
EBIT	-117	10	93	119	113	212	281	361
Investment income	0	0	0	0	0	0	0	0
Operating Profit	-117	10	93	119	113	212	281	361
Operating margin (%)	-42.4%	2.5%	18.1%	21.6%	20.0%	23.5%	28.7%	33.6%
Interest	-35	-35	-35	-35	-35	-105	-105	-105
Profit Before Tax	-152	-25	58	84	78	107	176	256
PBT margin (%)	-55.1%	-6.3%	11.3%	15.3%	13.8%	11.9%	18.0%	23.8%
Cumulative PBT	-152	-177	-119	-35	43	151	327	584
Tax	0	0	0	0	-16	-23	-37	-54
Profit After Tax	-152	-25	58	84	62	85	139	203
PAT margin (%)	-55.1%	-6.3%	11.3%	15.3%	10.9%	9.4%	14.2%	18.8%
Cumulative PAT	-152	-177	-119	-35	27	112	251	454

healthy forward booking for this year and next, Rick believes these assumptions are reasonable.

   ◻ An assumed doubling in staff costs, spread across room cleaning, waiting, cooking, and spa services, with no increase in the bar, reception, accounts, or gardens.

   ◻ A major marketing campaign is planned for both 2015 and 2016.

   ◻ 100 percent debt finance is assumed for the time being for the $1 million to be raised.

   ◻ The forecasts show operating margin rising from around 20 percent today to around 33 percent by 2018, a reflection of an almost doubled revenue stream spread across an overhead base that's increasing much more slowly—indeed, just 50 percent higher at the end of the period than budgeted for 2014.

From the cash flow forecast (Table 7–10), Rick observes that The Gorge should be throwing off, on average, more than $300,000 a year cash from operations in the three years following the Phase II investment.

And from the balance sheet forecast (Table 7–11), Rick notes with some satisfaction that the book value of owner equity should exceed $1 million by the end of the forecast period.

TABLE 7–10. The Gorge Inn's cash flow forecast.

The Gorge Inn & Oriental Spa:	Cash Flow Forecast, 2014-18							
		Actual		Budget		Forecast		
$000	2011	2012	2013	2014	2015	2016	2017	2018
Profit After Tax	-152	-25	58	84	62	85	139	203
Depreciation	101	101	101	101	101	185	185	185
Operating Cash Flow	-51	76	159	185	163	269	324	387
Change in Working Capital								
Change in inventory (increase = -)	-1	0	0	0	0	-1	0	0
Change in a/c receivable (increase = -)	-23	-10	-10	-3	-1	-28	-6	-8
Change in a/c payable (increase = +)	11	0	1	0	1	6	0	0
Net change (increase = -)	-12	-10	-9	-3	0	-23	-6	-8
Cash Flow from Operations	-63	66	150	182	162	246	318	380
(= Sales receipts less expense payments)								
Capital Expenditure								
Buildings and works	-996	0	0	0	-1030	0	0	0
Equipment	-15	0	-4	-9	-15	-2	0	-5
Vehicles	-30	0	0	0	0	0	-10	0
Total	-1041	0	-4	-9	-1045	-2	-10	-5
Cash Flow Pre-Financing	-1104	66	146	173	-883	244	308	375
Financing								
Mortgage taken on property	500	0	0	0	1000	0	0	0
Share capital Paid In	550	0	0	0	0	0	0	0
Cash Surplus for Year	-54	66	146	173	117	244	308	375
Cash Surplus (Cum)	-54	11	157	331	448	692	1000	1375
Net Cash Inflow to Shareholders	-604	66	146	173	117	244	308	375
Net Cash Inflow to Shareholders (cum)	-604	-539	-393	-219	-102	142	450	825

Since he has assumed all-debt financing, Rick addresses the risk of a rising interest rate. A 3 percent rise would mean an extra $30,000/year in interest charges, which Rick believes would be adequately covered by the cash generated from operations. But the bankers will want to take into account market and strategic risks, too, which will be addressed in the next chapter.

TABLE 7–11. The Gorge Inn's balance sheet forecast.

The Gorge Inn & Oriental Spa:	Balance Sheet Forecast, 2014-18							
	Actual			Budget	Forecast			
$000	31.12.11	31.12.12	31.12.13	31.12.14	31.12.15	31.12.16	31.12.17	31.12.18
Current Assets								
Inventory	1	1	2	2	2	3	3	3
Accounts receivable	23	33	42	45	46	74	81	88
Other (deposits, prepaid etc)	0	0	0	0	0	0	0	0
Cash	-54	11	157	331	448	692	1000	1375
Total	-31	45	201	378	496	769	1084	1466
Capital Assets								
Net fixed assets at start year	1041	940	843	751	1695	1596	1422	1242
less depreciation during year	-101	-101	-101	-101	-101	-185	-185	-185
Net fixed assets at end year	940	839	742	650	1594	1412	1237	1058
Other (e.g. investments, intangibles)	0	0	0	0	0	0	0	0
Total	940	839	742	650	1594	1412	1237	1058
TOTAL ASSETS	909	884	943	1028	2090	2181	2321	2524
Current Liabilities								
Accounts payable	11	11	12	13	13	19	20	20
Provision for taxation	0	0	0	0	0	0	0	0
Short-term loans due in 12 months	0	0	0	0	0	0	0	0
Total	11	11	12	13	13	19	20	20
Long-term Liabilities								
Long-term debt	500	500	500	500	1500	1500	1500	1500
Pension obligations	0	0	0	0	0	0	0	0
Total	500	500	500	500	1500	1500	1500	1500
Owner Equity								
Share capital paid up	550	550	550	550	550	550	550	550
Income statement b/f	0	-152	-177	-119	-35	27	112	251
Income statement this year	-152	-25	58	84	62	85	139	203
less dividends paid	0	0	0	0	0	0	0	0
Income statement c/f	-152	-177	-119	-35	27	112	251	454
Total	398	373	431	515	577	662	801	1004
TOTAL LIABILITIES	909	884	943	1028	2090	2181	2321	2524

Checklist on Financials and Forecasts

Draw up a set of financial forecasts rooted in a strategic context. You want your backers to see that your analyses of market demand and supply (Chapters 3 and 4) and your firm's strategy and resources (Chapters 5 and 6) translate rationally into the numbers of this Chapter 7.

Therefore, you must produce:

- *A forecast income statement* that shows sales framed in a market demand context and profit margins in an industry competition context

- *A forecast cash flow statement* in which the capital expenditure needed to drive the profit growth in the income statement will be evident and framed in the analysis of resource development (from Chapter 6)

- *A forecast balance sheet* that shows how your forecasts can be achieved with the assumed capital structure (the balance of debt and equity)

Finally, set out the big financial risks and opportunities that may impact on your business plan.

P.S. Here's a plea to you, the reader. Please do not load the business plan with irrelevant financial detail. In particular:

- Do not lay out monthly financial forecasts unless yours is a startup. Even then, you may only need this data for the first three months; after that, show the data by quarter to the end of the year, and by year thenceforth.

- Do not burden your backer with spurious accuracy in your forecasts. Sales in three years time will emphatically not be $1,654,729.53—so don't say that. They will also not be $1,654,729 and most probably not "$1,655 thousand." They may perhaps be on the order of $1.66 million. Three or a maximum four significant figures are all that are needed to convey the sense of whether or not your plan is backable.

Less is more. Less detail yields more clarity.

8

RISK, OPPORTUNITY, AND SENSITIVITY

When written in Chinese, the word crisis *is composed of two characters. One represents danger, and the other represents opportunity.* —John F. Kennedy

YOU'RE ALMOST there. You have set out the market context in which your firm exists, how it is positioned in that market, and how your strategy will deploy the firm's resources over the next few years. You have developed a set of financial forecasts that are consistent with that scenario.

All you need do now is set out what could go wrong with these forecasts, on the one hand, and what could go even more right with them.

In other words, what are the risks and opportunities behind those forecasts? And how likely are those risks and opportunities to occur? And, if they did happen, what impact would they have?

The good news is that you've already done the work. Not some of it, not even much of it, but all of it. At the end of each chapter of your business plan, you identified the risks and opportunities you have encountered. And not just any old risks and opportunities, but the big ones.

Back in Chapter 3 we defined a big risk (or opportunity) as one where:

- Likelihood of occurrence is medium (or high) and impact is high.

- Likelihood of occurrence is high and impact is medium (or high).

You have gathered all these big risks and opportunities along the way, relating to market demand (Chapter 3), industry competition (Chapter 4), your firm's competitive position (Chapter 5), your firm's resources (Chapter 6), and your financial forecasts (Chapter 7). All you need to do now is assemble them, weigh them, and address the key question: Do the opportunities surpass the risks?

And we have just the tool to help you with that.

Meet the Suns & Clouds Chart

Vaughan Evans first created the Suns & Clouds chart in the early 1990s. Since then he has seen it reproduced in various forms in reports by his consulting competitors. (They say imitation is the sincerest form of flattery, but he still kicks himself that he didn't copyright it back then!)

The reason it keeps getting copied is that it works. It manages to encapsulate in one chart conclusions on the relative importance of all the main issues in the business plan. It shows, diagrammatically, whether the opportunities (the suns) outshine the risks (the clouds). Or vice versa, when the clouds overshadow the suns. In short, one chart tells you whether your plan is backable. Or not.

The chart (see Figure 8-1) forces you to view each risk (and opportunity) from two perspectives: how likely it is to happen, and how big an impact it would have if it did happen. You don't need to quantify the impact, only have some idea of the theoretical, relative impact of each issue on the value of the firm.

In the chart, risks are represented as clouds, opportunities as suns. The more likely a risk (or opportunity) is to happen, the further to the right you should place it along the horizontal axis. In Figure 8-1, risk D is the most likely to happen, and risk B the least likely.

The bigger the impact a risk (or opportunity) would have if it were to happen, the higher you should place it up the vertical axis. In the same chart, opportunity B would have the largest impact and opportunity C the smallest.

For each risk (and opportunity), you need to place it in the appropriate position on the chart taking into account *both* factors—its likelihood and impact.

FIGURE 8–1. The Suns & Clouds chart.

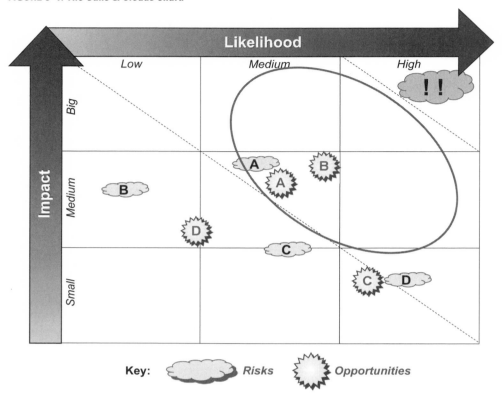

Don't worry if things don't make that much sense initially. This chart changes with further thought and discussion. Always. Arguably its greatest virtue is that it serves as a stimulus to discussion. A strategy consultant may give a PowerPoint presentation of 100 slides, facing no more than a question or two for clarification every now and then. Then, when the Suns & Clouds chart comes up, toward the end of the presentation, it can remain on-screen for a half hour or more. It stimulates discussion and provokes amendment. A client may choose to debate for 15 minutes the precise positioning of one risk, or opportunity, and *what can be done to shift its position favorably*.

Remember, you cannot be exact in this chart. Nor do you need to be. It is a pictorial representation of risk and opportunity, designed to give you a *feel* for the balance of risk and opportunity in your business.

It is up to you whether you include a Suns & Clouds chart in your business plan, but 99 percent of plans won't have anything like it. If you include it, yours will be distinctive, special, and backer-sensitive. But if you're grilled on it, will you be able to respond vigorously?

Whether you include the chart or not doesn't matter. The critical thing is the thought process. You must try and visualize the balance of risk and opportunity inherent in your plan. You must be conscious of the *big* risks and the *big* opportunities, as distinct from the myriad of lesser issues. You must screen out the background chatter and let the metaphorical voices of the main proponents of risk and opportunity be heard—and may the most convincing ones win.

This, after all, is what your backers will do. They, or their advisers, may well use a tool like the Suns & Clouds chart, but regardless of whether or not they do, you can be certain that is how they will be thinking. They will be assessing risk and opportunity. That's their job. It's what they do, day in, day out. Whether analytically or instinctively, that's how your backer thinks.

And you must be prepared to answer from the same perspective.

> **TOP TIP:** *The last of the seven Cs that make for a good business plan is to be convincing. It is in your analysis of risk and opportunity where you need to be just that. If you can convince your reader that the opportunities facing your business outshine the risks, you may have a backer.*

What the Suns & Clouds Tell You

Take calculated risks. That is quite different from being rash.

—George S. Patton

The Suns & Clouds chart tells you two main things about how backable your plan is: whether there are any extraordinary risks (or opportunities), and whether the overall balance of risk and opportunity is favorable.

EXTRAORDINARY RISK

Take a look at the top right-hand corner of the chart in Figure 8–1. There's a heavy thundercloud there, with two exclamation marks. That's a risk that is both very likely and very large. It's a showstopper risk. If your backer finds one of them in your plan, that's it. It's unbackable.

The closer a cloud gets to that thundercloud, the worse news it is. Risks that hover around the diagonal (from the top left to the bottom right corners) can be handled, as long as they are balanced by opportunities. But as soon as a cloud starts creeping toward that thundercloud—for example, around where opportunity B is placed—that's when your backer starts to get itchy feet.

But imagine a bright shining sun in that spot where the thundercloud is. That's terrific news, and your backers will be falling over themselves to invest.

It's not unusual for a backer to find a showstopper risk. Think of the excellent ABC-TV program *Shark Tank* (or *Dragon's Den*, which airs in Canada and the U.K.). Most aspiring entrepreneurs leave with no investment. Often it's just one risk that turns off the sharks. It may be disbelief that anyone would buy such a product or service. Or that the entrepreneur has been trying for so long, or has invested so much, for such little result. Or the product is too costly to yield a profit. Each is a risk that the sharks see as highly likely and having a large impact. Each is a top right-hand corner thundercloud, a showstopper.

Some risks are huge, but most are unlikely to happen. That's not to say that they won't happen. The unlikely can happen. But these are not showstopper risks. They are top left-hand corner risks. If we worried about the unlikely happening, we would never cross the road. Certainly no backer would ever invest a penny!

In the fall of 2001, one of the authors and his colleagues were advising a client on whether to back a company involved in airport operations. After the first week of work, they produced an interim report and a first-draft Suns & Clouds chart. In the top left-hand corner box, they placed a risk entitled "major air incident." They were thinking of a serious air crash that might lead to the prolonged grounding of a common class of aircraft. It seemed unlikely but would have a very large impact if it happened. The tragic events of 9/11 came just a few days later. They never envisaged anything so catastrophic, so inconceivably evil, but at least they had alerted their client to the extreme risks involved in the air industry. The deal was renegotiated and completed successfully.

THE BALANCE

In general, for most investment decisions, there's no showstopper risk. The main purpose of the Suns & Clouds chart will then be to present the *balance* of risk and opportunity. Do the opportunities surpass the risks? Given the overall picture, are the suns more favorably placed than the clouds? Or do the clouds overshadow the suns?

The way to assess a Suns & Clouds chart is to look first at the general area above the diagonal and in the direction of the thundercloud. This is the area covered in Figure 8–1 by the parabola. Any risk (or opportunity) there is worthy of note: It is at least reasonably likely to occur and would have at least a reasonable impact.

Those risks and opportunities below the diagonal are less important. They are of low to medium likelihood and of low to medium impact. Or they are not big enough risks or opportunities, or not likely enough to happen, to be of major concern.

A backer will look at the pattern of suns in this area of the parabola and compare it with the pattern of clouds. The closer each sun and cloud to the thundercloud, the more important it is. If the pattern of suns seems better placed than the pattern of clouds, your backers will be comforted. If the clouds overshadow the suns, they will be concerned.

In Figure 8–1, there are two clouds and two suns above the diagonal. But risk D lies outside the parabola. The best-placed element is opportunity B. Risk A and opportunity A more or less balance each other out, likewise for the other risks and opportunities. Only opportunity B is distinctly clear of the pack. The opportunities seem to surpass the risks. The business looks backable.

One of the best features of the Suns & Clouds chart is that it can be made dynamic. If the balance of risk and opportunity shown on the chart is unfavorable, you may be able to do something about it—and the chart will show this clearly.

For every risk, there are mitigating factors. Many, including those relating to market demand and competition, will be beyond your control. But you may be able to transfer that risk, at least in part, through insurance. Risks relating to your firm's competitive position, however, you may well be able to influence. There may be initiatives you can undertake to improve competitiveness and lower the probability of occurrence and/or impact. Some risks, indeed, may be wholly within your firm's control. You may even be able to eliminate them from the chart.

Likewise, there may be opportunities where your firm's chances of realizing them can be enhanced through an initiative that bolsters probability and/or impact.

Risk mitigation or opportunity enhancement in the Suns & Clouds chart can be illuminated with arrows and target signs. They'll show where your firm should aim and remind you that it's a target. It will improve the overall balance of risk in your plan.

How Material the Girl? Madonna and Risk

Suppose you're an investor. It's 1982 and you show up at a grubby studio in downtown Manhattan to meet a young woman with grandiose aspirations of stardom. Ms. Ciccone is a dancer who can sing a bit. She's a hard worker, but she's hard up. She's been scraping a living in New York City for five years, through a succession of low-paid jobs, including nude modeling.

She has made some progress as an entertainer. She has worked with a number of modern dance companies, been a backup dancer on a world tour, and played vocals and drums with a rock band, the Breakfast Club. She has written and produced a number of solo disco and dance songs and signed a singles deal with Sire Records. Her first single, "Everybody," written by herself and for which she received $5,000, has become quite a hit on the dance charts and in the clubs. However, it has made no impact on the Billboard Hot 100.

Would you have backed her? On the basis of the Suns & Clouds alone, possibly not—see Figure 8–2. Music trends were moving in other directions. "Everybody" was a successful single only in the small niche of club music. She might have followed that up with another single or two, even an album. But they too might have found just a niche following. She was basically a dancer, with a rather screechy voice. She dressed and looked sexy, but so did loads of other dancers.

But you may have seen something else. One opportunity (sun 3) may have stood out. You would have spent some time with her and caught a glimpse of what many people later came to recognize. It's a relentless drive, evidenced by her painstaking buildup of performing experience in the last few years. A steely professionalism. An extrovert bordering on the exhibitionist, with a readiness to blend her very person with her image. Boundless ambition. This quality was special. You may well have backed her on this basis alone.

FIGURE 8–2. Would you have backed Madonna in 1982?

Risks

1. Dance scene led by black bands (e.g., Kool and the Gang, Michael Jackson)
2. Moving to new pop (e.g., Human League, Men at Work)
3. Female artists more into soul (e.g., Diana Ross) or ballads (e.g., Olivia N-J) than rock (e.g., Tina Turner)
4. Madonna's high-energy dance music pitch too narrow a market
5. Madonna has limited singing talent

Opportunities

1. "Everybody" had niche club following; might be follow-up singles
2. Likewise with a first album
3. Madonna seems highly driven and committed to self-promotion
4. She could be packaged for new pop video market of MTV
5. Madonna could create new genre of white, female, dance rock

One year later and her Suns & Clouds chart (Figure 8–3) would have changed beyond recognition. Her first album, *Madonna*, reached the top 10 in the album charts and five of its singles became hits. One of them, "Holiday," went on to sell 12 million copies. The main risks concerning the breadth of her appeal would have evaporated. The main opportunity—namely, her potential to carve out a new genre of white, female dance-rock music with huge popular appeal—was now looking not just conceivable but likely.

If you hadn't backed her the year before, you wouldn't be able to afford to now. Opportunities were unbounded.

Fast-forward now to 1992. In the interim, albums such as *Like a Virgin*, *True Blue*, and *Like a Prayer* had kept Madonna at the top of the

FIGURE 8–3. Would you have backed Madonna one year later?

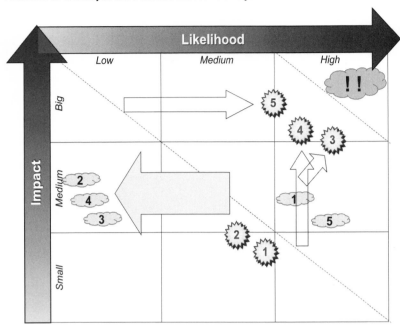

Risks

1. Dance scene led by black bands (e.g., Kool and the Gang, Michael Jackson)
2. Moving to new pop (e.g., Human League, Men At Work)
3. Female artists more into soul (e.g., Diana Ross) or ballads (e.g., Olivia N-J) than rock (e.g., Tina Turner)
4. Madonna's high-energy dance music pitch too narrow a market
5. Madonna has limited singing talent

Opportunities

1. "Everybody" had niche club following; might be follow-up singles
2. Likewise with a first album
3. Madonna seems highly driven and committed to self-promotion
4. She could be packaged for new pop video market of MTV
5. Madonna could create new genre of white, female, dance rock??

charts. She had even received critical acclaim for her role in a movie, *Desperately Seeking Susan.*

Then along came *Sex*, a coffee-table book of photographs featuring Madonna in an array of sexually explicit poses. It was damned by the media as narcissistic, some said pornographic. *Erotica* soon followed, an album that met with similar disdain. The video accompanying the (successful) lead single was withdrawn from MTV. Then Madonna took the leading female role in a movie *Body of Evidence*, a smuttier take on *Basic Instinct*. It flopped.

Had Madonna blown it? Had her star waned? Were these ventures into sexual explicitness just a sad, final fling for an entertainer who had passed her sell-by date?

Would you have backed her then? Could she ever recover from such a critical mauling, from an apparent obliteration of her fan base?

Could she ever generate again the kind of multimillion-dollar income stream she had achieved in the 1980s?

You may well have backed her. For all the risks, the dominant feature in Madonna's latest Suns & Clouds chart would have been her consistent strategy. If that could be encapsulated in one sentence—which a good strategy should be—it could have been:

> **To build on her capabilities in the performing arts through sustained investment of cash, time, and energy in image reinvention and self-publicity.**

That strategy may have dragged down her fortunes in 1992, but surely it could just as easily yank them up again in years to come? And perhaps she may have learned some lessons from the debacle and become a trifle more circumspect in her future reinventions. Her chart may have looked like Figure 8–4.

FIGURE 8–4. Would you have backed Madonna ten years later?

Risks

1. Pop music dominated by youth and boy bands
2. Madonna's music style now dated
3. Her image tarnished by multimedia ventures into explicit sex

Opportunities

1. All media coverage has value
2. The public loves to forgive
3. Madonna remains highly driven and committed to self-promotion
4. Her strategy of self-reinvention should ride her through the ups and downs

The one thing you know for sure in the world of entertainment is that performers must keep their names in the headlines and their faces on the front covers of magazines, whether in praise or condemnation. Any news is good news. No news is obscurity. In her year of sexual exhibitionism, Madonna had been very much the news. All she had to do next was reinvent herself again, preferably into something less controversial—an Argentinean folk heroine, perhaps, or an Eastern mystic, or an all-American girl, or a devoted mother, or a lady of the manor, whatever—and she could postpone her sell-by date indefinitely.

The strategy was brilliant. You would surely have backed her. She would go on to achieve the highest-grossing concert tour by a female artist ever, the controversial *Confessions* tour. Later she would break that record again with her *MDNA* and *Sticky & Sweet* tours. A material girl indeed.

BANKERS AND INVESTORS SEE DIFFERENT SKIES

The Suns & Clouds chart can be shown to any backer, whether your board, investor, or lender. But they will view it from different perspectives.

Bankers will focus on the clouds. They will want to know what can go wrong. Then they'll want to know what can go seriously wrong. They may even want to know what happens when everything goes wrong at the same time.

Your investors will also be interested in the clouds, but they will focus on the suns. They'll want to know what you can do to shift these suns up and to the right.

Same chart, different perspectives. The risks and opportunities faced by the entrepreneur translate into the risks and returns analyzed by the financiers. Bankers like low risk for which they are prepared to accept a relatively low return. Investors seek a higher return, for which they are prepared to accept higher risk.

It's all there on the Suns & Clouds chart.

Sensitivity Testing

The y-axis in the Suns & Clouds chart specifies impact on cash flow, or impact on value. But the chart is only looking for relative impact, in the sense that one risk will have a greater impact than another.

But your backers may be interested in specific impact. They may want you to quantify one or more risks or opportunities and put actual figures on them.

Indeed, you would be wise to preempt your backer's question and prepare some quantified impacts in advance. This is *sensitivity testing*. You test the financial statements to see how they change relative to a specific risk or opportunity or a general adjustment.

This is easy to do, assuming you have built up your financial forecasts in Excel or with special software. You should be able simply to plug in an amended value for the parameter in your spreadsheet and see the impact ripple down to the bottom line on your financial statements.

Pull out three or four big risks, assign specific, quantitative impacts to them, and observe the effects on your income statement and cash flow forecasts. Also stick in a couple of general risks beloved by bankers, such as operating costs up by 5 percent or expenditure on a key capital project up by 20 percent. Then take a look at the output and see how sensitive the financial forecasts are to these scenarios. (We'll revisit our fictional case study in a little bit, where Table 8–1 shows an example of sensitivity analysis for The Gorge Inn.)

Finally, you may choose to prepare a "downside case" for your banker, one where you combine two, three, or more risks and examine their cumulative impact. But beware. No matter how conservative and unlikely that your downside case may happen, the guys on the bank's credit committee will go further. They will assume bigger impacts on more risks, until your income statement resembles a battleground.

> **TOP TIP:** Stay realistic in your sensitivity testing. In the old days, that was taken for granted. Each test took many minutes of manual calculation, so only meaningful tests were contemplated. Nowadays, with electronic spreadsheets, any test can be done in a millisecond. Don't do tests on improbable values or scenarios—they will aggravate your backer. Stick to reasonably likely scenarios.

So, go gently in your downside case. And balance it with an upside case, where the opportunities in your Suns & Clouds chart materialize and/or have a bigger impact than in your base-case financial forecasts.

At the end of the day, your base-case forecasts are what you believe are most likely to happen. They have been drawn up coherently in a market and competitive context. Stand by them, defend them resolutely against undue pessimism, and counter the latter by pointing out similarly irrational optimism.

THE GORGE INN AND ORIENTAL SPA BUSINESS PLAN, 2014: RISK, OPPORTUNITY, AND SENSITIVITY

Rick and Kay Jones are quite surprised when they set out their Suns & Clouds chart. All during the process of drawing up the business plan, Kay has been diligent in teasing out of Rick the main risks, whether arising from market demand and competition or The Gorge's strategy, resources, and financials.

They have tried to envision how a banker would view things and believe they have been conservative, much more so than when they started the venture four years before. Yet when they draw up their Suns & Clouds chart (Figure 8–5), it looks so sunny, so favorable. Have they overdone it, they wonder?

FIGURE 8–5. Risks and opportunities facing The Gorge Inn.

Risks

1. Double-dip dents market demand
2. Spa fad wanes
3. A direct copy new entrant emerges
4. The Gorge's concept fades
5. Phase II construction costs up 20%
6. Phase II occupancy buildup slower than forecast
7. Interest rate up 3%

Opportunities

1. Market demand maintains growth
2. Focused marketing of The Gorge's proven concept
3. The Gorge spa attains profitability
4. New complementary services or products
5. Replicate concept elsewhere

They think not. Most of the risks they have identified have been of low probability and/or low impact. They have not been big risks. Only one risk seems to merit placing to the right of the diagonal, a slower buildup of occupancy than in the plan (cloud 6 in the chart).

On the other hand, there is one opportunity (sun 2) that shines all on its own—The Gorge concept, proven in Phase I, is poised to be rolled out and made more financially viable in Phase II.

Other opportunities that offset cloud 6 are the transformation of The Gorge's spa services to a profitable segment in their own right (sun 3), rather than a loss leader for the accommodation segment, and the introduction of complementary services and products (sun 4), such as day trips, sporting trips, and aromatherapy products.

Finally, there is the opportunity (sun 5) to replicate The Gorge's success. Rick and Kay have already identified a large B&B business in the North Cascades National Park that would be ideal and whose owners are planning to retire in a couple of years. Even if the timing of that deal doesn't work out, there will be other properties on the market when the time is right.

The Gorge is a lovely business. It has a healthy income statement, assets that the most conservative of bankers will lend against, and forecast cash flows that more adventurous bankers and equity investors would find attractive.

Whether or not this is a business that can attract 100 percent debt finance for this Phase II investment is an altogether different issue. While opportunities seem to outshine risks, it is also a business that is highly geared operationally—in other words, it has a high proportion of fixed cost. That's good news when things go well, not so good when things go poorly.

Rick figures that bankers will need to see some stress testing of certain key parameters, especially those flagged in the Suns & Clouds chart. He undertakes some sensitivity testing, as shown in Table 8–1.

TABLE 8–1. The Gorge Inn and Oriental Spa: Sensitivity testing.

$000	Profit Before Tax		Cash Flow	
	2016	2018	2016	2018
Business plan	107	256	244	375
Sensitivity tests				
Construction costs up 20%	94	243	247	377
Occupancy rates down 15%	-6	113	164	273
Both of the above tests	-19	100	167	276

The impact on profit before tax (PBT) from inflated Phase II construction costs of 20 percent seems limited and containable, Rick thinks—and, of course, there is only a minor cash flow impact in later years resulting from higher depreciation/lower tax.

But if occupancy rates turn out to be 15 percent below plan—for example, 51 percent in 2016 instead of the forecast 60 percent—the impact is much greater. The income statement in 2016 drops into the red and the profit forecast for 2018 is halved. Cash flow, however, remains positive, though shrunken.

Rick can show that such a drop is unlikely. A 51 percent overall occupancy rate in 2016 would imply a level of just 23 percent in the new rooms of Phase II (compared with a forecast 44 percent in the business plan), and The Gorge managed to achieve 39 percent occupancy in its first year of operations.

However, Rick understands that bankers tend to look at things rather more gloomily. They may view the risk of a slower buildup of occupancy (cloud 6) as having a higher probability. It will be quite a challenge to get 100 percent debt financing, he figures, but he'll give it a go.

◻ ◻ ◻ ◻ ◻ **THINKING OUT OF THE BOX** ◻ ◻ ◻ ◻ ◻

Succeeding in Business

A great attitude is not the result of success; success is the result of a great attitude.

—*Earl Nightingale*

Business is an art as well as a science. It is a matter of practical experience, judgment, foresight, and luck. To be successful in business, you must master the basics of business success.

Fortunately, all business skills are learnable. You can learn anything you need to learn, to achieve any goal you can set for yourself. There are no limits except the limits that you place on your own imagination.

There are three major reasons that businesses fail. They are:

1. Lack of money
2. Lack of knowledge
3. Lack of support

By mastering the basics of business success, you will gain the knowledge necessary to acquire the support and money you need for your business.

The way to succeed as a large company is to think and act like a small, flexible, entrepreneurial company. The way to succeed as a small or medium-size company is to think like, and use the same tools and strategies used by, large companies.

There are seven key areas of activity that are responsible for business success:

1. *Marketing*: the ability to determine and sell the right product to the right customer at the right time
2. *Finance*: the ability to acquire the money you need, and account for the money that you receive

3. *Production*: the ability to produce products and services at a high enough level of quality and consistency over time

4. *Distribution*: the ability to get your product or service to the market in a timely and economic fashion

5. *Research and development*: the ability to continually innovate and produce new products, services, processes, and responses to competition

6. *Regulation*: the ability to deal with the requirements of government legislation at all levels

7. *Labor*: the ability to recruit, train, and motivate the people you need to drive your business

Knowledge is power. Specialized knowledge, or skills in a vital area, can increase the likelihood of business success. Therefore:

◻ Learn all you can; never tell all you know. Control of vital information is a form of power.

◻ Aim to acquire superior knowledge in your chosen market niche.

Thousands of companies have been studied to discover the reasons for business failure. Here are the reasons, in order of importance. How many of these descriptions apply to you?

◻ *Lack of direction*. Business owners fail to establish clear goals or create plans to achieve those goals. They fail to develop a complete business plan before starting operations.

◻ *Impatience*. When business owners try to accomplish too much too soon, or expect to get results far faster than is possible, they grow impatient. Remember this old rule: Everything costs twice as much and takes three times as long as expected.

◻ *Greed*. When business owners try to charge too much and make a lot of money in a short period of time, it leads to business failure.

◻ *Taking action without thinking*. The business owner acts impetuously and makes costly mistakes that eventually cause the business to fail.

◻ *Poor cost control*. The business owner spends too much, especially at the beginning, and drains down all the funding raised before achieving profitability.

◻ *Poor quality of product*. Shoddiness makes it difficult to sell products, and extremely difficult to get repeat business.

◻ *Insufficient working capital*. The business owner fails to understand the crucial difference between revenue and cash inflow or is overoptimistic in working capital assumptions, expecting immediate, positive cash flow.

- *Bad or nonexistent budgeting.* The business owner fails to develop written budgets for operations that include all possible expenses.

- *Inadequate financial records.* The business owner fails to set up a bookkeeping or accounting system at the beginning.

- *Loss of momentum in the sales department.* Lower than expected sales, hence gross profit, makes it harder to cover fixed overhead costs.

- *Failure to anticipate market trends.* The business owner does not recognize changes in demand, customer preferences, or the economic situation.

- *Lack of managerial ability or experience.* The business owner does not possess or understand the important skills of running a business.

- *Indecisiveness.* The business owner is unable to make key decisions in the face of difficulties; decisions are delayed or improperly made because of concern for the opinions or feelings of other people.

- *Poor human relations.* Interpersonal difficulties lead to strained relations and perhaps conflict with staff, suppliers, creditors, or customers.

- *Diffusion of effort.* The business owner tries to do too many things, which results in a failure to set priorities and focus on high-value tasks.

Businesses also are successful for specific, identifiable reasons. They succeed when they have:

- A product or service well suited to the needs and requirements of the market

- A complete, robust business plan developed before commencing business operations

- A complete market analysis conducted before producing or offering the product or service

- Complete development of advertising, promotional, and sales programs

- Tight financial controls, good budgeting, and accurate bookkeeping and accounting, all backed by an attitude of frugality

- A high degree of competence, capability, and integrity on the part of key staff

- Good internal efficiency, time management, and precise job descriptions, accompanied by clear and measurable output and responsibilities.

- Good communication among the staff and an open-door policy

- Strong momentum in the sales department and a continued emphasis on marketing the product or service

- Concern for the customer as a top priority at all times

- Determination, persistence, and patience on the part of the business owners

Business success is attainable if you avoid the reasons for business failure and continually focus on improving in the areas that are responsible for business success.

What one action are you going to take immediately for succeeding in business as the result of what you have learned here?

□   □   □   □   □   □   □   □   □   □   □   □   □   □   □   □   □   □

Checklist on Risk, Opportunity, and Sensitivity

Set out and explain the big risks and opportunities facing the achievement of your business plan. Weigh them according to two criteria:

1. Likelihood of occurrence

2. Impact on cash flow if they do occur

Use the Suns & Clouds tool to chart the risks and opportunities. You do not have to include the chart in the plan, but nonetheless you should do the assessment for yourself.

Assure your backer of two fundamentals on the nature of the risk:

1. There is no showstopper risk in your plan.

2. On balance, opportunities to beat your plan surpass the risks faced.

Finally, quantify certain key risks and opportunities and assess their impact on the financial forecasts in a sensitivity analysis. Show that your cash flow forecasts remain robust and able to withstand the impact of reasonable adverse assumptions derived from specified risks.

Show that your plan is robust and backable.

CONCLUSION AND EXECUTIVE SUMMARY

Drive thy business or it will drive thee. —Benjamin Franklin

YOU ARE all but there! All that is left now is to prepare a conclusion and an executive summary. And possibly an investment highlights section. These sections must be punchy. They should knock out your backer!

Conclusion
This is the fun bit. All, yes, all the hard work has already been done. In each chapter you've had to do some serious research and thinking—about market demand, competition, strategy, resources, financials, and risk.

All you need to do now is take your headline conclusions from each of those chapters and weave them into a coherent story line that puts the case for obtaining backing in full context. In half a page.

You should set out the story line as **the overall conclusion on why your business is worthy of backing** (in which you summarize—in bold—the main findings from the headlines below):

- *Market demand prospects*. State your conclusions on what's going to happen to market demand, by key business segment (Chapter 3).

- *Competition*. Your conclusions on whether competition is intense and set to intensify (Chapter 4).

- *Strategy*. Your conclusions on your firm's current competitive position and its strategy for further developing competitive advantage (Chapter 5).

- *Resources*. Your conclusions on the resources your firm will deploy to implement that strategy and meet its goals (Chapter 6).

- *Financials and forecasts*. Your conclusions on how your firm will grow revenues and operating margin over the next few years (Chapter 7).

- *Risk, opportunity, and sensitivity*. Your conclusions on why opportunities for your firm outshine risks in your plan (Chapter 8).

You can either develop these conclusions into a half page of normal text or just write one overall conclusion supported by six bulleted sectional conclusions (as done here).

If you choose the latter format, make it super-concise. Force yourself to get right to the point. Each bullet point should be no more than one sentence. It can have a couple of commas, with some backup qualifying phrases, if necessary, maybe even a dash or a colon. But keep it to just the one sentence.

The more long-winded you make this story line, the more difficult it will be for the backer to see how you have derived your overall conclusion. The conclusion itself should also be just the one sentence. It should answer the question: *Why is this plan worthy of backing?*

> **TOP TIP:** Save the best until last. Make your conclusion punchy. And remember the seven Cs—make it clear, crisp, concise, consistent, coherent, credible, and convincing.

**THE GORGE INN AND ORIENTAL SPA BUSINESS PLAN, 2014:
CONCLUSION**

Rick has come to the end of his business plan for The Gorge, Phase II. He has thoroughly enjoyed working on it; he has relished every page and imbued it with a passion for the business. Here is his crisp, concise six-bulleted conclusion:

> The Gorge Inn and Oriental Spa is distinctive, well placed in a growing market, and poised to become a leading, highly profitable provider of spa services in the Columbia River Gorge, with opportunities to exploit a proven concept outshining risks of construction cost overrun or slower buildup of occupancy:
>
> - *Market demand prospects.* The overnight visitor market in the Columbia River Gorge has bounced back from the 2009 downturn and should grow at around 4 percent/year over the next few years to around $105 million in 2018.
>
> - *Competition.* The industry is competitive, with low barriers to entry, but with the most highly differentiated businesses thriving, with above-average occupancy levels.
>
> - *Strategy.* The Gorge is distinctive in its stunning location and Oriental-themed offering; has achieved a favorable competitive position in three years, with room occupancy budgeted at 75 percent in 2014; and is poised to become a leading provider of spa services in the Columbia River Gorge with the planned Phase II investment.
>
> - *Resources.* The $1.05 million Phase II investment will add 16 rooms to The Gorge's current 17-room capacity, plus a swimming pool, and involve a doubling of staff and a return to the marketing levels of the early days of Phase I.
>
> - *Financials and forecasts.* The Gorge sales are forecast to almost double by 2018, greatly surpassing the planned 50 percent increase in overhead and boosting profitability from 2014's budgeted 21.6 percent operating margin to 34 percent.
>
> - *Risk, opportunity, and sensitivity.* The opportunity to exploit The Gorge's proven concept outshines the main risks of construction cost overrun or a slower-than-anticipated occupancy buildup.

That should do the trick, Rick thinks. Time to collar the bank manager . . .

Executive Summary

The executive summary, which will become Chapter 1 of your business plan, is an extended version of the conclusion, no more, no less.

It should have the same overall conclusion, but instead of one sentence per bullet, it should have a couple of paragraphs for each.

The executive summary should be two pages of text, with perhaps three or four entries, including tables and/or charts. At six paragraphs per page, that gives an average of two paragraphs per bullet. One or two bullets might merit more than two, others less.

Again, remember that you must be clear, concise, and convincing in your executive summary.

Don't fall into the trap of dismissing the executive summary as a boring exercise. You are presenting a case for why your firm is worthy of gaining backing. Your case will be well researched and analyzed, but it must also be well presented. Nowhere is presentation more important than in the executive summary; after all, it will be the first few pages that everyone reads. Some senior decision makers will read nothing else.

Spend time on the executive summary; nurture it, hone it, and edit it remorselessly, even give it to a professional to edit. It may be the best investment you make.

Once perfected, the executive summary becomes Chapter 1 of your business plan.

Let's take another look at the executive summary of The Gorge Inn case study, first presented in Chapter 1 of this book. Hopefully it will give you an idea of how to make your plan crisp, coherent, convincing . . . and backable!

THE GORGE INN AND ORIENTAL SPA BUSINESS PLAN, 2014: EXECUTIVE SUMMARY

The Gorge Inn and Oriental Spa ("The Gorge") is a destination with a difference. It is set overlooking the stunning Columbia River Gorge in the Pacific Northwest of the United States and yet offers visitors a touch of the Orient in its room decor, cuisine, and spa. It has 17 rooms for rent, most with views over the canyon, with spa and restaurant facilities offering a menu of Western and Oriental selections to both overnight and day visitors.

It turned over $513,000 in 2013, having grown by 36 percent/year since 2011, and operating margin is expected to top 20 percent in 2014. Further investment of $1.05 million in a 16-room extension and swimming pool is forecast to double sales by 2018 and boost operating margin to 34 percent. Opportunities to exploit a proven concept outshine risks of cost overrun or slower buildup of occupancy.

The Gorge has three main business segments—rooms, catering, and spa. Room revenues have been growing fastest, at 45 percent/year, with spa revenues (20 percent of total) slower (at 18 percent/year) because of the increasing patronage of nonresident visitors from the start and subsequent capacity limitations, to be eased with the planned Phase II development.

The overnight visitor market in the Columbia River Gorge has bounced back from the 2009 downturn to an estimated $86 million in 2013 and is forecast to grow at around 4 percent/year to $105 million by 2018. Key long-term drivers are the growth in the U.S. population and per capita incomes; the propensity of Americans to take multiple short breaks; investment in state visitor attractions, such as scenic road and off-road cycling routes; and targeted marketing spend led by Travel Oregon. The main short-term driver is the economic cycle.

There are many excellent resorts, hotels, inns, B&Bs, and spas throughout Oregon. The industry is competitive, with low barriers to entry, but with the most highly differentiated businesses thriving and enjoying repeat customers. Occupancy rates in Columbia River Gorge hotels are a shade higher than elsewhere in Oregon. Spa facilities are not widespread in rural Oregon and are found primarily at the luxury resorts, but there are many good spas in Portland, the "City of Roses," which is just 35 miles from The Gorge. Restaurants offering Oriental cuisine, particularly Chinese, Thai, and Vietnamese, can also be found in Portland, along with its famed food cart pods and microbreweries.

The Gorge Inn is distinctive in two main ways: It enjoys a spectacular location atop one of the most beautiful canyons in North America, and it has an Oriental theme. The theme is understated, with a hint of the Orient applied to the bedroom decor and Oriental treatments available, in addition to standard ones, at the spa. Oriental cuisine is offered in the restaurant, but so too is Western fare. The customer is given the choice. In the three years since opening in December 2010, occupancy rates at The Gorge have grown from 39 percent to 56 percent to 71 percent and are budgeted conservatively for 75 percent in 2014. Restaurant take-up by overnight visitors has risen to 35 percent of visitor nights and spa occupancy 26 percent, both above budget.

Rick and Kay Jones bought the property in 2009 for $715,000, against which they took on a mortgage of $500,000 and spent a further $280,000 of their own funds on renovation. The owners work full-time in the business and employ a staff of three full-time workers, with part-time help added as appropriate. Spa professionals are contracted as required.

The business broke even at the operating profit level during 2012, the second year of operations, and achieved a profit before tax of 11 percent in 2013, budgeted to rise to 15 percent this year. The owners believe that profitability will be greatly boosted with the planned Phase II expansion, costing $1,050,000 for a new building with 16 rooms and an outside heated swimming pool. Overheads, other than financing costs, will rise by 50 percent, but revenues, once occupancy rates return to today's levels by (conservatively) 2018, will have almost doubled.

Operating margin, assuming no change in directors' remuneration, is forecast to reach 34 percent by 2018 and profit before tax 24 percent. The speed of growth will continue to yield challenges of cash flow, and the owners will look to their backer to provide the necessary flexibility of finance.

The key risks to this plan are a slower buildup of occupancy, perhaps occasioned by a double-dip recession; the opening of direct competition; a peaking of interest in the offering or insufficient awareness; slippage in construction work; and the health of the owners—all of which are examined in depth in the plan and found to be containable.

Upside opportunities lie in raising occupancy rates higher than in the plan through marketing that's focused on exploiting a proven concept; the introduction of new, complementary services or products; liftoff in the spa segment's profitability; and the acquisition of another site (Phase III), like one provisionally identified in the North Cascades National Park in Washington State, to replicate the Oriental spa concept in the state next door.

In conclusion, The Gorge has established itself as a serious player in the Oregon tourist industry, offering visitors something very special. It is now poised, through this expansion, to become a leading player in spa services in Oregon and to achieve healthy profitability. Its owners seek a financial partner who shares this vision.

Investment Highlights

If the purpose of your business plan is to raise equity finance, and especially if you are seeking to sell your company, you might consider including a section on investment highlights.

But take care. Financiers and their advisers treat investment highlight sections with suspicion. They can reek of a sales spiel. Potential backers may well skim through them and move on to the plan proper.

Investment highlight sections are common. They are often found in a Confidential Information Memorandum (CIM), a document typically put together in an auction situation by the corporate finance adviser to the vendor of part or all of a company's equity.

The CIM itself is a sale document. Good ones will transpose what is in management's business plan into a CIM format, while retaining the balance found in a good business plan. Risks will be addressed and measures to mitigate them set out. They will not be swept under the carpet.

A bad CIM is a miserable affair. It reads like the sale particulars of a dodgy estate agent. Everything that is good about a company will be in there, and exaggerated. Anything not so good will be absent. It will resemble the classic sales pitch that waxes lyrical about the spacious rooms of this detached Prairie Box house, but omits mentioning that it is located alongside a four-lane highway. Or it may state that the house "might benefit from some updating," meaning the roof needs to be retiled and the interior gutted, with the electrical, heating, plumbing, and plastering all best redone before you even think of redecorating.

If a CIM is bad, imagine what its investment highlights section is like! It is the hardest sell section of a hard sell document! We have seen some horrors over the years. How about these examples (suitably disguised):

- "ABC addresses a booming market, one that has doubled in the last three years." Yes, and it was on the verge of falling off a cliff due to imminent overcapacity in undersea transatlantic cables!

- "CDE is the only U.K.-based producer in this engineering segment." Yes, all others had withdrawn from the market because of a structural inability to compete with low-cost, well-engineered product from the Far East.

- "FGH is the leading player in the dental segment of this market." Yes, but demand for this product by dentists was limited and accounted for all of 3 percent of the company's sales.

If you are going to insert an investment highlights section, here are some tips:

- *Don't reproduce the executive summary.* Keep your investment highlights short and sharp; restrict yourself to a maximum of ten bullet points. These bullets should highlight the key reasons why a backer would choose to inject scarce resources into your company rather than somewhere else.

- *Don't have a separate chapter.* Just drop a text box into the middle of the executive summary chapter; the investment highlights section will of course duplicate some of what is in the executive summary, but both must be stand-alone elements, one summarizing the business plan and one calling out the highlights from a backer's perspective.

- *Don't mislead.* If you're found out, you'll have no deal, no matter how good your company is, how sound your business plan, or how attractive the return on investment.

Let your investment highlights section be a brief venture into sales blurb (albeit in a soft, understated tone) in an otherwise rational, factual, and balanced business plan.

THE GORGE INN AND ORIENTAL SPA BUSINESS PLAN, 2014: INVESTMENT HIGHLIGHTS

Rick Jones is hoping to raise the funds needed for the Phase II project from his bank. He recognizes, however, that his bank manager may well demand more of an equity cushion in case things veer from plan.

Rick is prepared therefore to insert a separate text box into the executive summary chapter of his business plan. Reticent as they are to part with 15 percent to 20 percent of the family equity in The Gorge, Rick and Kay are prepared to pay that price to see Phase II get off the ground. These investment highlights should do the trick, he figures, because this story line is not too hard a sell but nevertheless compelling.

Investment Highlights

The Gorge Inn and Oriental Spa business exhibits these attractive value drivers:

- A distinctive tourism offering in an area of outstanding natural beauty
- Steadily growing market
- 75 percent room occupancy rate after four years of operation
- Proven management
- Phase II investment of $1.05 million in extra room capacity and a swimming pool
- Poised to become the leading spa provider in the area
- Sales forecast to almost double by 2016
- Operating profit forecast to rise by 2016 to $360,000, a margin of 34 percent, up from 15 percent in 2012
- Potential to replicate concept elsewhere

The owners are seeking to raise $350,000 in equity finance in exchange for a minority shareholding. This represents an exceptional investment opportunity.

10

MONITORING AND EVALUATING

In preparing for war, I have always found that plans are useless but planning is essential.
—Dwight Eisenhower

YOU WROTE your plan; you won the backing. Great, but is that it? It's best not to think that's the end of it. You may want to monitor your plan for a while and then set aside time after a few years to evaluate it properly. There will be lessons to be learned for next time. And hopefully, this evaluation won't reveal you to have been someone prone to crafting pie-in-the-sky plans!

Monitoring Your Plan

In Chapter 1, we counseled against the use of business planning as a managerial tool for small and medium-size businesses (SMBs). That approach is fine in large organizations that are prepared to devote the required resources for a month or more each year to researching and analyzing markets, customers, competitors, resources, financial model assumptions, risk and sensitivity, and so on. It is not workable when resources are limited.

Nevertheless, if yours is an SMB and you developed a business plan for a specific purpose—typically to obtain backing, whether from your board, a bank, or an investor—it is still worthwhile to monitor it. You spent many hours drawing up the plan—the least you can do is see to what extent things have turned out as predicted.

Indeed, it may be useful to monitor performance against the plan to keep your backer informed of progress. At the very least this monitoring would consist of comparing key financial results with forecasts. It would be better to compare the underlying business drivers of those results—like occupancy and average achieved room rate, in the case of The Gorge Inn—with what was forecast.

After a year or so, however, this monitoring will be usurped, to a large extent, by the budget process. Once the new budget is in place, results over the following year will tend to be assessed in relation to the budget, not the old business plan, which is becoming a document past its sell-by date.

By the third year, the business plan will be regarded as a historical curiosity. Monitoring will be a superfluous exercise, but evaluation will not.

Evaluating Your Plan

If you needed to draw up a business plan for some specific purpose—possibly to obtain backing from your board or an external financier—chances are that you will need to do so again one day.

That may be in just a couple of years' time, if things go badly and there's a need for restructuring, or if things go extremely well and you need further capital for expansion. Or you are looking to expand by acquisition or alliance. It may be that you won't need to dust off your business plan and write a new one for another five years.

Whatever the case, you may well have to do this exercise again. So you need to know what you did right and what went wrong this time.

The way to do that is through a structured evaluation process, best done after three years, but sooner if a new business plan is needed within that period.

The evaluation should be carried out by someone independent of the initial business planning exercise. No vested interests should be at stake. It should focus on examining the outturn of key parameters forecast in the plan.

A summary of the evaluation process is shown in Table 10–1. The important points in the evaluation process are as follows:

▫ *Key parameters*. Select only those parameters that have a significant bearing on the outcome of your financial forecasts. For example, you might choose to compare the actual cost of premises rental with that forecast, but you won't review your forecast of paper clip costs.

▫ *Reasons*. If things turned out significantly different from forecast, why? Where did you go wrong?

▫ *Lessons*. The main point of the exercise is, of course, to discern what lessons can be learned for next time. Next time around, what should you do differently in the plan process? How can your forecast be made more accurate? What extra research or analysis would be beneficial?

TABLE 10–1. Evaluation of a business plan after three years: An example.

Key Parameter	Forecast	Actual	Reasons for Variance	Lessons
Market growth, 2014–2016	3.0%/yr	2.2%/yr		
Number of competitors	5	4		
Average unit pricing growth	2.5%/yr	1.9%/yr		
Customer return ratio	36%	41%		
Sales growth	6.3%/yr	7.8%/yr		
Operating margin, 2016	16.4%	14.2%		
Total capital expenditure, 2014–2016	$1.6m	$1.8m		

Monitoring your business plan can be regarded as an option. Evaluation should not be. It is not a time-consuming process. It can be carried out in just a few days. And the lessons may be illuminating and very useful for the next time, or if you are asked by the boss to write a business plan—by the end of the week!

TOP TIP: "If only I had done this, thought of that . . ." Evaluations work. Lessons are better learned late than never. Try to get it right next time!

Beware These Characters!

We have met some of these characters along the way, in various chapters. But it's useful to gather them together here at the end of the book to remind you of what not to do. Hopefully, when you and your colleagues do an evaluation of your business plan in three years' time, you won't go down in your firm's history as a dreamer, a loner, a magician, a macho man, a delusionist, or a shotgunner.

THE DREAMER

This is the guy who lays out a set of sales forecasts that bear no relation to the market demand forecast and/or how the firm is positioned in the market. We met him in Chapter 7, when looking at RandomCo's sales forecasts, and assessed his forecasts as wild. He's the kind of guy who forecasts 14 percent/year sales growth in a business segment even though market demand is shrinking, his firm is no more than reasonably positioned, and there are no plans to launch new products or services or enter new markets.

The dreamer's forecasts bear no relation to the market environment in which his firm operates or to his firm's competitive standing. He's unbackable.

THE LONER

This is the person whose business plan has a single sentence—not even a paragraph, let alone a chapter—on competition. Competition doesn't matter. She identifies a market and her firm will serve it. No one else matters, no competitor exists, no new entrant will arrive. Hers will be the sole provider to this market. If others do arrive, customers will be disdainful, since the newcomers won't have what it takes to compete. Only her firm counts.

The loner thinks her firm alone can serve the addressed market. Others are irrelevant. She's unbackable.

THE MAGICIAN

This is the clever guy who has forecast sales reasonably, consistent with both market demand and his firm's competitive position, but he has forecast his cost base to grow at a fraction of his sales growth rate. He believes he can use his purchasing skills to drive down direct costs and, as far as he is concerned, overhead expenses are too high at present. By forecasting them to remain flat while sales grow, he is being conservative. As for capital expenditure, who needs it? The company should do fine with its aging capital equipment for a few more years and, if space gets a bit tight in the plant, they can always improve the production process flow. Operating margin is thus forecast to grow dramatically year on year.

The magician thinks he can grow sales without deploying the resources, and costs, needed to serve them. Even if he has a sound market development case, he risks rejection by backers because of his unrealistic cost and margin forecasts. He may be unbackable.

THE MACHO MAN

This is the turnaround guy (or gal) extraordinaire. No matter that profits took a bit of a dive last year. This year profits are going to bounce back and rise exponentially thenceforth. His are the fabled "hockey stick" forecasts. Everything that could go wrong went wrong last year. Everything that can go right will go right in years to come. And why? Because he has taken charge; he's the new CEO. He'll sort everything out. He'll remotivate the sales staff, make the production staff more efficient, and the R&D staff more market-focused. The firm will have world-class leadership for the first time ever. Him!

The macho man may be right. Some hockey sticks do turn out as forecast. But the odds are not on his side, and his backers will be wary indeed of his manifold claims. They will examine his track record with a fine-tooth comb. And they will cross-examine him on every sentence and number in his business plan, that is, if they can bear sitting alongside him that long.

THE DELUSIONIST

This person has completed a rigorous, thoroughly researched, and analyzed assessment of the market opportunity. She has explained convincingly why it would be unlikely that more than four companies will enter the field. And she has set out in minute detail why her firm will remain at least as competitive as any other competitor on the assumption that others copy and follow her company's consistently innovative policies. Her sales forecasts assume conservatively no more than a one in four market share by Year 5. Her expense forecasts are individually well argued and seem reasonable. And yet her forecasts show an operating margin of 40 percent in Year 5.

She is deluded. The sales volume forecasts may well prove correct, so too the cost forecasts. But what about pricing? Can she assume that competitors won't price more competitively than her firm in order to gain share faster? Ultrahigh operating margins tend to get shaved back through competitive pricing by either the incumbents or a new entrant, or through escalating marketing costs, or high salary demands, or a mixture of all. She may well win her backing, but not on the terms suggested by her business plan.

THE SHOTGUNNER

This guy is good. He started a business from scratch, survived the early ups and downs, and now has a healthy, tidy little business. But he is not enamored of that final adjective. He wants to grow, and grow fast. There is little scope for expanding his current business as is. But it could be replicated in another location. Or he could try introducing a new product line, aimed at a different customer group. Or he could try doing something similar with a different product group entirely. Given his track record, he could well succeed in any one of these strategic directions.

The problem is that his business plan shows investment in all three directions. Forecast profit by the end of Year 3 shows a doubling, with each new direction contributing its share. It won't happen. He is going to be stretched in so many directions he will have to be the Fantastic Four's Mister Fantastic to catch all the balls. His plan is unbackable, but he might not be. If he can be persuaded to select one strategy, to focus, he may be backable. He must become a rifleman, not a shotgunner.

□   □   □

When you write your business plan, don't be a dreaming, lonesome, macho, deluded, shotgun-toting magician. Be realistic. Gain the respect of your backer. Get that funding.

Good luck!

■　■　□

EPILOGUE
12 HOT POTATOES

We shall either find a way or make one.　—Hannibal

HERE ARE some final thoughts before you remove the "draft" from your business plan.

You have set out your vision and plans for your company's future over the next few years clearly, crisply, concisely, consistently, coherently, credibly, and convincingly. You have, throughout the process, tried to address the questions you think a backer needs answered. That is why your business plan is distinctive. It is geared toward your backer's concerns, not necessarily yours.

But things change. Your backers concerns may change.

Happily, one thing doesn't change, not at all. The recommended structure of your plan—built around market demand, competition, strategy, resources, financials, and risk—is economically rational and no different from the structure we used or advised clients to use ten, twenty, or more years ago.

It is the content of each chapter that may need to change with the times. Are your backers' concerns evolving? To what extent will they be influenced by hot business trends of the day or by the winds of political and economic change?

This book has examined some of the issues affecting businesses at the time of writing. Over time these issues may change. When writing your plan, bear in mind which issues may have become hotter for your backer and which may have cooled.

Take another look through your plan. Should you add a section here, a paragraph or sentence there, to reflect the "hot potatoes" of the day?

Here are a dozen issues that financial backers are currently hot on, and in some cases have been for a number of years. Each of these issues may be worthy of further thought when finalizing the relevant chapters of your business plan:

1. The credit crunch and its aftermath (Chapter 3 on market demand)

2. The price of oil (Chapter 3)

3. Global competition (Chapter 4 on competition)

4. Going international (Chapter 5 on strategy)

5. Acquisitions (Chapter 5)

6. Raw material supplies and prices (Chapter 6 on resources)

7. Outsourcing (Chapter 6)

8. Offshoring (Chapter 6)

9. Carbon footprint (Chapter 6)

10. Corporate social responsibility (Chapter 6)

11. Social media marketing (Chapter 6)

12. Tax avoidance (Chapter 7 on financials)

The Credit Crunch and Its Aftermath

The credit crunch of 2007–11, which led to the financial crash of autumn 2008, severe recession in North America and Europe, and the sovereign debt crisis in the Eurozone, has scarred the OECD (Organization for Economic

Co-operation and Development) economies. At the time of this writing, economic recovery is still tentative and economic forecasters exhibit little cheer.

One thing is agreed. The prolonged, steady upward march of economic growth seen in the 2000s is a thing of the past. Unlike in middle-income economies such as the BRIC countries (Brazil, Russia, India, and China), where rapid economic growth resumed quickly, short-term economic prospects in the OECD countries are unexciting, with low growth at best.

But such predictions mask great variation by sector and by companies within sectors. Some sectors have done relatively well through the economic downturn, including telecommunications and other technology-driven areas, electronic media, domestic tourism, casinos, sports, chocolate and other comfort foods, renewable energy, even business start-ups. Others have taken a beating, like retail (other than discount stores), property and construction, automotive, print media, and the catering trade.

Has your sector been hit hard by recession? Or were you exposed to customers in sectors hit hard by recession? Have some competitors fared relatively well through recession? How? What are the prospects for recovery, given a backdrop of slow resumption of GDP growth? What are the risks of your sector faring adversely in the aftermath of recession? Conversely, what are the opportunities?

Your backer will want to know in detail how recession impacted your business and how it will fare in the future against a backdrop of unspectacular economic recovery.

The Price of Oil

The price of oil has become exceptionally volatile in the last few years. From the mid-1980s to the mid-2000s, oil prices were relatively steady in real terms, averaging around US$35 to $40/barrel (Brent crude oil spot price in US$, as of April 2011), with a short-lived spike of $60 during the Gulf War of 1991. Real prices doubled between 2004 and 2007, driven by demand growth in the BRIC countries, then more than doubled again in one year, peaking at over $140 in July 2008, before plummeting post-crash back to around $40 by the end of the year. In 2009–10, prices jumped again to around the $80 level and, driven by the uncertainties surrounding the Arab Spring, topped $100 again in the first quarter of 2011. The Libyan revolt and further tension between Iran and the West held prices high through to late 2012, averaging around $110.

Industry observers believe such volatility has become the new norm. How does this affect your business? Rising oil prices have a stagflationary effect on oil-importing countries; they dampen macroeconomic growth and raise prices. This double whammy affects most businesses because it constrains revenue growth and raises operating costs. Is your business sensitive to oil price rises? Very sensitive? Former Saudi oil minister Sheikh Yamani suggested in April 2011 that if the regional political unrest spread to Saudi Arabia, oil prices could leap to $200 to $300. "I don't expect this for the time being," he said encouragingly, then added, "but who would have expected Tunisia?" How will your business cope?

Global Competition

The world is getting smaller: a cliché, yes, but also a fact. Competition can now come from any direction. It can come from a player in a low-cost country or from a domestic or foreign player now producing in a low-cost country. It can come from a domestic distributor buying from a medium-cost country. It can even come from a player in a high-cost country offloading surplus production.

Backers are aware of this global competition. High up on their checklist is always "the threat from Asia." One of the authors advised a North American engineering company whose market was shared between a dozen or so domestic producers for decades. Out of the blue, two Korean companies, building on their larger scale in the Far East, entered the marketplace competitively and gained 25 percent market share in three years. And South Korea is no longer a low-cost country. What will happen when Chinese producers get around to targeting the market? The company needed to refocus on the quality of its product and service and lower its cost base, and do it quickly.

Where is tomorrow's competition going to come from in your industry? How will you respond?

Going International

This issue can be seen as the flipside opportunity to the global competition risk. The world is getting smaller, so why don't you help it along? To what extent can your firm's sustainable competitive advantage in your domestic market be translated into foreign markets—Latin America, the multicountry but single market European Union, or the Middle East?

And why not into Asia? Is it time to stop looking at the Far East as a threat and instead see it as an opportunity—a vast market ready to be tapped with highly differentiated, preferably branded product or services? Think of the Chinese market penetration achieved by GM, Gap, Mary Kay, or Kentucky Fried Chicken. Why not your firm, too?

Acquisitions

Private equity backers always have one eye on bolt-on acquisitions when they invest in a company. If a company is worth investing in—in other words, it is soundly placed in reasonably attractive markets—there may well be scope for buying into less well-placed companies in the same markets or well-placed companies in related markets. The economics should be favorable as long as the synergies achieved, whether in revenue enhancement or cost savings, are greater than the premium paid to gain control.

Which of your competitors could be strengthened though your firm's control? Into which related markets could your firm's strengths be transferred? Think on Microsoft's acquisition of Bungie Software in 2000, creators of the science fiction video game franchise, Halo. Microsoft bought Bungie's game development strengths and transferred its own marketing and distribution strengths. Halo became a major propellant of Microsoft's multibillion-dollar Xbox business. Are there other companies where you could add value? Who could add value to your company?

Raw Material Supplies and Prices

It is not just oil prices that have become more volatile in recent years. Virtually all commodities, hard and soft, experience price volatility. Prices of metals—aluminum, copper, iron ore, tin, zinc—tripled or thereabouts between the first half of the 2000s and 2006–08, plunged post-crash in 2008, and promptly bounced back to pre-crash levels in 2010. The overwhelming driver has been the appetite for resources created by the voluminous economic growth of the BRIC countries.

Meanwhile, prices of soft commodities have followed a similar trend. The price of maize averaged around $100/metric ton in 2000–05, before tripling to $287 in June 2008, tumbling to around $160 in 2009–10, and shooting up again to more than $300 in spring 2011. Again, a main driver has been rising demand from BRIC consumers, but as important has been the diversion of 40 percent of the U.S. corn crop to biofuels.

Other agricultural commodities (e.g., cotton, wool, rubber, and hides), food commodities (vegetable oils, meat, seafood, sugar, bananas, and oranges), and beverage commodities (coffee, tea, and cocoa) have shown similar rising price trends. It's small wonder that the world's largest commodities trader, Glencore, floated in May 2011 on the London Stock Exchange at the staggering valuation of $60 billion.

In a world of relentlessly growing demand and increasing scarcity, it's hard to see commodity prices returning to the levels and relative stability of the early 2000s.

What impact have rising commodity prices had on your business? To what extent have you been able to pass price increases on to your customers? In an environment of growing scarcity, have you had any difficulties, to date, in obtaining sufficient supplies of certain raw materials? Are you likely to in the future? What contingency plans do you have for such a situation? Your backer needs to know.

Outsourcing

Outsourcing of production and processes has long been with us. But in any one industry there is seldom any uniformity in the areas or degree of outsourcing. Some firms outsource more than others. Why? What should be the optimal extent of outsourcing?

We often come across manufacturing companies that have successfully outsourced production of most components, even modules of components, and yet, when asked why a competitor manages to undercut them on price, the manager replies: "They do everything in-house, like we used to 20 years ago. They make all their components on ancient equipment, long depreciated, so their cost base is lower than ours."

This is a strategic misconception. What about the extra labor costs, the lower productivity, the opportunity costs of the space? The rationale for outsourcing production is to concentrate production of a particular component in a specialized plant, which can use the very latest machinery to produce top-quality, high-volume, low-cost components. If that competitor can make that same component cheaper, with no loss of quality, then the outsourcer would have no business. The answer is probably more straightforward—the company needs to improve its purchasing procedures and negotiating skills.

It is the same with the outsourcing of processes. More often than not, many processes are now outsourced—for example, IT services—for very similar reasons to outsourcing production, namely, the acquisition of a top-quality, low-risk IT capability at a lower unit cost than doing it in-house.

But there are many processes that are not universally outsourced; for example, the claims management process undertaken by insurance companies. Some do, others don't, some do only for technically difficult areas, like drains insurance claims.

To what extent does your firm outsource production or processes? How does it compare with your competitors? How does the degree of outsourcing impact your relative competitive position? How is that likely to change in the future?

Offshoring

Offshore outsourcing, or "offshoring," in grim new business-speak, is merely an extension of outsourcing, only the outsourcer is located overseas, typically in a low-cost country. Again, offshoring can apply both to production and other processing links in the value chain, but the cost advantages can be much higher than same-country outsourcing—albeit sometimes at the expense of delivery times or customer service.

Offshoring often gets bad press. It can lead to a significant loss of jobs in the short term, with distressing socioeconomic consequences. In the longer term, however, at its best, it leads to a more competitive firm and hence a greater chance of that firm prospering, or just surviving and thereby maintaining employment, in the years ahead.

Offshoring is most evident in the transfer of production facilities to lower-cost countries such as Mexico or China, but IT offshoring has also been prevalent. Think of the outsourcing of call centers or technical help desks to countries such as India, the Philippines, or Turkey by telephone, personal computer, or Internet service companies. Some consumers may resent the time lags and occasional misunderstandings that occur when talking to customer service representatives who are far distant from them, geographically and culturally, but these same consumers are seldom prepared to pay the extra tariff charged by companies that guarantee home-country-based customer support.

Two more recent trends have been pulling in opposite directions: The offshoring of R&D by high-tech or science-based firms to science-rich countries, such as the former Soviet Union or India, has been offset by *reshoring* back to the United States some manufacturing or IT outsourcing—reflecting the greatly increasing labor and other resource costs of doing business in countries such as China.

In the previous example of the engineering company that needed to lower its cost base to fight off global competition, the company moved to buy certain components from a joint venture partner in low-cost India and set up a green-field plant in medium-cost Thailand to manufacture for the export market. It is on the right track.

To what extent does your firm offshore production or processes today? With what advantages or disadvantages? And in the future?

Carbon Footprint

It is not enough these days for a company to ensure that it is compliant with all environmental regulations on air pollution, noise, and waste disposal. The world has woken up to global warming and the influence of human activity. Organizations are expected to exercise greater control of their carbon footprint.

Eyebrows have been raised in the media over President Obama having his Chicago-based barber flown in every two weeks. Imagine, say, if the local press got wind of a story of you or your marketing director hiring a private jet to go to a conference a hundred miles away?

Your backers will want to know that your firm is aware of carbon footprints sensitivities. They will also want to hear how your firm has taken steps to lower its carbon footprint, at the same time cutting out waste and extravagance and thereby reducing cost. A paragraph or two in your business plan should suffice.

Corporate Social Responsibility

Corporate social responsibility, or corporate citizenship, or sometimes just termed *sustainability*, has evolved. Ten years ago, it was seen as a nice-to-have aspect to the way an organization conducted business. Nowadays, each company is expected to be cognizant of its interaction with all its stakeholders—employees, customers, suppliers, the community, government—and to be able to demonstrate that it makes a positive impact on society.

The United Nations Global Compact asks companies "to embrace, support, and enact, within their sphere of influence, a set of core values in the areas of human rights, labor standards, the environment, and anticorruption," and sets out in great detail ten principles within these four areas.

There is no need to undertake an audit of your firm's performance against the UN's ten principles in your business plan. Your carbon footprint is one area, already discussed, that falls within the UN's environmental principles. Other areas you may consider addressing are the firm's interaction with labor unions, suppliers (fair trade?), charities, the community, and, certainly, the environment (for which there is a specific section in Chapter 6 of your plan).

If your firm's competitive position depends to an extent on its ethical positioning—as, for example, The Body Shop—you may wish to consider building into your forecasts the so-called triple bottom line, whereby you give prominence to environmental and social performance as well as financial. But remember that if your business plan is for the purpose of raising external finance, financial performance will still need to be convincing and, for most investors, preeminent.

Social Media Marketing

Social media is a hot potato, important for many business-to-business companies and vital for consumer-facing businesses. Internet and social media marketing have developed rapidly and can be critical to success.

Today, advertisers often aim to create such a buzz that consumers click onto YouTube on their smart phones to catch up on an advertisement they may have missed. Other campaigns are even more creative—like the Jimmy Choo "Trainer Hunt," the Innocent "Tweet and Eat Cheap," and the La Senza "Nudist Beach" campaigns. In each case, consumers were encouraged to click proactively on Facebook or Twitter to attain the promised benefits, thereby prompting the campaign to go viral—and meanwhile creating a subliminal element of bonding between consumer and vendor.

How does your firm exploit Web 2.0? Do you at least send out a regular e-newsletter? Do you have a blog or two, clickable via your WordPress website? And plenty of photos? And moving pictures, accessible via your website and YouTube? Best of all, an app?

And how about social media, especially LinkedIn, Facebook, Twitter, and the like? Is yours the kind of business that could "go viral"? Be warned: Some do, but most don't. And your backers will be wary. If your backers are age 35 or older, chances are that they will be suspicious of marketing plans that are overly reliant on social media. They may choose to treat any social media liftoff as upside and grill you instead on your plans for the traditional four Ps marketing approach: product, place, promotion, and pricing (see Chapter 6).

Tax Avoidance

Public finances have been exceptionally tight since the credit crunch. Governments are seeking to tighten rules on tax avoidance to bolster their coffers. There's a crackdown on tax evasion. Do your financial forecasts rely on any clever tax-minimizing financial structures? Are they vulnerable to reinterpretation of existing rules? Or to future legislation? Your backers will expect you to have taken professional advice.

◻   ◻   ◻

That's a dozen hot potatoes. The list is not exhaustive. Some backers may have others. New ones will arise. Keep an eye as much on the general business pages as your trade press. What other hot potatoes could affect your business? Your backer may ask you how you plan to handle them. Be ready.

APPENDIX A

Deriving Competitive Position

The trouble with the rat race is that even if you win you're still a rat. —Lily Tomlin

In this appendix, you will assess how your firm measures up to the competition. You will conclude what your firm's competitive position is, both now and over the next few years. And you will do this assessment for each of your main business segments.

This appendix sets out a systematic way of deriving competitive position, as opposed to the shortcut listing of your firm's strengths and weaknesses discussed in Chapter 5.

You will go through three stages, for each of your firm's main segments:

1. Identify and weight customer purchasing criteria (CPCs): what customers need from their suppliers—that is, you and your competitors—in each segment.

2. Identify and weight key success factors (KSFs): what you and your competitors need to do to satisfy these customer needs and run a successful business.

3. Assess your competitive position: how you rate against those key success factors relative to your competitors.

We'll start, as always, with the customer.

Customer Purchasing Criteria

What do customers in your business's main segments need from you and your competitors? Are they looking for the lowest possible price for a given level of product or service? Or the highest-quality product or service irrespective of price? Or something in between?

Do customers have the same needs in your other business segments? Do some customer groups place greater importance on certain needs?

What exactly do they want in terms of product or service? The highest specifications? Fastest delivery? The most reliable? The best technical backup? The most sympathetic customer service?

Customers' foremost needs from their suppliers are called customer purchasing criteria (CPCs). For business-to-business (B2B) companies, CPCs typically include product quality (including features, performance, and reliability), product range, delivery capabilities, technical support, customer service, relationship, reputation, and financial stability. And, of course, price.

For business-to-consumer (B2C) companies, CPCs tend to be similar, although typically with less emphasis on product range and financial stability. Depending on the product or service being offered, the consumer will place varying importance on quality, service, and price.

CPCs can usefully be grouped into six categories. They are customer needs relating to the:

1. *Effectiveness* of the product or service

2. *Efficiency* of the service

3. *Range* of products or services provided

4. *Relationship* with the producer or service provider

5. *Premises* (only applicable if the customer needs to visit the service provider's premises)

6. *Price* of the product or service

These needs can be conveniently remembered, with perhaps a faint suggestion of a cult science fiction movie, as the E2-R2-P2 of customer purchasing criteria.

Let's look briefly at each in turn.

E1: EFFECTIVENESS

The first need of any customer from any product or service is that the job gets done. You, the customer, have specific requirements on the features, performance, and reliability of the product or service you need. You want the job done. Not half-done, not overdone, just done.

You want a crew cut. You as the customer go to the service provider, the barber. He gives you a crew cut. You pay and go home. Job done.

You may have other requirements, like how long it takes him to cut your hair, the interaction you have with the barber, whether he also offers a wet shave, how clean the barbershop is, or how reasonable his price. But the most basic requirement is that he is effective at giving you a crew cut. At getting the job done.

Suppose, however, that it's not a crew cut you want, but the cool cut sported by some movie star. Now you get a bit more demanding. You'll want your barber, or hairstylist, to be competent technically at delivering such a haircut, to know about the pros and cons of upkeep for such a haircut, and to have done a few of these cuts before—you don't want to be a guinea pig, not with your hair!

You'll place more importance on job effectiveness.

What constitutes product or service effectiveness for the customers of your business? How important is it to your customers, relative to other purchasing criteria? Is it of high, low, or medium importance?

E2: EFFICIENCY

The second main customer purchasing criterion is efficiency. The customer wants the job done on time.

All customers place some level of importance on efficiency for all types of service. You may not care if your crew cut takes 10, 15, even 30 minutes, but you would care if it took all Saturday afternoon and you missed the big football game.

Different customer groups may place different levels of importance on efficiency for the same service. How much emphasis do your customers place on the efficiency of your service? How important is it relative to other criteria? High, low, medium?

R1: RANGE

Then there is the range of products or services provided. This is an area that customers may find important for some products or services, even most important, and for others it's of no importance at all.

Let's return to the example of a hair salon. No self-respecting hairstylist would offer anything less than haircuts, perms, and colorings. But is that enough? Would customers prefer a salon that can also offer techniques such as hair relaxing, straightening, and braiding? How important to the salon's target customer group is the range of services provided?

At the other extreme lies the functional barbershop. If most customers only want a crew cut, they're going to look for a barbershop that is effective and efficient, and where the barber is a good guy. If the barber were also to offer head massage, big deal! Yet to some customers, the head massage may be the unique offering that draws them through the door.

How important a criterion is product range to your customers? High, low, medium?

R1: RELATIONSHIP

Your barber gives a good crew cut, and he does it quickly. But do you like the guy? Is he the sort of guy you feel comfortable with having his hands on your head? Do you want your barber to chat or stay quiet? How do you want to interrelate? Does it matter to you if he seems bored and disinterested? Or would you prefer him to be interested and enthusiastic?

Never underestimate the relationship component in providing a service. A successful builder knows how to keep the homeowner as content as possible during the work on a new extension. He'll try to ensure minimum disruption to everyday living—no wheelbarrows crossing the living room carpet—and he'll be of good cheer at all times. He knows that his business depends on personal referrals. If the stay-at-home spouse tells a neighbor that the contractor is not only a good builder, but an okay guy to have around under trying circumstances, his chances of converting the next sale are greatly improved.

How much emphasis do your customers place on personal relationships? High, low, medium?

P1: PREMISES

This criterion only applies to those businesses, typically services, where the buying decision may be influenced by the environment.

Think of hair salons again. If you're aiming for the rich and famous, then you'll need a presence in an upmarket street downtown. And it had better be spectacular. If you're going for the middle-class, suburban housewife, you should be located on the main shopping street and your salon should be clean and tasteful. Premises should be appropriate for the pocket of the customer.

Do you need a storefront for your business? What do customers expect of your premises? How important a criterion is it relative to others? High, low, medium?

P2: PRICE

This is the big one. Set your prices sky-high and you won't have many customers.

Think about the buying decisions you make regularly and the influence of price. For nonessential services, we tend to be more price sensitive. When your eight-year-old son's hair is flopping over his eyes, you look for a barber. He has little interest in his appearance (for the time being!), so you look around for the cheapest barber. But how cheap are you prepared to go? Would you take him to a barbershop that is (literally) dirt cheap, where the combs are greasy, the floor is covered with hair, and the barber is a miserable so-and-so? Probably not. You set minimum standards of service and then go for a reasonable price.

For essential services, we tend to be less fixated with price. When your central heating system breaks down in the middle of winter, will you go for the cheapest service engineer? Or will you call around your friends and acquaintances to find someone who is reliable, arrives when he says he will, fixes it with no fuss, and charges a price that is not exactly cheap but at least is no rip-off?

What are your customers' pricing needs? How important is pricing relative to other purchasing criteria? High, low, medium? Very high?

Finding Out CPCs

All this is very well in theory, but you may be asking, "How do you know what customers want?" Simple. Ask them!

It doesn't take long. You'd be surprised how after just a few discussions with any one customer group a predictable pattern begins to emerge. Some customers may consider one need very important, while others just call it important. But it's unlikely that another will say that it's unimportant. Customers tend to have similar needs.

The comprehensive way to find out customer needs is through structured interviewing, where you ask a selected sample of customers a carefully prepared list of questions.

In developing a strategy for your business, a customer survey is an essential input. If you haven't done one recently, you would be well advised to conduct one as preparation for your business plan. Appendix B shows how structured interviews are done.

Finally, you must also find out how your customers' needs are likely to change in the future. If they believe one purchasing criterion is highly important now, will it be as important in a few years' time? You need to know.

Key Success Factors

We define key success factors (KSFs) as what producers or service providers like you need to do to succeed in a marketplace. They are what your firm needs to get right to satisfy the customer purchasing criteria of the last section *and* run a sound business.

Typical KSFs are product (or service) quality, consistency, availability, range, and product development (R&D). On the service side, KSFs can include distribution capability, sales and marketing effectiveness, customer service, and post-sale technical support. Other KSFs relate to the cost side of things, such as location of premises; scale of operations; state-of-the-art, cost-effective equipment; and operational process efficiency.

To identify which are the most important KSFs for each of your main business segments, you need to undertake these steps:

- Convert CPCs into KSFs:
  - Differentiation-related
  - Cost-related

- Assess two more KSFs:
  - Management
  - Market share

- Apply weights to the KSFs.

- Identify any must-have KSFs.

Let's look briefly at each step.

CONVERT CPCS INTO KSFS

Here we convert the customer purchasing criteria we researched in the last section into key success factors. In other words, we need to work out what your business has to do to meet those CPCs.

This is fairly straightforward for those CPCs that are related to how competitors differentiate their products or services from others, so-called differentiation-related KSFs. A KSF can often seem similar to, even the same as, a CPC.

Suppose, for example, that you as a customer want your hair salon to be good at coloring. That's one of your needs. So the stylists need to be skilled at coloring. That's a KSF.

But KSFs generally tend to take a different perspective from CPCs. Here's an example. When you call up your Internet service provider technical help desk, you as a customer need someone who can understand and fix your problem. The associated KSFs for the technician are an appropriate technical qualification, subsequent completion of relevant training, experience of handling this and similar problems, and communication skills.

Here's another example. When you jump on the city tour bus in Acapulco, Barcelona, or Kyoto, you expect to be able to understand clearly what the tour guide is saying. The customer need is clarity of communication. The associated KSFs are proficiency in the language of delivery and clear communication skills.

When converting a CPC, you may find that the associated KSF can sometimes be the same as you've already associated with another CPC. In other words, one KSF can sometimes be sufficient to meet two or more CPCs. Returning to the tour guide, for example, another customer need may well be rapport with the guide. Rapport will be greatly eased through fluency in the language of delivery. In this example, one KSF, language proficiency, serves two CPCs, namely 1) clarity of communication and 2) rapport.

What are the main differentiation-related KSFs in your business? How important are they? Of high, low, medium, medium-high, or low-medium importance?

There's one CPC that needs special attention, and that's price. Customers of most services expect a competitive price. Producers need to keep their costs down. Price is a CPC, cost-competitiveness a KSF.

In a competitive service business like car repair, middle-income customers tend to be sensitive to price, among other needs, such as quality of work and integrity. A small car repair proprietor will therefore try to keep the rental costs of his premises down by locating his garage well off Main Street, maybe off the side streets, too, and onto some commercially zoned land alongside the railway line.

Other determinants of cost-competitiveness in your business could include cost of materials, use of subcontractors, outsourcing of business processes, and overhead control, including not just premises, but numbers of support staff, remuneration levels, and IT systems.

And size may matter. Other things being equal, the larger the business, the lower costs should be for each unit of business sold. These are "economies of scale" and they apply not just to the unit cost of materials or other variable costs, where a larger business will benefit from negotiated volume discounts, but also overheads.

Think of two hair salons competing against each other on Main Street. One has double the amount of space of the other and serves on average 80 customers a day, compared with the smaller salon's 40-customers-a-day average. They are thus similarly efficient and they charge similar prices. But the larger salon has lower rental costs *per customer* because of a discount negotiated with the landlord on the second commercial unit rented. The larger salon also pays lower marketing costs *per customer*, since advertising space in the Yellow Pages or in local glossy magazines costs the same per column inch for both salons, irrespective of how many customers the advertiser serves.

What are the main cost-related KSFs in your business? Cost of materials? Use of subcontractors? Premises? Overhead control? Economies of scale? How important are they?

ASSESS TWO MORE KSFS

So far, we've derived two sets of KSFs from the CPCs discussed in the previous section: differentiation-related and cost-related. There are two more sets to be considered: management and market share.

How important is management in your business? We discussed your firm's managerial capabilities in greater depth in Chapter 6 on resources, but here you need to identify how important management is in general in your industry. Think about whether a well-managed company, with a superb sales and marketing team reinforced by an efficient operations team, but with an average product, would outperform a poorly managed company with a superb product in your industry.

Management needs to be added as a differentiation-related KSF. And that will include management for sales and marketing, the lifeblood of any small or medium-size business. How important is management as a KSF in your business?

There's one final KSF—an important one—that we need to take into account that isn't directly derived from a CPC. This is your firm's market share. The larger the market share, the stronger should be the provider.

A high market share can manifest itself in a number of different competitive advantages. One such area is in lower unit costs. But we've already covered this point under economies of scale in cost-related KSFs, so we must be careful not to double count.

Market share is an indicator of the breadth and depth of your customer relationships and your business reputation. Since it is more difficult to gain a new customer than to do repeat business with an existing customer, the provider with the larger market share typically has a competitive advantage—the power of the incumbent.

For example, if your hairstylist fulfills all your customer needs—does excellent hairstyling, has relaxing premises, provides rapport (aka gossip!), and offers a reasonable price—the fact that one or two of your friends are chatting about the superb new stylist who has just set up shop farther down the street will not necessarily tempt you away from your usual provider. Why switch? Your stylist would be most upset, especially when she has done nothing to deserve such disloyalty. This is the power of the incumbent. Customers don't like switching, unless they are sorely tempted (the pull factor) or forced to move because of deficient quality of product or service (the push factor). Keep the service quality levels high and your customers will tend to stick with the provider they know.

It can even be costly to switch, for example, if your service provider offers you loyalty discounts. Sometimes it's costly in terms of time to switch. If you change Internet service providers, you face the hassle of having to notify all your contacts of your new e-mail address. Sometimes it's costly in emotional terms to switch, as we saw with the hairstylist. The higher the switching costs, the greater the power of the incumbent.

Incumbency tends to rise in importance as a KSF where customers rely on their service provider for historical continuity. It's easier to change your shoe repairer, even your hairstylist, than to change your psychiatrist or your accountant. The latter two service providers have built up useful knowledge about you, whether it's your mind or your double-entry books. If you were to switch to another provider, it may take a long time for the new provider to build up the relevant understanding of you as an individual or business.

How great is the power of the incumbent in your business? How important is market share as a KSF?

APPLY WEIGHTS TO THE KSFS

You've worked out which are the most important KSFs in your business. Each one has been ranked in order of importance. Now you need to weight them.

A simple quantitative approach works best. Don't worry; you won't have to compute a weighting of, say, 14.526 percent. That would be horribly phony accuracy. But it's helpful to derive a percentage for the weighting, whether to the nearest 5 percent or even 10 percent, so that in the next step you can easily total up and rate your overall competitiveness relative to your peers.

So that 14.526 percent would become simply 15 percent. No more accuracy than that is needed. How do you apply these weights? There are two ways: methodically or eyeballing.

If you want a methodical approach, take a look at the example in the sidebar, "A Systematic Approach for Deriving KSF Weightings."

If you would prefer to eyeball it, to get a rough-and-ready answer, start from this guideline: market share 20 percent, cost factors 30 percent, management and differentiation factors 50 percent. Then adjust those percentages to what you have found to be critical to success in your business. And make sure that however you jiggle them, they still add up to 100 percent.

A Systematic Approach for Deriving KSF Weightings

Here's a step-by-step systematic approach to weighting KSFs:

- Use judgment on the power of the incumbent to derive a weighting for market share of i percent, typically in the range of 15 percent to 25 percent.

- Revisit the importance of price to the customer. If you judged the customer need of medium importance, give cost-competitiveness a weighting of 20 percent to 25 percent. If it's of low importance, 15 percent to 20 percent. If highly important, 35 percent plus. If yours is a commodity business, it could be 40 percent to 45 percent, with a correspondingly low weighting for relative market share. Settle on c percent.

- Think about the importance of management factors to the success of your business, especially marketing. Settle on m percent, typically within a zero to 10 percent range.

- You've now used up a total of $(i + c + m)$ percent of your available weighting.

- The balance (namely, 100 percent minus the total from the previous steps) will be the total weighting for differentiation factors, as follows: $100 - (i + c + m) = D$ percent.

- Revisit the list of KSFs relating to differentiation issues, excluding price, which has already been covered. Where you've judged a factor to be of low importance, give it a KSF score of 1. Where high, 5. If a factor rates in between, use a prorated weighting (e.g., medium/high would be a 4).

- Add up the total score (T) for these differentiation-related KSFs (excluding price).

- Assign weightings to each differentiation KSF as follows: Weighting (percent) = KSF Score * D/T.

- Round each of these numbers up or down to the nearest 5 percent.

- Adjust further if necessary so that the sum of all KSF weights is 100 percent.

- Eyeball the numbers for sense, making final adjustments.

- Check that the sum is still 100 percent.

Once you've eyeballed the weightings in general, you need to assess to what extent these weightings differ for each of your business segments. In particular, different customer groups can often place a different emphasis on price, so cost-competitiveness may be more of an issue in one segment than in others. Other customers in other business segments may be more concerned about product quality or customer service. You need to know.

IDENTIFY ANY MUST-HAVE KSFS

There is one final wrinkle. But it may be crucial.

Is any KSF in your business so important that if you don't rank highly against it, you shouldn't even be in business? You simply won't begin to compete, let alone succeed? You won't win any business, or you won't be able to deliver on the business you win? In other words, it is a must-have KSF, rather than a mere should-have.

Must a business in your marketplace have, for example, the right ISO classification to win future orders in a competitively intensifying environment? Must it deploy the new cost-revolutionary range of capital equipment? Must your product incorporate a particular new feature?

Are any of the KSFs in your business must-haves? Bear this in mind when you assess your competitive position in the next section.

Rating Performance for Competitive Position

Now you are ready to rate how your business performs against each of the KSFs identified previously. You'll then compute a weighted average rating and see how your overall position compares against competitors.

You should determine this rating for each of your main business segments, since your position in one may be very different from in others. Then you should consider how your position is likely to change in each segment over the next few years and what you can do to improve it over time.

Finally, you need to do a reality check. Do you by any chance rate poorly against one of the must-have KSFs? If so, that may mean you don't get past first base. You shouldn't be in this business.

WHO ARE YOUR PEERS?

The first thing to decide is who to compare yourself with. Sometimes that seems like a no-brainer. Often it requires a little more thought.

Take a simple example. For the owner of one of three hair salons on a suburban shopping street, the comparison may seem obvious. She judges herself against the other two. But some of her potential customers may have their hair done in the city during lunch breaks or after work. Others may get it done when they do their weekly grocery shopping at the out-of-town supermarket. They are competitors, too.

Don't be stingy. If you think another provider is serving clients who could potentially be yours, rate them, too. Remember, this section is the easy bit. It takes just a few minutes to have a first shot at rating each competitor.

DERIVING COMPETITIVE POSITION

How do you compare with your peers? Are you more competitive? Less competitive? What's your competitive position? And theirs?

To draw up your competitive position, all you need to do is rate yourself against each of the KSFs drawn up in the previous step. If you use a numerical rating system, alongside the percentage weighting system you've already drawn up, your competitive position will emerge clearly. A simple rating system of 0 to 5 is suggested.

If you perform about the same as your peers against a KSF, give yourself a score in the middle, a 3 (*good/favorable*). If you perform very strongly, rate yourself a 5 (*very strong*). Poorly, a 1 (*weak*). If you perform not quite as well as most others, give yourself a 2 (*tenable*). Better than most, a 4 (*strong*).

Now do the same for each of your competitors against that KSF. Who's the best performer against this KSF? Do they merit a rating of 5, or are they better but not that much better than others, for a 4?

Continue this rating against each KSF.

If you are using Excel, your competitive position falls out at the bottom of the spreadsheet (see the example of The Gorge Inn in Chapter 5). In the old days, it had to be done by hand—either by adding things up in one's head or using a calculator. For youngsters today, that must be hard to imagine.

Excel makes things so much easier. But beware. The old manual approach encouraged you to think very carefully about each rating, because you really didn't want the hassle of having to do the calculation all over again. With Excel you do no calculating, so sloppy thinking incurs no time penalty. It's a trap, well known in financial planning these days. Think carefully.

Algebraically, your overall rating is the sum of each rating (r) against each KSF multiplied by the percentage weighting (w) of the KSF. If there are n KSFs, your overall rating will be (r1 * w1) + (r2 * w2) + (r3 * w3) + . . . + (rn * wn). As long as the percentage weightings add up to 100 percent, you will get the right answer.

IMPLICATIONS FOR FUTURE MARKET SHARE

The main use of competitive position is to give your backers some idea of how your business is likely to fare over the next few years in relation to the market as a whole.

If your firm's competitive position turns out to be around 3, or good/favorable, your backer will expect you, other things being equal, to be able to grow your business in line with the market over the next few years. In other words, to hold market share.

If your competitive position is 4 or above, they will expect you to be able to beat the market and gain market share, again, other things being equal. Suppose they have already concluded that your Chapter 3 forecast of market demand growth of 10 percent a year seems reasonable. With a competitive position of 4, they'll feel more comfortable if your plan is to grow business at, say, 12 percent to 15 percent a year.

If your competitive position is around 2, however, your backers will be less confident about your business prospects. It is more likely you'll underperform the market and they'll be especially worried if your plans show that you are outperforming the market! They will wonder if they are backing the right horse.

Finding Out Performance Ratings

The first step is to do it yourself. Over the years or, if you've only just started in business, over several months, you will already have had occasional feedback from your customers: "Great piece of work" generally means you've done something right. "No way am I gonna pay you for that!" suggests the opposite.

Have a go at rating your business yourself. Then stick a question mark against those ratings where you are a little unsure on your performance. Investigate those ratings one or two at a time. Next time you are with a customer, throw in this comment: "By the way, you know that job we did for you a couple of months ago—were you happy with the turnaround time? Did you expect it to be quicker?" Gradually you'll be able to start removing the question marks and firm up your rating.

While rating your own company's performance, you should also be comparing it with your competitors. All performance is relative, so if you give yourself a rating of 3 against one KSF, it will be relative to a competitor that you rate as a 4, or another a 2. Do a first draft of rating your competitors at the same time that you are rating your own performance. Again, stick in question marks against the numbers where you are unsure. Then start throwing in the odd question with your customers, like: "What about Company B? Do they turn things around as fast as we do?" Gradually the question marks on your competitors' ratings should also disappear.

The methodical way to derive ratings is through structured interviewing. This is what management consultants do on behalf of their clients to derive primary information on business strategy, marketing, or due diligence assignments. A structured interviewing program differs from the more casual approach of collecting occasional feedback in two respects: You select a representative sample of interviewees, and you draw on a prepared questionnaire.

The advantage of a structured interviewing process is that it will, in time, give you all you need to know. There are two disadvantages. First, it takes up the time of your customers. There's a risk that you'll leave your customers thinking that you've just wasted a quarter or half hour of their precious time. Second, you may be a bit sensitive about your customers knowing that you are doing a strategy review. You don't want them to think that you may be moving on to bigger and better things, leaving them in your wake. You also may not want your customers to think too hard about your service as compared with others, in case they suddenly realize they would be better off shifting to another provider!

These risks should, however, be containable as long as you prepare your story well in advance and try to make the experience as beneficial for the customer as for you.

For a detailed description on how to conduct a structured interview program with your customers, see Appendix B.

COMPETING BY SEGMENT

We've talked thus far as if your firm has only one business segment. How does your competitive position compare in each of your main product/market segments?

You need to apply the same process for each segment: identifying how customer purchasing criteria differ by segment, assessing key success factors for each, and deriving competitive position for each. You'll find that some ratings are the same; some are different. Take product quality, for example. Your rating against that KSF will be the same in each segment relating to a product group.

But the weighting of that KSF may well differ by customer group segment, thereby impacting your overall competitive position in each.

Ratings for some KSFs may differ by segment. For instance, your company may have an enviable track record in one segment, but you've only just started in another—rating a 5 in the first but only a 1 or 2 in the other.

COMPETING OVER TIME

So far your analysis of competitive position has been static. You've rated your current competitiveness and that of others. But that's only the first part of the story. What your backers also want to know is how your competitive position is likely to change over the next few years. They will want to understand the dynamics. Is it set to improve or worsen?

The simplest way to expand your analysis is to add an extra column to your chart representing your business in, say, three years' time. Then you can build in improvements in your ratings against each KSF. For the time being, these prospective improvements need to be both in the pipeline *and* likely to occur for your backer to be convinced. In Chapter 5 of your business plan, you looked at how you can proactively and systematically improve your competitive position, and how you can develop a strategy to bridge the gap with the ideal provider. But for now, you can just look at how your competitive position seems set to change naturally over the next few years.

Remember, however, that improved competitive position is a two-edged sword. Your competitors, too, will have plans. This is where analysis of KSF dynamics gets challenging—and intriguing. It's easy enough to consider where you are heading, but what are your competitors up to?

Try adding a couple of further columns representing your two most fearsome competitors as they may be in three years' time. Do you have any idea how they are planning to improve their competitiveness in the near future? What are they likely to do? What could they do? *What are you afraid they'll do?*

How is your competitive position likely to change over time? And what about your competitors?

GETTING PAST FIRST BASE

Previously in this chapter, we introduced the concept of the must-have KSF. Without a good rating in any must-have area, your business cannot even begin to compete.

Did you find a must-have KSF in any of your business segments? If so, how do you rate against it? Is your rating favorable or strong? Fine. Okay-ish? Your position is questionable. Weak? That's troublesome. A straight zero, not even a 1? You're out. You don't get past first base.

And what about in a few years' time? Could any KSF develop into a must-have? How will you rate then? Will you get past first base?

And even though you rate as tenable against a must-have KSF today, might it slip over time? Could it slide below a rating of 2, into tricky territory?

This may be a case of being cruel to be kind. It's better to know. The sooner you realize that you are in a wrong business segment, the sooner you can withdraw and focus resources on the right segments.

Structured Interviewing of Customers

Your most unhappy customers are your greatest source of learning. —Bill Gates

In Chapter 5, and in more detail in Appendix A, we recommended that a program of structured interviews of customers is the best and most methodical way to obtain the information needed to derive your firm's competitive position.

Here's how to do it:

- Select a representative range of customer interviewees.

- Prepare your story line.

- Create a concise questionnaire.

- Interview the customers, through e-mail, on the telephone, or face-to-face.

- Thank them and give them some feedback.

Choosing the Interviewees

The interviewees should represent a broad cross section of your business, including:

- Customers from each of your main business segments

- Your top six customers in terms of revenue

- Long-standing customers as well as recent acquisitions

- Customers who also use, or used to use, your competitors, so they can compare your performance from direct experience rather than conjecture

- Customers with whom you've had problems

- Would-be customers, currently using a competitor, but on your target list

- Former customers who switched to a competitor

That sounds like a lot, but be selective. Three to six customers for each main business segment should suffice. Aim for two to three dozen in all.

Preparing Your Story Line

Here's your opportunity to put a positive light on your business. Compare these two story lines:

Option 1: "Sorry to waste your time, but can I ask for your help in figuring out how well our company is performing?"

Option 2: "As you know, our company has been rather busy over the last couple of years. But we thought we should take some time out to ask some of our most important customers how their needs may be changing over time and to what extent we can serve those needs better."

Guess which line will get the better response *and* put your business in a favorable light? The first statement conveys a negative impression and is all about your firm and its needs. The second leaves a positive impression and addresses your customer's needs. Stick to the second!

Creating a Concise Questionnaire

The questionnaire needs care. It must be taken as a guideline, not as a box-checking exercise. It stays with you, and it doesn't get handed or e-mailed to the interviewee. It's a prompter to discussion, no more. It needs to be simple. And concise.

It should be in four parts: 1) the story line, 2) customer needs, 3) performance, and 4) the future.

1. *The Story Line.* The story line should be written out at the top of the questionnaire and memorized. It must be delivered naturally and seemingly spontaneously. Pausing on occasion or saying "um" or "er" will make it seem less rehearsed.

2. *Customer Needs.* What are your customers' purchasing criteria? And how important are they, now and in the future? You should allow your customers to draw up their own set of needs, but it's best to prepare your own list to use as a prompt, in case your customer runs out of answers or misses an obvious one. These are the main questions to put on your questionnaire:

- What are your main needs, your criteria, in buying this service? What do you expect from your providers?

- How important are each of these needs? Which are more important than others? How would you rank them?

- Will these needs become more or less important over time?

- Are any other needs likely to become important in the future?

3. *Performance.* You want to know how your firm and your competitors rate against those needs. Again, you should allow your customers to select who they think are the alternative providers of your service, but you should keep to one side a prompt list of your main competitors—which you may or may not choose to use. (No need to alert customers to a troublesome competitor that they're not yet fully aware of!)

Here are some performance-related questions to pose to your customers:

- How do you think our firm meets your needs? How do we perform?

- How do other providers perform? Do they better meet those needs than we do?

- Who performs best against your most important needs?

4. *The Future.* You want to have customers tell you how you can better serve their needs. Ask, "What should we be doing to better meet your needs and those of other customers?"

Conducting the Interviews

Interviews are best done face-to-face. Then you can see the nuances behind the replies—the shifting glance, the fidgeting, the emphatic hand gestures. But face-to-face interviews are the most time-consuming, unless you happen to be seeing your customer as part of your service delivery anyway.

If the interviews are done over the phone, they are best scheduled in advance. You can schedule your calls by e-mail or with a preliminary phone call.

After you've delivered the story line, add: "I wonder if you could spare five to ten minutes to discuss this issue with me. I know you're very busy, but perhaps we could set up a time later in the week for me to give you a call."

The call itself must be carefully managed. Don't launch into the question-naire without a warm-up. Ask the customer how things are going, how work is, how's the family, whatever. Then gently shift to the story line: "Well, as I was saying the other day . . ."

After you've finished the structured interview, don't forget the warm-down at the closing. Return to one of the topics you discussed at the outset and gently wind down the discussion, not forgetting to thank them sincerely for giving so freely of their valuable time.

Thanking Them and Providing Feedback

At a later time—a few hours, a day, a couple of days, or a week later, whenever you feel it is appropriate—thank your customer again, officially. By letter is best, but that may feel overly formal for you in this electronic world. E-mail is probably fine, but use your judgment.

The e-mail should be cheerful and full of sincere gratitude. If possible, it should contain a snippet of information that could be of interest or use to your customer. One or two sentences should suffice. It could pick up on one aspect of the discussion and draw a comparison to what another customer had to say on the same topic. You could give an indication of the results of your survey: "Interestingly, most customers seemed to think that track record was their most important need," or "Encouragingly, most customers seemed to think we were the most innovative service provider!"

■ ■ ■

You now have a process to follow for conducting structured interviews with your customers. Now all you have to do is compile the results of those inter-views, whether on a piece of paper, on an Excel worksheet, or simply in your head, and feed them into your ratings against each key success factor—for your firm and for each of your main competitors.

The intriguing thing, then, is to compare these customer-derived ratings with your first-draft, do-it-yourself ratings. You may be in for a surprise!

Templates for Creating Your Own Plan

A pessimist sees the difficulty in every opportunity; an optimist sees the opportunity in every difficulty.
—Winston Churchill

If you have been able to get this far in the book without picking up pen and pencil or typing on your keyboard to get going on your business plan, now is the time to start.

To help you on the way, we've included some templates for key graphics that you may choose to include in your plan. Please note that they are not intended to be self-explanatory. You will need to refer to the relevant chapter in this book for further instruction on how each graphic should best be used.

If your company is active in two or more key product/market segments, you will need to photocopy the charts for Chapters 3 to 5 and complete one for each main segment.

You will see that no particular graphic is suggested for Chapter 1 and Chapter 6, where the message tends to be more readily communicated using words and bullet points. Instead, we have included a one slide reminder of what needs to go in each of those two chapters.

In the next section, Appendix D, you will see many of these charts being used in context in two sample PowerPoint business plans, one for an established company in a service business and one for a start-up in manufacturing.

Your Plan Chapter 1: Executive Summary

Chapter 1 Content: Get Those Ducks in a Row!

Summary of Executive Summary	1 paragraph
Business Mix	
Market Demand Prospects	
Competition	
Strategy	2–3 paragraphs on each
Resources	
Financials and Forecasts	
Risk, Opportunity, and Sensitivity	
Conclusion	

Your Plan Chapter 2: Business Mix

Your Sales by Product/Market Segment

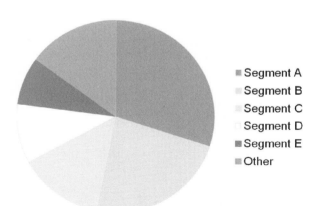

- Segment A
- Segment B
- Segment C
- Segment D
- Segment E
- Other

Your Plan Chapter 2: Business Mix

Your Plan Chapter 3: Market Demand

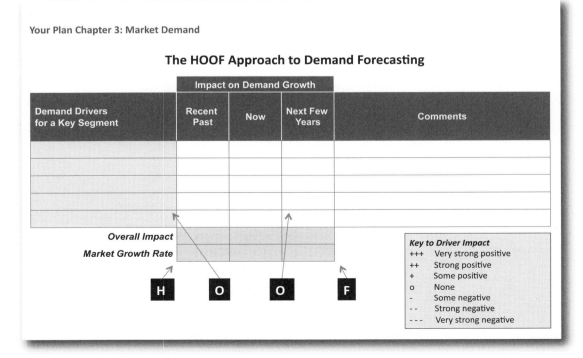

Your Plan Chapter 4: Industry Competition

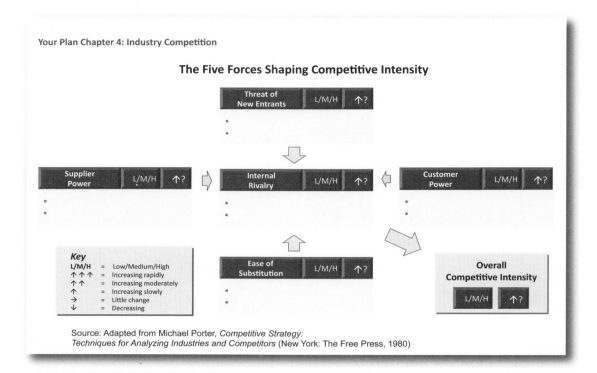

The Five Forces Shaping Competitive Intensity

Source: Adapted from Michael Porter, *Competitive Strategy: Techniques for Analyzing Industries and Competitors* (New York: The Free Press, 1980)

Your Plan Chapter 5: Strategy

Assessing Customer Purchasing Criteria

Customer Purchasing Criteria for a Key Segment	Importance (Low/Med/High?)	Change (→, ↑, ↓?)
Effectiveness		
Efficiency		
Relationship		
Range		
Premises		
Price		

Your Plan Chapter 5: Strategy

Deriving Key Success Factors

Customer Purchasing Criteria for a Key Segment	Importance (Low/Med/ High?)	Change (→, ↑, ↓?)	Associated Key Success Factors
Effectiveness · ·			· ·
Efficiency · ·			· ·
Relationship · ·			· ·
Range · ·			· ·
Premises · ·			· ·
Price			• Cost competitiveness • •

Your Plan Chapter 5: Strategy

Rating Your Competitive Position in a Key Segment

Key Success Factors for a Key Segment	Weighting (%)	Your Business Today	Competitor A	Competitor B	Competitor C	Your Business Tomorrow
Market Share						
Cost Factors:						
Management Factors:						
Differentiation Factors: Effectiveness						
Efficiency						
Relationship						
Range						
Premises						
Competitive Position	*100%*					

Key to Rating: 1 = Weak, 2 = Tenable, 3 = Favorable, 4 = Strong, 5 = Very strong

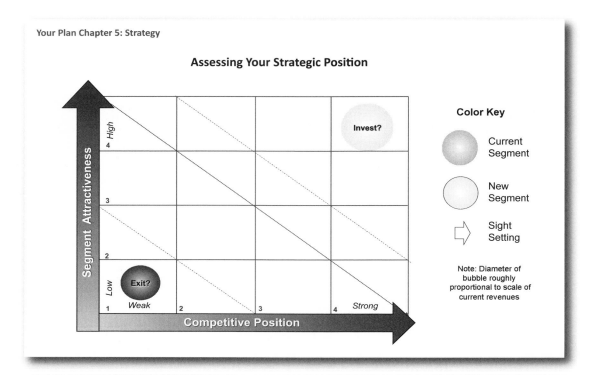

Assessing Your Strategic Position

Color Key

Current Segment

New Segment

Sight Setting

Note: Diameter of bubble roughly proportional to scale of current revenues

---

Chapter 6 Content

Management — One paragraph per key manager in plan, one-page bio in appendix

Marketing — Show in one page why yours is a market-driven organization, with supporting proof in appendix

Operations and Capital Expenditure
Supplies
Purchasing
Manufacture or Service Provision
R&D
Distribution, Storage, and Logistics
Customer Service and Technical Support
Systems & IT
Quality and Financial Control
Regulatory Compliance

A helicopter view of the resources and capex needed to meet your plan, with supporting detail, as appropriate, placed in appendices

Your Plan Chapter 7: Financials and Forecasts

Drawing Up Your Market-Based Sales Forecast

Business Segments	Revenues ($000)	Market Demand Growth (%/year)	Company Competitive Position (0–5)	Likely Revenue Growth (%/year)	Top-Down Revenues ($000)	Bottom-Up Revenues ($000)	Total Revenues ($000)
	Latest Year	Next Three Years	Next Three Years	Next Three Years	In Three Years	In Three Years	In Three Years
1	2	3	4	5	6	7	8
Source:	Chapter 2	Chapter 3	Chapter 5	Here in Chapter 7			
A							
B							
C							
Others							
Total							

Your Plan Chapter 7: Financials and Forecasts

Drawing Up Your Competition-Based Margin Forecast

Business Segments	Revenues ($000)	Profit ($000)	Profit Margin (%)	Competitive Intensity (Low-Med-High)		Planned Profit Margin (%)	Forecast Profit ($000)	Planned Profit Improvement Measures
	Latest Year	Latest Year	Latest Year	Latest Year	In Three Years	In Three Years	In Three Years	
1	2	3	4	5	6	7	8	9
Source:	Chapter 2			Chapter 4		Here in Chapter 7		Chapters 5 & 6
A								
B								
C								
Others								
Total								

Your Plan Chapter 7: Financials and Forecasts

Forecasting Your Income Statement

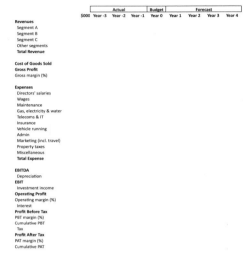

	Actual			Budget	Forecast			
$000	Year -3	Year -2	Year -1	Year 0	Year 1	Year 2	Year 3	Year 4

Revenues
Segment A
Segment B
Segment C
Other segments
Total Revenue

Cost of Goods Sold
Gross Profit
Gross margin (%)

Expenses
Directors' salaries
Wages
Maintenance
Gas, electricity & water
Telecoms & IT
Insurance
Vehicle running
Admin
Marketing (incl. travel)
Property taxes
Miscellaneous
Total Expense

EBITDA
Depreciation
EBIT
Investment income
Operating Profit
Operating margin (%)
Interest
Profit Before Tax
PBT margin (%)
Cumulative PBT
Tax
Profit After Tax
PAT margin (%)
Cumulative PAT

Your Plan Chapter 7: Financials and Forecasts

Forecasting Your Cash Flow Statement

	Actual			Budget	Forecast			
$000	Year -3	Year -2	Year -1	Year 0	Year 1	Year 2	Year 3	Year 4

Profit After Tax
Depreciation
Operating Cash Flow

Change in Working Capital
Change in inventory (increase = -)
Change in a/c receivable (increase = -)
Change in a/c payable (increase = +)
Net Change (increase = -)

Cash Flow from Operations
(= Sales receipts less expense payments)

Capital Expenditure
Buildings and works
Equipment
Vehicles
Total

Cash Flow Pre-Financing

Financing
Mortgage taken on property
Share capital paid In

Cash Surplus for Year
Cash Surplus (Cumulative)

Net Cash Inflow to Shareholders
Net Cash Inflow to Shareholders
(cumulative)

Your Plan Chapter 7: Financials and Forecasts

Forecasting Your Balance Sheet

$000	Actual			Budget	Forecast			
	End-Yr -3	End-Yr -2	End-Yr -1	End-Yr 0	End-Yr 1	End-Yr 2	End-Yr 3	End-Yr 4

Current Assets
Inventory
Accounts receivable
Other (deposits, prepaid, etc.)
Cash
Total

Capital Assets
Net fixed assets at start year
less depreciation during year
Net fixed assets at end year
Other (e.g., investments, intangibles)
Total

TOTAL ASSETS

Current Liabilities
Accounts payable
Provision for taxation
Short-term loans due in 12 months
Total

Long-Term Liabilities
Long-term debt
Pension obligations
Total

Owner Equity
Share capital paid up
Income statement b/f
Income statement this year
less dividends paid
Income statement c/f
Total

TOTAL LIABILITIES

Your Plan Chapter 8: Risk, Opportunity, and Sensitivity

Do Your Suns in Your Plan Outshine Your Clouds?

Sample Business Plans

Type 1: a growing business in services

The Gorge Inn and Oriental Spa

Type 2: a startup business in manufacturing

PermaRoll

The Gorge Inn
and Oriental Spa
Business Plan

April 2014

 Introduction

The Gorge Inn is a distinctive destination, operates profitably, and seeks co-funding to expand and become a leading player in spa services in Oregon

➢ The Gorge Inn and Oriental Spa ("The Gorge") is a destination with a difference: It is set overlooking the stunning Columbia River Gorge in the U.S. Pacific Northwest and yet offers visitors a touch of the Orient in its room decor, cuisine, and spa.

➢ It has 17 rooms for hire, most with views over the canyon, with spa and restaurant facilities offering a menu of Western and Oriental selections to both overnight and day visitors.

➢ The Gorge turned over $513,000 in 2013, with an operating margin of 18%.

➢ Phase II expansion is poised to start, costing $1.05m for a new building with 16 rooms and an outside, heated swimming pool.

➢ Revenues are forecast to almost double by 2018 and operating margin to reach 34%, making The Gorge a leading player in spa services in Oregon.

➢ This business plan aims to secure a financial partner who shares the owners' vision.

Contents

3

 Executive summary

The Gorge Inn will become a leading player after the Phase II project, with sales doubling, profitability enhanced, and opportunities outshining risks

2. *The business:* The Gorge Inn has progressed rapidly and above plan since opening in 2010.

3. *Market demand:* Market demand for travel in the Mt. Hood and Gorge area is forecast to grow at 4%/year to 2017.

4. *Industry competition:* Competitive intensity is medium to high, with the main risks being a copycat entrant or spas going the way of a fad.

5. *Strategy:* The Gorge is already a credible competitor to the Belmont in local spa services and will become a regional leader after the Phase II project.

6. *Resources*: The resource implications of The Gorge's strategy are in line with past experience and under control.

7. *Financials:* The Gorge is forecast to grow revenues to over $1m and operating margin to 34% by 2018.

8. *Risk:* Risks of fad, copycat, and slower buildup are outshone by opportunities such as the proven concept, spa profitability, and replication at another site.

4

Executive summary

Note: Use the Executive Summary as a divider page instead of the Contents page – it reinforces the upbeat story line and puts any concerns raised in perspective.

The Gorge Inn will become a leading player after the Phase II project, with sales doubling, profitability enhanced, and opportunities outshining risks

2. *The business:* The Gorge Inn has progressed rapidly and above plan since opening in 2010.

3. *Market demand:* Market demand for travel in the Mt. Hood and Gorge area is forecast to grow at 4%/year to 2017.

4. *Industry competition:* Competitive intensity is medium to high, with the main risks being a copycat entrant or spas going the way of a fad.

5. *Strategy:* The Gorge is already a credible competitor to the Belmont in local spa services and will become a regional leader after the Phase II project.

6. *Resources*: The resource implications of The Gorge's strategy are in line with past experience and under control.

7. *Financials:* The Gorge is forecast to grow revenues to over $1m and operating margin to 34% by 2018.

8. *Risk:* Risks of fad, copycat, and slower buildup are outshone by opportunities such as the proven concept, spa profitability, and replication at another site.

5

 The business Background

The Gorge Inn has progressed rapidly and above plan since opening in 2010.

➤ The Gorge is a destination with a difference:
- It is set overlooking the stunning Columbia River Gorge in the U.S. Pacific Northwest and yet offers visitors a touch of the Orient in its room decor, cuisine, and spa.
- It has 17 rooms for hire, most with views over the canyon, with spa and restaurant facilities offering a menu of Western and Oriental selections to both overnight and day visitors (see gallery in Appendix X).

➤ *Goals and objectives*: Our main goal is to give visitors a distinctive, treasured stay, thereby boosting the return rate, aimed to rise from 21% to 33% by 2018.

• *Strategy*: The early strategy of maximizing occupancy rates at the expense of average room price will be resumed following completion of the Phase II extension.

• *Resources and key da*tes: Following 8.15.11, our first day at 100% occupancy, marketing resources have been scaled down, but will need restoring in Phase II.

• *Financials*: Phase I work in 2009–10 turned out 17% over budget because of problems with the old building, but P&L growth has exceeded plan, with sales in 2013 reaching$513,000 (up 17% on plan) and operating margin 18% (14% in plan).

6

V<P **The business** Segments

2

The Gorge's revenues derive mainly from accommodation services, followed by spa and catering, and primarily from leisure visitors.

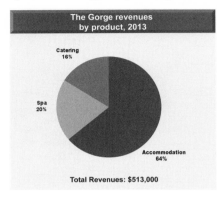

The Gorge revenues
by product, 2013

Catering
16%

Spa
20%

Accommodation
64%

Total Revenues: $513,000

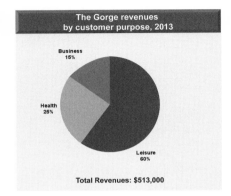

The Gorge revenues
by customer purpose, 2013

Business
15%

Health
25%

Leisure
60%

Total Revenues: $513,000

➢ Further product/market segmentation (to, say, revenues from business visitors on spa services) would add unnecessary complexity for this business.

7

V<P Executive summary

The Gorge Inn will become a leading player after the Phase II project, with sales doubling, profitability enhanced, and opportunities outshining risks.

2. *The business:* The Gorge Inn has progressed rapidly and above plan since opening in 2010.

3. *Market demand:* Market demand for travel in the Mt. Hood and Gorge area is forecast to grow at 4%/year to 2017.

4. *Industry competition:* Competitive intensity is medium to high, with the main risks being a copycat entrant or spas going the way of a fad.

5. *Strategy:* The Gorge is already a credible competitor to the Belmont in local spa services and will become a regional leader after the Phase II project.

6. *Resources*: The resource implications of The Gorge's strategy are in line with past experience and under control.

7. *Financials:* The Gorge is forecast to grow revenues to over $1m and operating margin to 34% by 2018.

8. *Risk:* Risks of fad, copycat, and slower buildup are outshone by opportunities such as the proven concept, spa profitability, and replication at another site.

8

V𝄞P **Market demand prospects**

Market demand for travel in the Mt. Hood and Gorge area is forecast to grow at 4%/ year to 2017, assuming no return to national recession as in 2009.

➤ The Gorge's addressed travel market in the Mt. Hood and Gorge area is estimated at $52 million for lodging plus $33 million on restaurants and $1 million on spa services, to total $86 million in 2013 (see sources and methodology in Appendix X).

➤ The market is forecast to grow at 4%/year to $101 million in 2017.

➤ Main long-term drivers have been per capita income growth, the growing propensity of Americans to take multiple short breaks, the steadily improving range of visitor facilities and attractions in the area (e.g., investment in scenic road and off-road cycling routes), and the targeted marketing carried out jointly by Travel Oregon and industry players.

➤ These drivers are expected to remain positive over the next few years.

➤ The main short-term driver was the 2009 recession induced by the financial crisis, from which U.S. travel as a whole managed to recover strongly in 2010–12 at 6.8%/year.

9

V𝄞P **Market demand prospects**

Market demand for travel in the Mt. Hood and Gorge area is forecast to grow at 4%/ year to 2017, assuming no return to recession as in 2009. *(continued)*

➤ Larger and higher-star hotels should fare better than the average during the economic recovery as visitors reverse their trading down behavior during the recession.

➤ Hotels offering special premium or niche facilities such as spas should fare likewise.

➤ The main risk facing Oregon hoteliers is a double-dip recession, sufficiently severe to contract the travel market again, as in 2009, but this is deemed to be of low likelihood.

10

Executive summary

The Gorge Inn will become a leading player after the Phase II project, with sales doubling, profitability enhanced, and opportunities outshining risks.

2. *The business:* The Gorge Inn has progressed rapidly and above plan since opening in 2010.

3. *Market demand:* Market demand for travel in the Mt. Hood and Gorge area is forecast to grow at 4%/year to 2017.

4. *Industry competition:* Competitive intensity is medium to high, with the main risks being a copycat entrant or spas going the way of a fad.

5. *Strategy:* The Gorge is already a credible competitor to the Belmont in local spa services and will become a regional leader after the Phase II project.

6. *Resources:* The resource implications of The Gorge's strategy are in line with past experience and under control.

7. *Financials:* The Gorge is forecast to grow revenues to over $1m and operating margin to 34% by 2018.

8. *Risk:* Risks of fad, copycat, and slower buildup are outshone by opportunities such as the proven concept, spa profitability, and replication at another site.

11

 Industry competition Occupancy

Occupancy rates in the Mt. Hood and Gorge area came down in 2009, but are likely to have recovered since to 2008 levels.

➤ Average hotel occupancy in Oregon in 2009* was 53.9%, down 7.7% on the 61.6% of2008—which compares with 55.1% nationwide, down 8.7% (see sources in Appendix X).

➤ Occupancy rates in the Mt. Hood and Gorge area were 56.1%, down 6.1% on the 62.2% of 2008—somewhat higher than for the state as a whole.

➤ Occupancy rates in the area are seasonal, with average rates ranging from 40% in December (48% in 2008) to 73% in August (81%).

➤ Average room rate for 2009 in the area was $79, compared with $86 for the state and $98 nationwide; revpar (revenue per available room) in Mt. Hood and Gorge was $44 in 2009.

➤ There is no indication of localized oversupply in the area.

> * No good data on occupancy have been readily available since 2009, but with the subsequent recovery in market demand and from anecdotal reportage, 2008–09 data can be taken as useful and indicative.

12

Industry competition Competitors

The Gorge faces an array of competitors, from luxury resorts to excellent B&Bs and Portland spas.

➢ Competitors are many (see details of offering and scale in Appendix X) and include:
  - Three top-of-the-range resorts, with golf courses, swimming and plunge pools, and luxurious spa facilities operating up in the hills above The Gorge, two on the Washington side of The Gorge and one on the Oregon side nestling in the foothills of Mt. Hood—as well as another such resort with a high-profile spa located in the Willamette Valley
  - One business-style hotel, owned by a chain, located at Cascade Locks and offering a fitness suite and good, basic spa facilities
  - Two first-class hotels, in Hood River and Crown Point, offering the option of limited spa services such as massage
  - A unique manor-style hotel-cum-hostel destination, featuring spa facilities as well as golf, pools, and craft and theater, located in Troutdale, close to Portland airport
  - Five first-rate B&Bs, one of which with a magnificent view over The Gorge on the Oregon side, another similarly sited on the Washington side, two located on the outskirts of towns (Portland and Hood River), and one near Troutdale—none of which offer spa services
  - Half a dozen first-class spas/wellness centers in Portland, two in particular with an Oriental influence

➢ All offer serious direct or indirect competition, but none mirrors the distinctiveness of The Gorge Inn and Oriental Spa.

13

 Industry competition Intensity

Competitive intensity is medium to high, with the main risks being a copycat entrant or spas going the way of a fad.

| Threat of New Entrants | High | ↑ |

- Low barriers to entry at bottom end of spa services, higher at top end, with high capital and running costs
- But new entrants spread the word

| Supplier Power | Low | → |

- Plenty of spa equipment suppliers
- Much available labor in Oregon

| Internal Rivalry | Med | → |

- Many players in Columbia River Gorge and elsewhere in Oregon
- But above-average demand growth in The Gorge niche

| Customer Power | High | → |

- Customers have plenty of choice where to take their break, whether in the Gorge area, Oregon, or beyond

Key
↑↑↑ = Increasing rapidly
↑↑ = Increasing moderately
↑ = Increasing slowly
→ = Little change
↓ = Decreasing

| Ease of Substitution | Med | → |

- Spas vulnerable to the next big thing in health vacationing

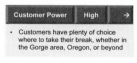

| Overall Competitive Intensity |
| Medium to High | ↑ |

Source: Adapted from Michael Porter, *Competitive Strategy: Techniques for Analyzing Industries and Competitors* (New York: The Free Press, 1980)

14

Executive summary

The Gorge Inn will become a leading player after the Phase II project, with sales doubling, profitability enhanced, and opportunities outshining risks.

2. *The business:* The Gorge Inn has progressed rapidly and above plan since opening in 2010.

3. *Market demand:* Market demand for travel in the Mt. Hood and Gorge area is forecast to grow at 4%/year to 2017.

4. *Industry competition:* Competitive intensity is medium to high, with the main risks being a copycat entrant or spas going the way of a fad.

5. *Strategy:* The Gorge is already a credible competitor to the Belmont in local spa services and will become a regional leader after the Phase II project.

6. *Resources*: The resource implications of The Gorge's strategy are in line with past experience and under control.

7. *Financials:* The Gorge is forecast to grow revenues to over $1m and operating margin to 34% by 2018.

8. *Risk:* Risks of fad, copycat, and slower buildup are outshone by opportunities such as the proven concept, spa profitability, and replication at another site.

15

 Strategy Customer purchasing criteria

The main purchasing criteria in spa services are the effectiveness of the treatment, the standard of the premises, and price.

Customer purchasing criteria in spa services

Spa Customer Purchasing Criteria		Importance	Change
Effectiveness	• Therapist capabilities	*High*	→
	• Understanding of benefits	*Low/Med*	→
	• Confidence in process	*Med*	→
Efficiency	• Effort	*Low/Med*	→
	• Timeliness	*Low*	→
Relationship	• Rapport	*Med*	↑
	• Enthusiasm	*Med/High*	→
Range	• Facilities	*Med/High*	→
	• Treatments	*Low/Med*	↑↑
Premises	• Cleanliness, hygiene	*High*	↑
	• Space, decor		
Price		*Med/High*	↑

16

Strategy Key success factors — 5

The winning provider of spa services will have highly skilled and experienced therapists, quality premises, a positive, upbeat culture, and tight control of costs.

Key success factors in spa services

Spa Customer Purchasing Criteria		Importance	Change	Associated Key Success Factors
Effectiveness	• Therapist capabilities • Understanding of benefits • Confidence in process	*High* *Low/Med* *Med*	→ → →	• **Therapist skills** • **Qualification** • **Track record**
Efficiency	• Effort • Timeliness	*Low/Med* *Low*	→ →	• **Availability** • **Work ethic** • **Delivery**
Relationship	• Rapport • Enthusiasm	*Med* *Med/High*	↑ →	• **People skills (communication)** • **Positive, upbeat culture**
Range	• Facilities • Treatments	*Med/High* *Low/Med*	→ ↑↑	• **Range of facilities** • **Range of treatments**
Premises	• Cleanliness, hygiene • Space, decor	*High*	↑	• **Spa quality premises**
Price		*Med/High*	↑	• **Cost-competitiveness**

17

 Strategy The Gorge's competitive position — 5

The Gorge is already a credible competitor to the Belmont in local spa services and could become a regional leader with the Phase II project.

The Gorge Inn competitive position in spa services, Mt. Hood and Gorge area

Key Success Factors	Weighting	The Gorge Inn	Belmont	Best American	Reina's	The Gorge Phase II
Market Share	15%	1.5	4	2	2.5	2.5
Cost Factors: Overhead control, Scale economies	25%	3.5	2	3	3	4
Management Factors: Marketing	10%	1.5	4	5	3	2
Differentiation Factors: Effectiveness—Standard of therapists	10%	5	4.5	3	4	5
Efficiency—Work ethic, Delivery	5%	5	4.5	3	4	5
Relationship—Communication, Attitude	10%	5	4	3	5	5
Range—Facilities, Treatments	10%	2	5	2	4	3.5
Premises—Hygiene, Décor, Space	15%	4	5	4	4	4.5
Competitive Position	*100%*	**3.3**	**3.8**	**3.1**	**3.5**	**3.9**

Key to Rating: 1 = Weak, 2 = Tenable, 3 = Favorable, 4 = Strong, 5 = Very strong

Selected competitors: The Gorge Inn and Oriental Spa; Belmont Hot Springs Resort & Spa, Mt. Hood; Best American Cascade Hotel, Cascade Locks; Reina's Spa, Troutdale

18

Strategy The Gorge's strategy

The Gorge is poised to exploit strategic success to date with the Phase II project.

➤ The Gorge has come from nowhere to be a credible player in its niche by:
  - Offering the overnight visitor an experience somewhat out of the ordinary—clean, crisp, comfortable accommodation spiced with a hint of the Orient, with stunning views over the Columbia River Gorge
  - Offering the diner the choice of traditional American fare or home-cooked, delicately spiced Oriental cuisine, with the same lovely views
  - Creating a spacious, relaxing environment, a high quality of therapy, and a culture of service and enthusiasm in its spa services, factors that counterbalance the limited range of facilities offered compared with leading local competitors
  - And, on the other hand, keeping a tight control over overheads

➤ The Gorge's occupancy rates provide evidence:
  - Average room occupancy of 71% by Year 3 of operations, well above the area average

➤ Completion of the two-phase strategy could make The Gorge one of the leading providers of spa services in the Columbia River Gorge area, not in terms of scale or market share, *but of competitive position, hence profitability.*

➤ Strategic risks are low: The Gorge will offer in Phase II more of the same successful formula of Phase I; it seems unlikely that this concept, so successful so far, will become dated and of lesser appeal over the next five years.

19

 Executive summary

The Gorge Inn will become a leading player after the Phase II project, with sales doubling, profitability enhanced, and opportunities outshining risks.

2. *The business:* The Gorge Inn has progressed rapidly and above plan since opening in 2010.

3. *Market demand:* Market demand for travel in the Mt. Hood and Gorge area is forecast to grow at 4%/year to 2017.

4. *Industry competition:* Competitive intensity is medium to high, with the main risks being a copycat entrant or spas going the way of a fad.

5. *Strategy:* The Gorge is already a credible competitor to the Belmont in local spa services and will become a regional leader after the Phase II project.

6. *Resources:* The resource implications of The Gorge's strategy are in line with past experience and under control.

7. *Financials:* The Gorge is forecast to grow revenues to over $1m and operating margin to 34% by 2018.

8. *Risk:* Risks of fad, copycat, and slower buildup are outshone by opportunities such as the proven concept, spa profitability, and replication at another site.

20

Resources 6

The resource implications of The Gorge's strategy are in line with past experience and under control.

➤ Management—Rick and Kay Jones, unlike three years earlier, are now proven managers in hotel and spa services (see bios in Appendix X) and, with Kay's connections, envisage no difficulties in recruiting a spa manager with an Oriental heritage.

➤ Marketing—more of the same, but for 33 rather than 17 rooms (see Appendix X):
  - Local and regional advertising
  - Attendance at regional promotions
  - Competitive pricing off-season and other special packages, such as during weddings
  - [NEW] Partnering with successful spa hotels elsewhere, giving them a cut on business referrals, and offering the customer variety in where to stay next time

➤ Operations—no serious constraints (Appendix X):
  - Same supplies, purchasing process, provision of services, systems (the reservation system has worked very well after the inevitable teething problems), controls, compliance
  - Planning permits now secured and same building contractor for Phase II as for Phase I
  - Environment, health, and safety record good so far (see Appendix X)

➤ Resource risk—under control:
  - Slippage or construction cost inflation—two months' delay and 10% contingency already in plan
  - Health of owner managers—insurance taken, but in worst case the business is now highly salable

21

VP **Executive summary**

The Gorge Inn will become a leading player after the Phase II project, with sales doubling, profitability enhanced, and opportunities outshining risks.

2. *The business:* The Gorge Inn has progressed rapidly and above plan since opening in 2010.

3. *Market demand:* Market demand for travel in the Mt. Hood and Gorge area is forecast to grow at 4%/year to 2017.

4. *Industry competition:* Competitive intensity is medium to high, with the main risks being a copycat entrant or spas going the way of a fad.

5. *Strategy:* The Gorge is already a credible competitor to the Belmont in local spa services and will become a regional leader after the Phase II project.

6. *Resources:* The resource implications of The Gorge's strategy are in line with past experience and under control.

7. *Financials:* The Gorge is forecast to grow revenues to over $1m and operating margin to 34% by 2018.

8. *Risk:* Risks of fad, copycat ,and slower buildup are outshone by opportunities such as the proven concept, spa profitability, and replication at another site.

22

Financials and forecasts Historics

7

The Gorge has achieved satisfactory profitability since its launch in late 2010.

The Gorge Inn income statement and key parameters, 2011–14

US$000	2011 Actual	2012 Actual	2013 Actual	2014 Budget
Average no. of rooms available	*17*	*17*	*17*	*17*
Average achieved room rate ($)	*64.1*	*69.5*	*73.9*	*75.5*
Average room occupancy	*39.2%*	*55.9%*	*71.4%*	*75.0%*
Revenues - Accommodation	155	240	326	354
- Catering	45	65	82	87
- Spa	76	92	105	109
- Total revenues	**276**	**397**	**513**	**550**
EBITDA	-16	111	194	220
Operating profit	-117	10	93	119
Operating margin (%)	**-42.4%**	**2.5%**	**18.1%**	**21.6%**
Profit before tax	-152	-25	58	84

Source: Appendix X

23

 Financials and forecasts Historics

7

The Gorge has achieved satisfactory profitability since its launch in late 2010.
(continued)

➤ Occupancy of 39% in 2011 outperformed the planned 25–30% and has since grown to 71%, with 2014 forecast to reach 75%.

➤ AARR has been nudged up by 7.5%/year since 2011, with budget 2014 showing a further 3% increase to almost $80 and revenues reaching $550,000.

➤ Breakeven at operating margin was achieved in early 2012 and at the bottom line toward the end of the year, both ahead of plan; operating margin grew to 18% by 2013 and should reach 22% in 2014.

➤ Following financing of a $500,000 mortgage and owner equity of $550,000, no further cash has been injected; it has been operationally cash positive since 2012.

➤ By end-2013, the book value of owner equity reached $431,000 and seems set to exceed the $550,000 invested by 2015; this takes no account of the enhancement in the value of the property since purchase and renovation.

24

Financials and forecasts Forecasts

The Gorge is forecast to grow revenues to over $1m and operating margin to 34% by 2018.

The Gorge Inn income statement forecasts, 2013–18

US$000	2013 Actual	2014 Budget	2015 Forecast	2016 Forecast	2017 Forecast	2018 Forecast
Average number of rooms available	17	17	17	33	33	33
Average achieved room rate ($)	73.9	75.5	79	70	72	74
Average room occupancy	71.4%	75.0%	75%	60%	65%	71%
Revenues - Accommodation	326	354	368	506	564	633
- Catering	82	87	87	135	145	159
- Spa	105	109	109	263	273	284
- Total revenues	513	550	564	904	982	1076
EBITDA	194	220	214	397	466	546
Operating profit	93	119	113	212	281	361
Operating margin (%)	**18.1%**	**21.6%**	**20.0%**	**23.5%**	**28.7%**	**33.6%**
Profit before tax	58	84	78	107	176	256

Source: Appendix X

25

 Financials and forecasts Forecasts

The Gorge is forecast to grow revenues to over $1m and operating margin to 34% by 2018. *(continued)*

➢ The Gorge revenues are forecast to double over 2013–18, despite some conservative assumptions:
- An assumed 10% drop in average achieved room rate and a 20% drop in occupancy rate once the new accommodation capacity comes on stream in 2015; given how full the inn has been in recent months and the healthy forward booking for this year and next, these assumptions seem reasonable

➢ Operating margin is forecast to rise from 2013's 18% to 33%, likewise with conservative assumptions:
- An assumed doubling in staff costs, spread across room cleaning, waiting, cooking, and spa services, with no increase in the bar, reception, accounts, or gardens
- A major marketing campaign planned for both 2015 and 2016
- 100% debt finance assumed for the $1 million to be raised

➢ The enhanced profitability reflects the impact of doubled revenues spread across an overhead base that's increasing more slowly; a more productive use of the existing and Phase II asset base.

26

Financials and forecasts Forecasts

The Gorge is set to outpace the market, with or without Phase II.

The Gorge market contextual revenue forecasts, 2013–18

Business Segments	Revenues ($000)	Market Demand Growth (%/year)	Company Competitive Position (0–5)	Likely Revenue Growth (%/year)	Top-Down Revenues ($000)	Phase II-derived Revenues ($000)	Total Revenues ($000)
	2013	2013–18	2013–18	2013–18	2018	2018	2018
1	2	3	4	5	6	7	8
Source:	Chapter 2	Chapter 3	Chapter 5	Here in Chapter 7			
Accommodation	326	3-4%	3.6 to 3.9	5%	416	217	633
Catering	82	2-3%	3.3 to 3.5	3%	95	64	159
Spa	105	4-5%	3.5 to 4.1	7.5%	151	133	284
Total	**513**			**5.2%**	**662**	**414**	**1076**

Source: Appendix X

 Financials and forecasts Forecasts

The Gorge is set to outpace the market, with or without Phase II. *(continued)*

➤ When placed in a market context, The Gorge is well placed to beat the market even in the absence of the Phase II building program.

➤ It would do so in two main ways:
- Growing accommodation revenues faster than the market, due to its strong competitive position—this would be done more by nudging up room rates than through higher occupancy, since The Gorge already enjoys high occupancy.
- Deriving a higher share of revenues from spa services, for both overnight and outside guests, even in the absence of the Phase II facilities, as The Gorge's range of services continues to develop and becomes better known.

➤ Over three-fifths of revenues by 2018 would be derived from the existing business, with the balance from the Phase II development.

Financials and forecasts Forecasts

The Gorge is forecast to generate an average of $300,000 cash each year following Phase II development.

The Gorge Inn cash flow forecasts, 2013–18

US$000	2013 Actual	2014 Budget	2015 Forecast	2016 Forecast	2017 Forecast	2018 Forecast
Profit before tax	58	84	78	107	176	256
Depreciation	101	101	101	185	185	185
Operating cash flow	159	185	163	269	324	387
Change in working capital	-9	-3	0	-23	-6	-8
Cash flow from operations	**150**	**182**	**162**	**246**	**318**	**380**
Capital expenditure	-4	-9	-1045	-2	-10	-5
Cash flow pre-financing	146	173	-883	244	308	375
Mortgage	0	0	1000	0	0	0
Cash surplus for year	**146**	**173**	**117**	**244**	**308**	**375**
Cash surplus (cumulative)	157	331	448	692	1000	1375

Source: Appendix X

29

 Financials and forecasts Forecasts

The Gorge's owner equity should exceed $1m by 2018.

The Gorge Inn balance sheet forecasts, 2013–18

US$000	2013 Actual	2014 Budget	2015 Forecast	2016 Forecast	2017 Forecast	2018 Forecast
Current assets – cash	157	331	448	692	1000	1375
Current assets – total	201	378	496	769	1084	1466
Capital assets	742	650	1594	1412	1237	1058
Total assets	**943**	**1028**	**2090**	**2181**	**2321**	**2524**
Current liabilities	12	13	13	19	20	20
Long-term liabilities	500	500	1500	1500	1500	1500
Owner equity	*431*	*515*	*577*	*662*	*801*	*1004*
Total liabilities	**943**	**1028**	**2090**	**2181**	**2321**	**2524**

Source: Appendix X

30

VKP   Executive summary

The Gorge Inn will become a leading player after the Phase II project, with sales doubling, profitability enhanced, and opportunities outshining risks.

2. *The business:* The Gorge Inn has progressed rapidly and above plan since opening in 2010.

3. *Market demand:* Market demand for travel in the Mt. Hood and Gorge area is forecast to grow at 4%/year to 2017.

4. *Industry competition:* Competitive intensity is medium to high, with the main risks being a copycat entrant or spas going the way of a fad.

5. *Strategy:* The Gorge is already a credible competitor to the Belmont in local spa services and will become a regional leader after the Phase II project.

6. *Resources:* The resource implications of The Gorge's strategy are in line with past experience and under control.

7. *Financials:* The Gorge is forecast to grow revenues to over $1m and operating margin to 34% by 2018.

8. *Risk:* Risks of fad, copycat, and slower buildup are outshone by opportunities such as the proven concept, spa profitability, and replication at another site.

31

VKP   Risk, opportunity, and sensitivity   8

Risks of fad, copycat, and slower buildup are outshone by opportunities such as the proven concept, spa profitability, and replication at another site.

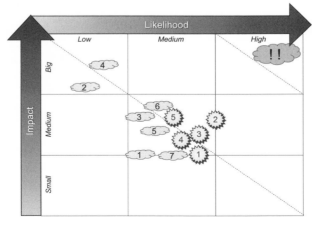

Risks

1. Double-dip dents market demand
2. Spa fad wanes
3. A direct copy new entrant emerges
4. The Gorge's concept fades
5. Phase II construction costs up 20%
6. Phase II occupancy buildup slower than forecast
7. Interest rate up 3%

Opportunities

1. Market demand maintains growth
2. Focused marketing of The Gorge's proven concept
3. The Gorge spa profitability
4. New complementary services or products
5. Replicate concept elsewhere

Risk, opportunity, and sensitivity

Risks of fad, copycat, and slower buildup are outshone by opportunities such as the proven concept, spa profitability, and replication at another site. *(continued)*

➢ The major risk is a slower buildup in occupancy than forecast (Cloud 6), but …
  - The forecast has taken a 15% hit in occupancy between 2015 and 2016, dropping from 75% to 60% …
  - …which is a little higher than Year 2's 55%...
  - … and despite an assumed drop in AARR of 11% from $79 to $70

➢ And The Gorge is no startup—it is now a proven concept (Sun 2).

➢ Other promising opportunities stand out:
  - The transformation of The Gorge's spa services to a profitable segment in their own right (Sun 3), rather than a loss leader for the accommodation segment
  - The introduction of complementary services and products (Sun 4), such as day trips, sporting trips, and aromatherapy products

➢ Finally, there is the opportunity (Sun 5) to replicate The Gorge's success:
  - A large B&B business in the North Cascades National Park has been identified that would be ideal, and whose owners are planning to retire in a couple of years
  - Even if the timing of that deal doesn't work out, there will be other properties on the market when the time is right

33

 Risk, opportunity, and sensitivity

The plan is reasonably sensitive to lower occupancy rates, but such levels are considered most unlikely.

➢ We understand that this business is operationally highly geared, so have conducted appropriate sensitivity tests:
  - The impact on profit before tax (PBT) from inflated Phase II construction costs of 20% seems limited and containable—and there is only a minor cash flow impact in later years resulting from higher depreciation/ lower tax.
  - If occupancy rates turn out to be 15% below plan—for example, 51% in 2016 instead of the forecast 60% — the impact is greater; the income statement in 2016 drops into the red and the profit forecast for 2018 is halved; cash flow, however, remains positive, though shrunken.
  - Such a drop is most unlikely; a 51% overall occupancy rate in 2016 would imply a level of just 23% in the new rooms of Phase II (compared with a forecast 44% in the business plan) and The Gorge managed to achieve 39% occupancy in 2011, its first year of operations.

The Gorge Inn business plan sensitivity tests, 2016 & 2018

$000	Profit Before Tax		Cash Flow	
	2016	2018	2016	2018
Business plan	107	256	244	375
Sensitivity tests				
Construction costs up 20%	94	243	247	377
Occupancy rates down 15%	-6	113	164	273
Both of the above	-19	100	167	276

34

Conclusion

Note: Repeat the conclusion of the Executive Summary!

9

> The Gorge Inn will become a leading player after the Phase II project, with sales doubling, profitability enhanced, and opportunities outshining risks.

35

 Appendices

X. Image gallery

X. Market research data

X. Competitor data

X. Competitive position data

X. Management bios

X. Marketing plan

X. Operations data

X. Environment, health, and safety data

X. Financial data

Note: These appendices are not shown in this book, since the level of detail contained would be pertinent only to the sample business plan and not to that of the reader's business.

36

PermaRoll
Business Plan

April 2014

Author note: I worked briefly in this interesting niche industry in the mid-2000s. It makes for a good case study since the manufactured output and its market can be readily envisaged by the reader, unlike so many niche industries. In reality, the new material, design, production process, and lifetime product guarantee already existed in the industry in the 2000s, but let us imagine that it was PermaRoll founder, Randy King, who developed, patented, and marketed this product in his Atlanta garage in the 2010s. Names of all market players have been changed and their market shares and competitive positioning juggled.

 Introduction

PermaRoll is a start-up producer of innovative, top-end clutches for roller shades and is seeking to raise $1m to invest in scaling up production.

➤ PermaRoll Inc., based in a garage workshop in Atlanta, GA, produces an innovative, top-end clutch/operating system for use in alternative window coverings ("AWCs") such as roller shades or Venetian blinds, as opposed to curtains and draperies.

➤ It started two years ago and is owned and managed part-time by Randy King.
  - A management consultant with Alfred S. Short, formerly with the clutch division at AWC leader, Thompson Adams; he is a mechanical engineer and an MBA from McDonough.
  - One full-time employee, Juan Lopez, an engineer, and one contracted salesperson, Suzanne Wong.

➤ Patent protection has been filed for both PermaRoll's product and production process.

➤ Pitches to potential customers have been promising, with many believing there to be a distinct gap in the market for such a highly engineered, dependable product.

➤ Management believes PermaRoll is ready to move beyond the pilot phase and into the first stage of production and marketing, aiming through this business plan to raise an initial $1m.

Contents

1. *Executive summary*

2. *The business*

3. *Market demand prospects*

4. *Industry competition*

5. *Strategy*

6. *Resources*

7. *Financials and forecasts*

8. *Risk, opportunity, and sensitivity*

2

 Executive summary

PermaRoll has a sustainable competitive edge in the top-end AWC market, with opportunities to gain share outshining the main risk of customer stickiness.

2. *The business:* PermaRoll will focus manufacturing initially on clutches for alternative window coverings, highly engineered for superior ease of use and reliability.

3. *Market demand:* PermaRoll's initial addressed market recovered to $75m in 2012, with growth forecast at 3.5%/year.

4. *Industry competition:* Competition will be less intense at the top end of the market, as long as a new entrant has a sustainable competitive edge.

5. *Strategy:* PermaRoll's top-end product has been well received by target customers and should enable a market foothold to be gained, grown, and defended.

6. *Resources*: A CFO will be hired to bolster PermaRoll's management team.

7. *Financials*: PermaRoll sales should reach $3m by Year 4, with peak funding requirement < $1m.

8. *Risk*: Opportunities to gain business beyond the plan forecasts outshine the key risks of customer stickiness and competitor retaliation.

3

Executive summary

> Note: Use the Executive Summary as a divider page instead of the Contents page – it reinforces the upbeat story line and puts any concerns raised in perspective.

PermaRoll has a sustainable competitive edge in the top-end AWC market, with opportunities to gain share outshining the main risk of customer stickiness.

2. *The business:* PermaRoll will focus manufacturing initially on clutches for alternative window coverings, highly engineered for superior ease of use and reliability.

3. *Market demand:* PermaRoll's initial addressed market recovered to $75m in 2012, with growth forecast at 3.5%/year.

4. *Industry competition:* Competition will be less intense at the top end of the market, as long as a new entrant has a sustainable competitive edge.

5. *Strategy:* PermaRoll's top-end product has been well received by target customers and should enable a market foothold to be gained, grown, and defended.

6. *Resources:* A CFO will be hired to bolster PermaRoll's management team.

7. *Financials:* PermaRoll sales should reach $3m by Year 4, with peak funding requirement < $1m.

8. *Risk:* Opportunities to gain business beyond the plan forecasts outshine the key risks of customer stickiness and competitor retaliation.

4

The business

PermaRoll will focus manufacturing initially on clutches for AWCs, highly engineered for outstanding ease of use and reliability.

➤ Clutches and operating systems for alternative window coverings today have evolved much and many are now sophisticated, reliable items of equipment.

➤ PermaRoll has developed a clutch system specifically for the top end of the market.
  ▪ Fiberglass super-reinforced nylon material to give superior strength
  ▪ Internal spring technology enabling demonstrably superior balance, tort, and smoothness...
  ▪ ...and that minimizes friction and abrasion—see Appendix X: The PermaRoll technology
  ▪ A more automated assembly process that minimizes future risk of product failure—see Appendix X: The PermaRoll production process

➤ The PermaRoll clutch should last "forever," unless abused—effectively until the user decides to refresh the look of the windows and replace the covering.

➤ This will have a major marketing benefit to the customer, who will feel confident in offering the consumer a lifetime guarantee for the clutch.

➤ The clutch will, however, cost more to produce than current top-end products—an estimated 15–20%, once minimum economic production levels are achieved.

5

The business

PermaRoll will focus manufacturing initially on clutches for AWCs, highly engineered for outstanding ease of use and reliability. *(continued)*

➤ PermaRoll management has conducted 27 interviews with potential customers, many of which have been highly promising—see Appendix X:
  ▪ Seven customers have expressed such enthusiasm for the product that they would be willing to build an extended guarantee into their marketing campaigns.
  ▪ Three customers have submitted formal Letters of Intent.
  ▪ One of these customers, Palazzo Venezia, number three in the top end of the market, intends to purchase a minimum of $350,000's worth in our first year of operations.

➤ We examine PermaRoll's competitive positioning in more detail in Chapter 5 and the derived revenue prospects in Chapter 7.

6

VP Executive summary

PermaRoll has a sustainable competitive edge in the top-end AWC market, with opportunities to gain share outshining the main risk of customer stickiness.

2. *The business:* PermaRoll will focus manufacturing initially on clutches for alternative window coverings, highly engineered for superior ease of use and reliability.

3. *Market demand:* PermaRoll's initial addressed market recovered to $75m in 2012, with growth forecast at 3.5%/year.

4. *Industry competition:* Competition will be less intense at the top end of the market, as long as a new entrant has a sustainable competitive edge.

5. *Strategy:* PermaRoll's top-end product has been well received by target customers and should enable a market foothold to be gained, grown, and defended.

6. *Resources:* A CFO will be hired to bolster PermaRoll's management team.

7. *Financials:* PermaRoll sales should reach $3m by Year 4, with peak funding requirement < $1m.

8. *Risk:* Opportunities to gain business beyond the plan forecasts outshine the key risks of customer stickiness and competitor retaliation.

7

Market demand prospects Alternative window coverings

Market demand for clutches for alternative window coverings recovered to $245m in 2012 and is forecast to grow at 3.25%/year to 2017.

➤ The U.S. wholesale market for all window coverings recovered to $6.2bn in 2012 and is forecast to grow at 3.5%/year, given the improved outlook for house building, the post-slump rebound in home moves, and economic recovery in general, to $7.4bn in 2017—see sources in Appendix X.

➤ The market for alternative window coverings ("AWCs") has grown share in recent years from 58% in 2000 to 61% in 2008 and is forecast to grow more slowly to 62% by 2017, yielding a market of $4.6bn—see sources in Appendix X.

➤ The market for clutches (and supporting equipment such as brackets), given typical wholesale prices (see Appendix X), is estimated at one-twentieth of that for AWCs plus an additional 10% for replacements and spares, or $245m in 2012.

➤ Given the tendency to trade up over time, the improved durability of better quality clutches, and hence the slower rate of growth of replacements and spares, the market for clutches is forecast to grow at 3.25%/year to $285m in 2017.

8

 Market demand prospects Top end

PermaRoll's initial addressed market can be estimated at $75m and is growing at 3.5%/year, with further potential in export markets.

➤ The top end of the U.S. market for AWC clutches can be classified by specific makers and distributors, and by the top-end ranges offered by full range producers:
  - Thompson Adams (overall market leader) with its top-end Elite and Prestige ranges—$18m
  - Rollershade (No 4 overall) with its top-end Style range—$14m
  - Palazzo Venezia—$10m
  - Louvers & Shades (No 2 overall) with its top-end Mediterranean range—$6m
  - Blindsforshow.com—$7m
  - Sausalito Style—$5m
  - Other—$15m
  - **Total U.S. market—$75m** (roughly 30% of the total U.S. AWC market)

➤ Post-recession trading up should drive top-end market growth a shade higher than for the overall AWC market—at 3.5%/year.

➤ PermaRoll intends to launch the product overseas from Year 3, where top-end AWC market sizes can be estimated roughly at:
  - Canada—$15m and Latin America—$20m
  - U.K.—$10m and Other Europe—$40m
  - Far East—$20m
  - **Total export markets—$105m**

9

Executive summary

PermaRoll has a sustainable competitive edge in the top-end AWC market, with opportunities to gain share outshining the main risk of customer stickiness.

2. *The business:* PermaRoll will focus manufacturing initially on clutches for alternative window coverings, highly engineered for superior ease of use and reliability.

3. *Market demand:* PermaRoll's initial addressed market recovered to $75m in 2012, with growth forecast at 3.5%/year.

4. *Industry competition:* Competition will be less intense at the top end of the market, as long as a new entrant has a sustainable competitive edge.

5. *Strategy:* PermaRoll's top-end product has been well received by target customers and should enable a market foothold to be gained, grown, and defended.

6. *Resources:* A CFO will be hired to bolster PermaRoll's management team.

7. *Financials:* PermaRoll sales should reach $3m by Year 4, with peak funding requirement < $1m.

8. *Risk:* Opportunities to gain business beyond the plan forecasts outshine the key risks of customer stickiness and competitor retaliation.

10

 Industry competition Competitors 4

PermaRoll is targeting the high end of the AWC clutch market, currently served by E-Z-Roll and ShadeLite.

➤ Today's AWC clutch producers fall into three camps (see details of offering, revenues, production facilities, number of employees, and strategy in Appendix X):
- Established independents, dominated by market leaders, E-Z-Roll and ShadeLite, with roughly 40% and 25% market shares, who have a range of products serving most categories, other than motorized AWCs, as well as more reliable, more expensive products catering for the top end of the market
- Low-cost country producers, such as Hi Ya in China, offering mixed quality product and serving primarily LCC AWC producers, but also U.S. producers with offshore facilities and increasingly targeting low-end U.S.-based AWC producers
- Two vertically integrated customers, the AWC market leaders, who produce some of their own clutches, primarily for the mass market, but also buy in most of their clutches; Thompson Adams makes an estimated one-third of its clutches in-house and Louvers & Shades 45%

➤ PermaRoll does not regard the latter two camps as direct competitors, now or in the near future, given entry barriers and PermaRoll's strategic focus.

➤ PermaRoll's direct competition will be at the top end of the range, the high-quality, well-engineered products of E-Z-Roll and ShadeLite.

11

Industry competition Intensity 4

Competition will be less intense at the top end of the market, as long as a new entrant has a sustainable competitive edge.

Competitive force	Mass market		Top end		Comments
	Intensity	Change	Intensity	Change	
Internal rivalry	High	↓	Med	→	• Only two main players at top end, but the same plus vertically integrated customers and low-cost producers for mass market • Easing with resumed growth
Threat of new entrants	High	↑	Low/Med	→	• More low-cost producers eyeing market, but capital and tech barriers protect at top end
Threat of substitutes	Low	→	Low	→	• Curtains and draperies have been around since the Middle Ages
Power of customers	High	→	Low/Med	→	• Integrated customers wield much bargaining power in mass market
Power of suppliers	Low	→	Low	→	• Suppliers are plentiful
Overall intensity	**Med/High**	→	**Low/Med**	→	• Competition is not intense at top end, but a new entrant must have an edge

12

 Executive summary

PermaRoll has a sustainable competitive edge in the top-end AWC market, with opportunities to gain share outshining the main risk of customer stickiness.

2. *The business:* PermaRoll will focus manufacturing initially on clutches for alternative window coverings, highly engineered for superior ease of use and reliability.

3. *Market demand:* PermaRoll's initial addressed market recovered to $75m in 2012, with growth forecast at 3.5%/year.

4. *Industry competition:* Competition will be less intense at the top end of the market, as long as a new entrant has a sustainable competitive edge.

5. *Strategy:* PermaRoll's top-end product has been well received by target customers and should enable a market foothold to be gained, grown, and defended.

6. *Resources*: A CFO will be hired to bolster PermaRoll's management team.

7. *Financials*: PermaRoll sales should reach $3m by Year 4, with peak funding requirement < $1m.

8. *Risk*: Opportunities to gain business beyond the plan forecasts outshine the key risks of customer stickiness and competitor retaliation.

13

Strategy Product positioning

PermaRoll has a product that appeals to the very top end of the range.

➤ PermaRoll's product is not for everyone; it is highly engineered, made from relatively costly material, and designed for ease of use and length of life; the mass market for alternative window coverings has no need for such a benefit.

➤ At the top end of the market, PermaRoll will compete with other, well-engineered product; winning new business will not be easy:
  ▪ The top-end products of E-Z-Roll and ShadeLite are very good.
  ▪ Many quality AWC producers will say they are happy with the clutches they have and be averse to switching.

➤ But PermaRoll's product (and production process) is distinctive and top-end customers will give PermaRoll at least a hearing:
  ▪ It uses state-of-the-art super-reinforced plastic material.
  ▪ Its design and spring technology enable superior balance, tort, and smoothness.
  ▪ Its more automated production process eliminates one area of weakness faced by the competition.
  ▪ It offers the customer the opportunity to reinforce its pitch that its AWC product is the very best on the market—including the extension of clutch guarantee from typically three years to product lifetime.

➤ And initial soundings are highly promising ... (PTO).

14

 Strategy Customer response

PermaRoll's product has been uniformly well received by top-end AWC producers, with three potential customers delivering Letters of Intent.

➤ PermaRoll management has conducted 27 interviews with 19 potential customers of the clutch, each operating at the top end of the AWC market—see Appendix X.

➤ All but one of the 19 customers gave positive and encouraging feedback, with only five saying that, though they admired the product, they saw no need to switch supplier over the next few years.

➤ Six customers were enthusiastic and would consider our pitch seriously, while another seven went further and said they would consider building the product and its extended guarantee into their marketing campaign.

➤ Three of these customers have provided formal Letters of Intent—see Appendix X.

➤ One of these customers, Palazzo Venezia, has expressed intent to purchase a minimum of 100,000 units in our first year of operations, at a value of $350,000.

15

Strategy Competitive position

PermaRoll management is under no illusion; competing in the early stages will be tough, with E-Z-Roll and ShadeLite so strongly ensconced in the market.

PermaRoll competitive position in clutches for top-end window coverings

Key Success Factors	Weighting	Perma Roll	E-Z-Roll	Shade Lite	Th'son Adams	Perma Roll Year 3
Market Share	25%	0	4	2.5	1	2
Cost Factors: Overhead control, scale economies	20%	2	4	3.5	3	3
Management Factors: Sales, marketing	10%	3	4	4	5	4
Differentiation Factors: Effectiveness—product quality, innovation	20%	5	4	4	3	5
Efficiency—delivery	10%	4	4	3	3	5
Relationship and service	10%	3	4	4	5	5
Range	5%	1	5	5	4	1
Premises	0%	0	0	0	0	0
Competitive Position	**100%**	**2.5**	**4.1**	**3.5**	**3.0**	**3.6**

Key to Rating: 1 = Weak, 2 = Tenable, 3 = Favorable, 4 = Strong, 5 = Very strong

16

 Strategy Competitive position

But PermaRoll's product should enable steady share growth and management will field competitive response stoutly to emerge stronger by Year 3.

➤ E-Z-Roll has few evident weaknesses: Its product is very good, it continues to bring out new products, its customer service and delivery are fine, and it enjoys economies of scale in production, sales, and marketing; ShadeLite is not far behind, though it has suffered recently from distribution hiccups—see Appendix X.

➤ But neither have PermaRoll's technology, nor can they have with patent protection imminent; they would love to have it—ShadeLite experimented three years ago with a similar technology but was unable to perfect the production process.

➤ They will be unhappy at PermaRoll taking some top-end share and may respond —initially with renewed sales effort, perhaps later in pricing (though this might be counterproductive); where they cannot respond is through offering a like product.

➤ PermaRoll is prepared for such a response—see sensitivity analysis of Chapter 8.

➤ PermaRoll's strategy of continuous improvement in production, delivery, and service should strengthen competitive position measurably by Year 3.

17

Executive summary

PermaRoll has a sustainable competitive edge in the top-end AWC market, with opportunities to gain share outshining the main risk of customer stickiness.

2. *The business:* PermaRoll will focus manufacturing initially on clutches for alternative window coverings, highly engineered for superior ease of use and reliability.

3. *Market demand:* PermaRoll's initial addressed market recovered to $75m in 2012, with growth forecast at 3.5%/year.

4. *Industry competition:* Competition will be less intense at the top end of the market, as long as a new entrant has a sustainable competitive edge.

5. *Strategy:* PermaRoll's top-end product has been well received by target customers and should enable a market foothold to be gained, grown, and defended.

6. *Resources*: A CFO will be hired to bolster PermaRoll's management team.

7. *Financials*: PermaRoll sales should reach $3m by Year 4, with peak funding requirement < $1m.

8. *Risk*: Opportunities to gain business beyond the plan forecasts outshine the key risks of customer stickiness and competitor retaliation.

18

 Resources 6

The resources required to drive PermaRoll's strategy have been identified, with a CFO to be hired and the main risk being fluctuating raw material prices.

➢ Management—Randy, to become full-time, will be CEO/CSMO; Juan will be COO (see bios in Appendix X) and, with our financial partner, we shall appoint a CFO.

➢ Sales and marketing—emphasis will be on further direct sales calls, by Randy and Suzanne, with limited marketing expense in trade journals and trade shows.

➢ Operations—detailed plans completed (see summary in Appendix X):
   ▪ 14,000 sq ft factory identified on outskirts of Atlanta, at $4/sq ft/year
   ▪ Capital equipment earmarked, including spring making machine and assembly machine
   ▪ Two fiberglass super-reinforced nylon (FSRN) suppliers lined up
   ▪ A transport operator lined up, another in discussions
   ▪ Aluminium bracket and other low-tech products lined up with sources in China

➢ Resource risk—limited, other than raw material pricing, which applies to all players:
   ▪ Plenty of factory space available in Atlanta area at present
   ▪ FSRN prices have followed the broad trends of petrochemical prices, but with somewhat lesser volatility
   ▪ Aluminium prices have steadied from the peak of $3,000 per tonne in mid-2008 and the trough of $1,300 in early 2009, hovering around $2,000 in the last two years
   ▪ Labor availability in Atlanta currently plentiful

19

Executive summary

PermaRoll has a sustainable competitive edge in the top-end AWC market, with opportunities to gain share outshining the main risk of customer stickiness.

2. *The business:* PermaRoll will focus manufacturing initially on clutches for alternative window coverings, highly engineered for superior ease of use and reliability.

3. *Market demand:* PermaRoll's initial addressed market recovered to $75m in 2012, with growth forecast at 3.5%/year.

4. *Industry competition:* Competition will be less intense at the top end of the market, as long as a new entrant has a sustainable competitive edge.

5. *Strategy:* PermaRoll's top-end product has been well received by target customers and should enable a market foothold to be gained, grown. and defended.

6. *Resources:* A CFO will be hired to bolster PermaRoll's management team.

7. *Financials:* PermaRoll sales should reach $3m by Year 4, with peak funding requirement < $1m.

8. *Risk:* Opportunities to gain business beyond the plan forecasts outshine the key risks of customer stickiness and competitor retaliation.

20

 Financials and forecasts Historic

PermaRoll has generated no revenues to date and has incurred cumulative expenses of $188k, financed by owner equity.

➤ PermaRoll has been operating out of an Atlanta garage for two years, with strategic focus on developing and testing an innovative clutch design for top-end AWCs.

➤ Expenses incurred have totaled $188k to date, with current run-rate $17k/month—see Appendix X:
  - Salary of one engineer (14 months): $76k
  - Fees for part-time salesperson (4 months): $19k
  - Salary of owner: $0k
  - Lease of premises: $0k
  - Machinery rental: $41k
  - Materials: $12k
  - Travel: $19k
  - Miscellaneous: $21k

➤ The venture has been funded thus far through seed capital provided by the owner.

➤ The forecasts assume receipt of funds and installation of equipment in leased premises in Year 0, with operations kicking off at start of Year 1.

21

Financials and forecasts Income forecasts **7**

Management forecasts PermaRoll to grow revenues to almost $3m by Year 4, with EBIT margin turning positive in mid-Year 2 to reach 23% by Year 4.

PermaRoll income statement forecasts, Years 1–4

US$000	Year 1 Forecast	Year 2 Forecast	Year 3 Forecast	Year 4 Forecast
No. of customers	*3*	*5*	*9*	*12*
Units sold (000)	*200*	*350*	*550*	*800*
Average unit revenue ($)	*3.50*	*3.50*	*3.50*	*3.50*
Revenues	**700**	**1225**	**1925**	**2800**
Gross margin (%)	57%	58%	60%	60%
Gross profit	397	715	1151	1680
Overheads	-696	-771	-881	-996
EBITDA	**-297**	**-61**	**274**	**684**
Depreciation	-34	-35	-35	-37
EBIT	**-331**	**-95**	**239**	**647**
EBIT margin (%)	**-47%**	**-8%**	**12%**	**23%**

Source: Appendix X

22

 Financials and forecasts Income forecasts **7**

Management forecasts PermaRoll to grow revenues to almost $3m by Year 4, with EBIT margin turning positive in mid-Year 2 to reach 23% by Year 4. *(continued)*

➢ PermaRoll should grow revenues to almost $3m by Year 4, despite conservative assumptions—see details in Appendix X:
  ▪ Only the three customers who have already submitted Letters of Intent assumed to generate revenues in Year 1, despite strong interest from others
  ▪ The two other customers in Year 1 are forecast at one-half the volumes of Palazzo Venezia each
  ▪ Year 2 assumes just two new customers, with little buildup in volume from existing ones
  ▪ Years 3 & 4 assumes sales and marketing effort now building momentum, rising to 12 customers, including two or three in export markets
  ▪ Average revenue per unit assumed to remain flat at the price provisionally agreed with Palazzo Venezia

➢ Gross margin is forecast to improve slowly as volumes grow (see Appendix X).

➢ Overhead expenses are high for low volumes in Year 1, but grow more slowly:
  ▪ Directors' salaries flat at $120k, but wages to rise from $400k in Year 1 to $725k in Year 4
  ▪ Lease of premises flat at $56k until Year 4 review

➢ EBIT margin inevitably in the red in Year 1, but moves into black by mid-Year 2 and should reach 23% by Year 4.

23

Financials and forecasts Market share forecasts

PermaRoll's market share gain assumptions seem reasonable and unlikely to result in significant competitive retaliation.

➤ The market size for top-end AWC clutches in the U.S. has been estimated at $75m and forecast to grow at 3.5%/year, reaching $86m by Year 4 (see Chapter 3).

➤ Market size should therefore increase by $11m between Year 0 and Year 4.

➤ Management forecasts PermaRoll sales of $2.8m in Year 4, or 25% of this increased market size, giving PermaRoll a market share by Year 4 of around 3%.

➤ Sales of the two main players, E-Z-Clutch and ShadeLite, will have increased in absolute terms by Year 4, even if their market shares may have been shaved:
- If E-Z-Roll grew with the market, holding share, its sales in Year 4 would rise from $30m to $34m.
- PermaRoll is forecast to take around $1.5m of E-Z-Roll's business in Year 4.
- But E-Z Roll's sales will still increase, from $30m to $32.5m, though its share will have slipped off 40%.

➤ PermaRoll's entry is thus not expected to lead to any price-led retaliatory response from the two main top-end players, though they may well sharpen up their sales and marketing tools.

24

 Financials and forecasts Cash flow forecasts

PermaRoll will continue to need cash as revenues grow fast, but the funding requirement should peak by mid-Year 3 at < $1m.

➤ Cash outflows are forecast to reverse by Year **3**:
- Working capital mounts as revenues build up, but EBITDA turns positive by mid-Year 2.
- Capex will be minor following initial outlay of $420k, including $180k on spring machine and $120k on assembly **machine**—see Appendix X.
- Peak **funding requirement** < $1m.

PermaRoll cash flow forecasts, Years 1–4

US$000	Year 0 Forecast	Year 1 Forecast	Year 2 Forecast	Year 3 Forecast	Year 4 Forecast
EBITDA		-297	-61	274	684
Change in working capital		-62	-84	-114	-142
Cash flow from operations		**-359**	**-145**	**160**	**542**
Capital expenditure	-420	-10	-20	-5	-25
Cash flow pre-financing	**-420**	**-369**	**-165**	**155**	**517**
Cash flow pre-financing (cumulative)	-420	-789	-954	-798	-281

Source: Appendix X

25

VP **Executive summary**

PermaRoll has a sustainable competitive edge in the top-end AWC market, with opportunities to gain share outshining the main risk of customer stickiness.

2. *The business:* PermaRoll will focus manufacturing initially on clutches for alternative window coverings, highly engineered for superior ease of use and reliability.

3. *Market demand:* PermaRoll's initial addressed market recovered to $75m in 2012, with growth forecast at 3.5%/year.

4. *Industry competition:* Competition will be less intense at the top end of the market, as long as a new entrant has a sustainable competitive edge.

5. *Strategy:* PermaRoll's top-end product has been well received by target customers and should enable a market foothold to be gained, grown, and defended.

6. *Resources*: A CFO will be hired to bolster PermaRoll's management team.

7. *Financials*: PermaRoll sales should reach $3m by Year 4, with peak funding requirement < $1m.

8. *Risk*: Opportunities to gain business beyond the plan forecasts outshine the key risks of customer stickiness and competitor retaliation.

26

VP **Risk, opportunity, and sensitivity**   8

Opportunities to gain business beyond the plan forecasts outshine the key risks of customer stickiness and competitor retaliation.

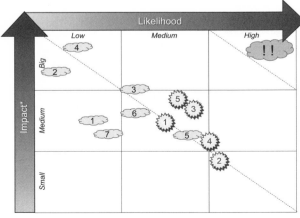

Risks

1. Double-dip recession
2. AWCs go out of fashion
3. Top two competitors retaliate
4. PermaRoll product failure
5. Customers won't shift supplier
6. Export customers won't shift
7. Operational hiccups

Opportunities

1. Economy recovers well
2. PermaRoll wins > 3 customers in Year 1
3. Share gain > 3% of U.S. top-end market by Year 4
4. Exports lift off
5. Pricing nudged up in Years 3–4 as product benefits realized

* Note: Impact on cash flow forecasts in business plan

Risk, opportunity, and sensitivity   8

Opportunities to gain business beyond the plan forecasts outshine the key risks of customer stickiness and competitor retaliation. *(continued)*

➢ The main risk to the plan is customer stickiness—they are happy with their current clutch, happy with their current supplier, and averse to switching to a new, more expensive product from a new supplier.

➢ This risk is mitigated by the evident customer benefits, customer response to date, three Letters of Intent, and conservative revenue forecasts.

➢ The other main risk of competitive retaliation is mitigated by the fact that competitors' sales will still grow, even if their top-end share slides a bit to PermaRoll—see Chapter 7.

➢ These risks are outshone by the main opportunities to grow beyond the conservative 3% market share target of the business plan ...

➢ ... and to nudge up pricing, at least in line with inflation, as the benefits to the customer in terms of a lifetime guarantee on the clutch become more widely appreciated.

28

 Risk, opportunity, and sensitivity   8

Due to working capital adjustments, peak funding requirement is not especially sensitive to lower (or, more likely, higher) revenue assumptions.

➢ A new venture such as PermaRoll is more sensitive to revenue assumptions than those for capital or operating costs, with the cost base relatively known and predictable:
  ▪ A 20% hit on PermaRoll revenues in each of Years 2–4 would have a major impact on EBITDA (49% down, if costs were not adjusted), but a lesser impact on peak funding requirement (up 16% to $1,105k), due to lower working capital requirements

➢ Management believes, however, that an upside scenario is more likely than such a downside, with a 20% revenue boost lowering peak funding requirement to $853k.

PermaRoll business plan sensitivity tests

$000	EBITDA		Peak Funding Requirement
	Year 1	Year 4	
Business plan	-297	684	954
Sensitivity tests			
Revenues down 20% in Year 1	-378	684	1033
Revenues down 10% in each of Years 2–4	-297	516	1004
Revenues down 20% in each of Years 2–4	-297	348	1105
Revenues up 20% in Year 1	-217	684	874
Revenues up 10% in each of Years 2–4	-297	852	903
Revenues up 20% in each of Years 2–4	-297	1020	853

29

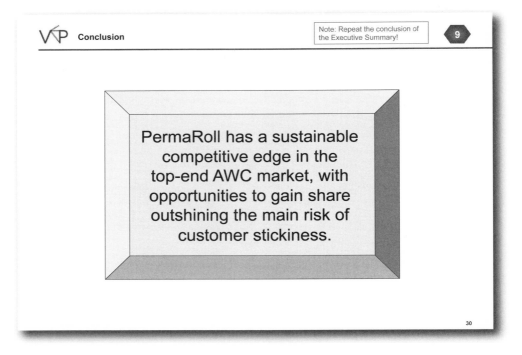

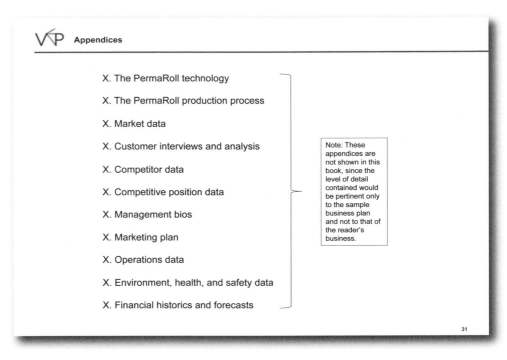

INDEX